Approaches to Teaching Hurston's *Their Eyes Were Watching God* and Other Works

Approaches to Teaching World Literature

For a complete listing of titles,
see the last pages of this book.

Approaches to Teaching Hurston's *Their Eyes Were Watching God* and Other Works

Edited by

John Lowe

The Modern Language Association of America
New York 2009

Library of Congress Cataloging-in-Publication Data

Approaches to teaching Hurston's Their eyes were watching God
and other works / edited by John Lowe.
p. cm. — (Approaches to teaching world literature, ISSN 1059-1133 ; 111)
Includes bibliographical references and index.
ISBN 978-1-60329-043-2 (hardcover : alk. paper) –
ISBN 978-1-60329-044-9 (pbk. : alk. paper)
1. Hurston, Zora Neale. Their eyes were watching God—Study and teaching.
2. Hurston, Zora Neale—Study and teaching.
3. African Americans in literature—Study and teaching.
I. Lowe, John, 1945-
PS3515.U789Z625 2009
813'.52—dc22 2009021403

Approaches to Teaching World Literature 111
ISSN 1059-1133

Cover illustration for the paperback edition:
Dixie Belles. Photograph by Fonville Winans. 1938. © Bob Winans

Published by The Modern Language Association of America
26 Broadway, New York, New York 10004-1789
www.mla.org

This volume is dedicated to the memory
of our cherished colleagues,
Nellie Y. McKay
and
Gay Wilentz

CONTENTS

Other Works by Hurston

ACKNOWLEDGMENTS

This volume has profited from many productive conversations with the contributors; I thank them all. My only regret is that our dear friends and colleagues Nellie Y. McKay and Gay Wilentz did not live to see our work in print, but we rejoice to have their final essays as part of our offering. Many other scholars have provided advice and encouragement as this collection progressed toward publication, among them Pam Bordelon, Keith Byerman, Keith Cartwright, Daryl Dance, Thadious Davis, Susan Donaldson, Sally Ann Ferguson, Joanne Gabbin, Mary Emma Graham, Lynda Hill, Fred Hobson, Dolan Hubbard, Joyce Marie Jackson, Suzanne Jones, Barbara Ladd, Veronica Makowsky, Deborah E. McDowell, Brenda Marie Osbey, Pearlie Mae Peters, Pete Powers, Joseph T. Skerrett, Jr., Reggie Young, and Rafia Zafar. I especially thank the comparative literature program at Louisiana State University and its director, Greg Stone, for funding the work of my invaluable research assistant, Erin Breaux, whose energy and eye for detail enriched every page of this volume. All of us thank our students, whose questions, comments, and curiosity have goaded us into a better understanding of Hurston, her texts, and the needs and interests of a new generation of readers.

The publications staff at the Modern Language Association could not have been more helpful. Over the years this project took shape, Joseph Gibaldi, David G. Nicholls, James C. Hatch, Sara Pastel, and, especially, Sonia Kane provided sound advice, editorial assistance, and firm support. Finally, as always, I thank my wife, June Conaway Lowe, for the best kind of motivational and inspirational tough love.

PREFACE

Zora Neale Hurston, once a forgotten writer, has risen from obscurity to take her place in the American literary canon. *Their Eyes Were Watching God*, her greatest achievement, enjoys wide popularity among general readers and has become a favorite of teachers at every level of instruction. Although it has finally and correctly come to be understood as a masterwork of African American and women's literature, it has also proved amenable to other subjects of inquiry, including studies of the 1930s, small-town life, folklore, regionalism, dialect theory, critical race theory, literary modernism, geographical aspects of place, and ecological theory. A film of the novel starring the Academy Award winner Halle Berry as Janie was created by Oprah Winfrey's production company and aired on national television. The book is also exhibit A for the cult of Zora, since Hurston has emerged as a kind of iconic figure on a par with Ernest Hemingway, Virginia Woolf, and F. Scott Fitzgerald. Several actresses have mounted one-woman shows impersonating Hurston, and her image has found a place on coffee mugs and in bookstore murals across the nation. Her hometown, Eatonville, Florida, has become a popular tourist destination and a state office building has been named in her honor. Eatonville sponsors the annual Zora! festival, and the professor Ruthe Sheffey, of Morgan State University, some years ago founded the Zora Neale Hurston Society, which publishes a journal and convenes academic conferences. Several of Hurston's plays have been staged, as have comedies and dramas based on her short fiction. Hurston was a character in the frame story of the 1991 Broadway production of the play she wrote with Langston Hughes, *Mule Bone*, and, more recently, the Arena Stage in Washington mounted a production of her three-act play *Polk County*, which she coauthored with Dorothy Waring. Hurston, the subject of much literary gossip and mythology, in her own time and now ours—especially as a kind of godmother of the Harlem Renaissance (even though most of her writing was done after the 1920s, the great period of that group's productivity)—sometimes seems in danger of her legend eclipsing her literary output.

Although a great deal of scholarly interest has been trained on *Their Eyes*, Hurston's other works have yet to attract a wide readership, and even *Their Eyes* needs a better scholarly apparatus that can assist teachers as they prepare to teach the novel. Accordingly, this volume situates Hurston's work against the African American, southern, and national cultures that engendered it; it assesses her success as short story writer, playwright, novelist, autobiographer, folklorist, and anthropologist. Concurrently it provides modes of classroom access to her other important book-length publications, her dramas, and her short stories. Because Hurston is taught in such a variety of courses, we have also tried to relate her to other writers of her time, to women's issues, literary modernism, relations between the sexes, humor, folk culture, and the new move to the literature of the global South, transnational studies, Atlantic studies, and the African diaspora.

The Novels

Their Eyes Were Watching God (1937), drenched in metaphor and cosmic imagery, alternates between mythic, sometimes romantic writing and pungent, dialect-driven folk expression. Although much of the narrative features a bright embroidery of humor, serious issues trace darker patterns, as characters rehearse slavery, Reconstruction, and the emergence of a rural folk into the modern, technological age. Janie's story, which is often read as a paradigm for a woman's search for identity, is firmly attached to a folk history based in Hurston's all-black hometown of Eatonville. The telling details of flora and fauna, hamlet commerce, and local custom seamlessly interlace with the overarching narrative of Janie's life: how she married three times, was schooled in folk culture, farmed on the Everglades "muck," survived a hurricane, killed her beloved husband, and underwent a subsequent murder trial. Acclaimed as Hurston's most important achievement by virtually all scholars, it receives the major focus of this volume.

Their Eyes was preceded in Hurston's literary output by *Jonah's Gourd Vine* (1934), a novel loosely based on her parents' marriage. John Pearson, a strapping mulatto, escapes from his backwoods hamlet after a fight with his stepfather, crossing the creek to meet the well-off Lucy Potts, who encourages him to get an education. They marry, John is called to preach, and he becomes a denominational leader in the state. He neglects Lucy and their growing family, however, and embarks on a string of adulteries. Lucy's death leads to John's marriage to one of his paramours, then divorce, and a final marriage with a genteel widow, just before his untimely death at a train crossing. The novel features much local idiom and humor, alongside soaring religious rhetoric, for John is a man of words, whose story has much to say about patterns of black masculinity, marital relations, and the role of religion in African American life.

Hurston, a protean writer, changed shape yet again in *Moses, Man of the Mountain* (1939), a retelling of the biblical saga in modern black dialect, with many anachronisms. Despite frequent surface levity, the novel explores serious subjects, such as slavery and exile, warring ethnicities, color prejudice, racial leadership, sibling rivalry, and nation building. Moses is figured as definitely Egyptian and as the greatest hoodoo man who ever lived. Although in conversation with God, his conjuring comes from African sources and mentors.

Seraph on the Suwanee (1948), a perplexing novel centered on the upward rise of a white Cracker woman, Arvay Henson, and her troubled marriage to the handsome, enterprising, but often sexist Jim Meserve, takes place against the backdrop of a booming Florida. Hurston explores orange growing, real estate development, the shrimp industry, and emerging tastes for black music among white Americans, as well as relations between black workers and white employers, new immigrants from the Caribbean and Portugal, consumer culture, and changing social mores. It also considers parent-child relationships in greater depth than her other novels.

The Nonfiction

Hurston's years of gathering folk materials, first for her graduate work at Columbia University and then later for the Federal Writers' Project, culminated in three books of folklore; two were published in her lifetime and are considered here. The third, *Every Tongue Got to Confess: Negro Folk-Tales from the Gulf States* (2001), does not feature a controlling narrator, unlike the other two volumes. The first of those, *Mules and Men* (1935), grew out of a long scholarly article on black folklore that Hurston published in an entire issue of *Journal of American Folklore*, a signal accomplishment at that time. Dissatisfied that too many readers could not access this work, she rewrote it, inserting herself as a narrating participant, resulting in a delightful work that reads like a novel, as Hurston crisscrosses the South, serving stints in Eatonville, Polk County, sawmill camps, and New Orleans, where she is initiated as a hoodoo priestess.

Tell My Horse (1938) follows Hurston as she does fieldwork in Jamaica, the Bahamas, and, most dramatically, Haiti, where she meets and photographs a zombie. Voodoo rites, practices, and beliefs are explained and dramatized. The book also features searching discussions of Haitian culture and politics and highlights the complex relation of the island nation to the United States, which had just concluded a long occupation of the island. Raising key issues of colonialism, imperialism, and transnational culture, the text also explores British racial stances, Afro-francophone culture and history, sexual mysteries and practices (especially in relation to religion), and New World forms of African religions.

Much controversy has swirled around Hurston's autobiography, *Dust Tracks on a Road*, since it first appeared, in 1942. Hurston's childhood is followed by a ten-year gap, and her marriages—if mentioned at all—get the briefest acknowledgment, as does the Harlem Renaissance. The work frustrates readers looking for a formulaic tell-all life story but provides rich rewards in its portrait of Hurston's aesthetics, her religious sensibility, her sense of philosophy and politics, and the moving description she provides of her mother, particularly at the time of her death. It also yields many insights into black communal life and social mores and is enlivened by buoyant, constantly creative language. The versions currently in print have restored excised chapters that editors viewed as overly critical of American institutions and political activities during the 1940s.

JL

Part One

MATERIALS

Editions and Anthologies

Their Eyes Were Watching God, long out of print, was reissued by the University of Illinois Press in 1978. Subsequently, Illinois reprinted *Moses, Man of the Mountain* and *Dust Tracks on a Road* in 1984. Harper Collins supplanted Illinois as Hurston's publisher in a paperback series edited by Henry Louis Gates, Jr., in the 1990s: *Their Eyes Were Watching God*; *Jonah's Gourd Vine*; *Mules and Men*; *Tell My Horse*; *Dust Tracks on a Road*; *Moses, Man of the Mountain*; *Seraph on the Suwanee*; the play Hurston cowrote with Langston Hughes, *Mule Bone: A Comedy of Negro Life*; and *The Complete Stories*. The last work does not include a short story that subsequently came to light, "Under the Bridge." A volume edited by Jean Lee Cole and Charles Mitchell collects her known plays, many of which were discovered years ago at the Library of Congress and are available on the Internet (Hurston, *Zora Neale Hurston Plays*). Hurston's short stories, essays, and portions of her novels appeared in the early Feminist Press anthology, *I Love Myself When I'm Laughing and Then Again When I'm Looking Mean and Impressive: A Zora Neale Hurston Reader* (A. Walker). In 1985, the Turtle Island Foundation published *Spunk: The Selected Short Stories of Zora Neale Hurston*. Her folklore has appeared in a variety of ways; the Harper Collins edition of *Mules and Men* was preceded by Indiana University Press's reprint in 1978. *The Sanctified Church*, also published by Turtle Island, collected twelve essays on folklore that did not appear in either *Tell My Horse* or *Mules and Men*. A second collection of essays on folklore, edited by Pamela Bordelon and including Bordelon's long biographical essay full of new information, appeared from Norton in 1999. Later, a third manuscript of folklore collected by Hurston was discovered at the Smithsonian in the 1990s and was published under the editorship of Carla Kaplan by Harper Collins in 2001 as *Every Tongue Got to Confess*. The Library of America brought out a two-volume collection of Hurston's work, under the supervision of Cheryl A. Wall, in 1995. The first volume contains her novels and stories, while the second features her folklore, memoirs, and other writings. Many kinds of anthologies have reprinted Hurston's short stories—usually "The Gilded Six-Bits" or "Sweat."

Courses and Contexts

Our survey of instructors revealed that *Their Eyes Were Watching God* is taught in high schools, junior colleges, and colleges across America. Its frequent inclusion in survey courses of American literature indicates its central place in the new American literary canon. The novel has also earned regular treatment in many African American literature courses, modernism seminars, women's studies classes (especially those concentrating on black feminist or womanist theory), ethnic literature surveys, and courses on American or African American humor. In the South, the novel has a secure place in courses on the region's literature and culture and often finds favor from southern history instructors. Hurston's other novels, however, are rarely taught, especially *Seraph on the Suwanee*. *Mules and Men* has for many years been a staple in American folklore syllabi. Recently, interest in the transnational South, the black diaspora, and global studies has made *Tell My Horse* a popular choice. *Dust Tracks on a Road* has enjoyed an increasingly prominent place in life writing classes, where it often receives interrogation as a nontraditional autobiography and is read in context with other American life stories, especially those by African Americans, such as *Up from Slavery*, *Black Boy*, and *I Know Why the Caged Bird Sings*.

The Instructor's Library

The respondents to our survey were asked to suggest reference and background works that they found useful when they taught Hurston's works.

Reference Works

The most commonly recommended reference works were Adele S. Newson, *Zora Neale Hurston: A Reference Guide*; Rose Parkman Davis, *Zora Neale Hurston: An Annotated Bibliography and Reference Guide*; and Robert W. Croft, *A Zora Neale Hurston Companion*.

Background Studies

Many respondents recommended reading Hurston's various essays and letters as useful background materials, especially explanations of folklore found in *Mules and Men* and Hurston's essays "How It Feels to Be Colored Me" and "Characteristics of Negro Expression." Several teachers use contemporary book reviews of Hurston's novels, particularly Richard Wright's acerbic "Between Laughter and Tears." Teachers who like to juxtapose Wright and Hurston favor June Jordan's essay on the pair, "Notes toward a Black Balancing of Love and Hatred." Alice Walker's moving essay "Looking for Zora," included in her anthology *In Search of Our Mothers' Gardens*, is used by many when teaching Hurston's works. Some instructors found treatments of the Harlem Renaissance such as Allon Schoener's *Harlem on My Mind* and David Levering Lewis's *When Harlem Was in Vogue* helpful. Many recommended Alain Locke's 1925 collection, *The New Negro*, which includes works by Hurston but also others by nearly all the movement's participants. Her overall role in the Harlem Renaissance is explored by Cheryl A. Wall in *Women of the Harlem Renaissance*. Other works cited included Melville Herskovits's *The Myth of the Negro Past* and the anthropological studies of Franz Boas and Ruth Benedict, Hurston's anthropology professors. One of the most useful studies of the period is Richard Gray's *Southern Aberrations: Writers of the American South and the Problems of Regionalism*. Beverly Robinson's "Africanisms and the Study of Folklore," in Joseph E. Holloway's *Africanisms in American Culture*, was praised for preparing students to recognize Hurston's use of folklore. Marjorie Pryse's introduction to her coedited (with Hortense Spillers) volume *Conjuring: Black Women, Fiction, and Literary Tradition* was also recommended. Hurston's folklore, one respondent mentioned, should be compared with Joel Chandler Harris's Uncle Remus tales. Another instructor felt that *Jonah* and *Their Eyes* could be foregrounded by a reading of selections from Booker T. Washington's *Up from Slavery*. Another teacher likes to assign chapter 5 of Henry Louis Gates's *The Signifying Monkey* to introduce and explain the concept of signifying. Situating *Their Eyes* in the tradition of the African American novel can be facilitated by consultation of Bernard Bell's *The African American Novel and Its Tradition*. One respondent likes to use N. Y. Nathiri's *Zora! Zora Neale Hurston: A Woman and Her Community*, whose pictures help students focus on Hurston's community. Steve Glassman and Kathryn Lee Seidel's *Zora in Florida* was also cited for this purpose.

Classic Essays on Their Eyes

Several essays not included in the books listed above were cited as helpful: Lorraine Bethel, "'This Infinity of Conscious Pain': Zora Neale Hurston and the Black Female Literary Tradition"; Sally Ann Ferguson, "Folkloric Men and Female Growth in *Their Eyes Were Watching God*"; Barbara Johnson, "Metaphor, Metonymy, and Voice in *Their Eyes Were Watching God*"; Missy Dehn Kubitschek, "'Tuh De Horizon and Back': The Female Quest in *Their Eyes Were Watching God*"; Mary Helen Washington, "Zora Neale Hurston: The Black Woman's Search for Identity."

Biographical Studies

Robert Hemenway's pioneering *Zora Neale Hurston: A Literary Biography* almost single-handedly brought Hurston back into the public consciousness. The product of many years of research, part of it undertaken in a battered camper across the rural South, the study profits immensely from Hemenway's deep knowledge of African American folk culture and anthropology. Hemenway tried to talk with almost everyone still alive who knew Hurston, and just in time, too, since many of them—particularly her siblings—died soon after talking with him. He treats virtually all her writing that was known at that time and raises most of the critical issues that dominate Hurston scholarship today.

Hemenway always said that a second biography of Hurston would someday be written by a black woman. Valerie Boyd's *Wrapped in Rainbows: The Life of Zora Neale Hurston* fulfilled that prophecy, when it was published in 2003. Although it presents some new facts—such as Hurston's heretofore unknown third marriage—it basically follows Hemenway's outline, correcting some of his facts but generally seconding his findings and assessments and giving perhaps a more positive overall evaluation of Hurston's literary legacy.

A much shorter biography, Mary E. Lyons's *Sorrow's Kitchen: The Life and Folklore of Zora Neale Hurston*, offers a more focused approach to Hurston's life than the longer biographies listed above. Pam Bordelon's long introductory essay to *Go Gator* adds valuable new information to the life as it was known at that time and uses new conversations with key relatives and information gleaned from the family bible. A children's biography, *Jump at de Sun: The Life Story of Zora Neale Hurston*, by A. P. Porter, is basic, readily comprehensible, and has the added attraction of a collection of pictures of Hurston and her various backdrops.

Several article-length biographies offer even shorter accounts of Hurston's life. Craig Werner's entry on Hurston in *Modern American Women Writers* combines key biographical fact with concise but acute criticism of her major work. John Lowe's version of Hurston's life and influence appears in *The History of Southern Women's Literature*. An extensive collection of Hurston's correspondence, *Zora Neale Hurston: A Life in Letters*, was edited and published by Carla Kaplan in 2002 and offers invaluable insights into her life and writings.

Critical Studies

Considering the ubiquity of Hurston's work in the nation's classrooms, there have been surprisingly few book-length studies of her work. There are many essays on *Their Eyes* but far fewer on the other novels, although recently *Seraph* has enjoyed some attention. The Hemenway biography offered the first set of sustained readings of her work and was soon followed by Lillie P. Howard's *Zora Neale Hurston*, a basic and useful reading of her major works. Karla Holloway's *The Character of the Word: The Texts of Zora Neale Hurston* was the first book-length study to employ critical-feminist theory to read Hurston's work. John Lowe, in *Jump at the Sun: Zora Neale Hurston's Cosmic Comedy*, ranges widely over most of Hurston's texts, archival manuscripts, and letters, showing how Hurston employed humor to map and dissect race, gender, and folk culture. Deborah G. Plant's *Every Tub Must Sit on Its Own Bottom: The Philosophy and Politics of Zora Neale Hurston* questions Hurston's supposed feminism, arguing instead that Hurston was a writer of resistance who had read widely in philosophical texts. Lynda Marion Hill's study, *Social Rituals and the Verbal Art of Zora Neale Hurston*, situated Hurston in the realm of performance. Pearlie Mae Fisher Peters's *The Assertive Woman in Zora Neale Hurston's Fiction, Folklore, and Drama* situates Hurston's female figures in the trajectory of black womanist fiction. Susan Edwards Meisenhelder's *Hitting a Straight Lick with a Crooked Stick* profits from archival research and suggests that much of Hurston's work proceeds from a trickster's ironic position. Tiffany Ruby Patterson's *Zora Neale Hurston and a History of Southern Life* foregrounds the writer's regional identity.

The following works were cited as containing valuable sections on Hurston: John F. Callahan, *In the African-American Grain: The Pursuit of Voice in Twentieth-Century Black Fiction*; Henry Louis Gates, Jr., *The Signifying Monkey: A Theory of Afro-American Literary Criticism*; Nathan Grant, *Masculinist Impulses: Toomer, Hurston, Black Writing, and Modernity*; Trudier Harris, *The Power of the Porch: The Storyteller's Craft in Zora Neale Hurston, Gloria Naylor, and Randall Kenan*; Lillie P. Howard, *Alice Walker and Zora Neale Hurston: The Common Bond*; Sharon L. Jones, *Rereading the Harlem Renaissance: Race, Class, and Gender in the Fiction of Jessie Fauset, Zora Neale Hurston, and Dorothy West*; Carla Kaplan, *The Erotics of Talk: Women's Writings and Feminist Paradigms*; Delia Caparoso Konzett, *Ethnic Modernisms: Anzia Yezierska, Zora Neale Hurston, Jean Rhys, and the Aesthetics of Dislocation*; Tom McGlamery, *Protest and the Body in Melville, Dos Passos, and Hurston*; Eric Sundquist, *The Hammers of Creation: Folk Culture in Modern African-American Fiction*; Cheryl A. Wall, *Women of the Harlem Renaissance*.

Useful critical anthologies and reading guides include Michael Awkward, *New Essays on* Their Eyes Were Watching God; Harold Bloom, *Zora Neale Hurston's* Their Eyes Were Watching God; Josie P. Campbell, *Student Companion to Zora Neale Hurston*; Robert W. Croft, *A Zora Neale Hurston Companion*; Gloria L. Cronin, *Critical Essays on Zora Neale Hurston*; Henry Louis Gates, Jr., and K. A. Appiah, *Zora Neale Hurston: Critical Perspectives Past and Present*; Steve Glassman and Kathryn Lee Seidel, *Zora in Florida*; Cheryl A. Wall, *"Sweat": Zora Neale Hurston*; and Cheryl A. Wall, *Zora Neale Hurston's* Their Eyes Were Watching God*: A Casebook*.

Recommended online resources include the special issue of *The Scholar and Feminist Online* devoted to Hurston (Monica L. Miller; http://barnard.columbia.edu/sfonline/hurston); the Zora Neale Hurston Festival of the Arts and Humanities (held every January; http://www.zorafestival.com); and the Zora Neale Hurston / Richard Wright Foundation (http://www.hurston-wright.org).

Some suggestions for Hurston works and bibliographies are *The Zora Neale Hurston Plays at the Library of Congress*; the *Mules and Men* e-project at the University of Virginia; *Harlem, 1900–1940*, the online exhibit from the Schomburg Center for Research in Black Culture; *Black Renaissance in Washington, D.C., 1920s–1930s*, the exhibit from the District of Columbia Public Library

(Martin); *African American Odyssey: A Quest for Full Citizenship*, an exhibit by the Library of Congress section on post–World War I society and the Harlem Renaissance; and *Rhapsodies in Black: Art of the Harlem Renaissance*, an online collection on art and culture during the Harlem Renaissance.

Part Two

APPROACHES

Introduction

John Lowe

This volume has been created to provide helpful insights for teachers as they present a masterwork in the classroom, as well as other works by Zora Neale Hurston that need to be better known and more often taught.

Hurston emerged on the literary scene during the Harlem Renaissance, one of the most important moments of American literary history. African Americans began "the great migration" to northern cities from the South during and after World War I, when restrictions on immigration and wartime demands for factory workers expanded opportunities for black laborers. Members of this workforce found little chance for advancement in the rural South's exploitative sharecropping system, which was augmented by racial segregation and lynching. While many major northern cities attracted black immigrants, New York City, the center for theater, art, dance, and, perhaps most important, publishing, naturally became a magnet for those who were artistically inclined. The availability of affordable housing in Harlem, along with the attraction of an existing black citizenry there, soon led to an artistic cluster nestled in the bosom of a supportive and hopeful black community.

Hurston, however, had left her native Florida before the war, traveling as a lady's maid with a Gilbert and Sullivan company. She enrolled in a series of schools, including Baltimore's Morgan State College, Washington's Howard University, and, finally, New York's Barnard College. Residence in three major northern cities expanded her horizons and acquainted her with leading literary and artistic figures who had migrated to the northeast from points across the nation. Hurston soon found that she could win friends, scholarship, and white patronage by regaling listeners with stories drawn from the folklore and daily life of her home state.

Eventually, her graduate studies in anthropology at Columbia with Franz Boas and Ruth Benedict sent her back south to gather folklore, which led to scholarly publications but also to short stories and novels based on the culture she had formerly taken for granted but now saw through the spyglass of anthropology.

It should not be supposed, however, that Hurston's South was a backward rural outpost. As Hurston makes clear in her last novel, Florida was being transformed by timber and turpentine industries, swamp drainage, real estate development, new railroads, tourism, expanded fisheries, and the growth of ports and cities. Immigrants from the Caribbean and elsewhere were radically transforming the state's population, at the same time that many black Floridians were heading north. Her South was changed yet again by the region's participation in World War II, new racial struggles, the *Brown v. Board of Education* decision, and the onset of the cold war. Although Hurston died in 1960, she was affected by all these events and contributed letters, essays, and articles about many of the issues to journals and local newspapers. Her trips to Haiti, Jamaica, the

Bahamas, and Honduras made her aware of the myriad connections between the South and what was south (and east) of the South and of the many links among cultures of the black diaspora that crossed national boundaries.

Students should also be aware that before and after the New Negro Renaissance of the 1920s, black writers had great difficulty publishing their work, a situation that persisted well into the 1960s. Although there was, as Langston Hughes said, a vogue for all things Negro during the 1920s (224), the Depression put a damper on the Harlem Renaissance, and publishers let books already published by black writers go out of print. Three writers, Richard Wright, Ralph Ellison, and James Baldwin, were exceptions to this trend and were widely read during the 1950s and 1960s. But Hurston was largely forgotten in those decades and only came back into print in the 1970s, through the efforts of Robert Hemenway and Alice Walker and the rising tide of interest in women's literature stemming from the women's liberation movement. Hurston and all black writers—particularly before Wright's *Native Son* created a market for "protest literature" in 1940—had to be aware of what she termed "what white publishers won't print."

The first set of essays in this volume concentrates on *Their Eyes Were Watching God* and provides quite varied approaches. Genevieve West's study of canon formation situates Hurston against several backdrops, including the literary and publishing scene she faced in the 1930s and the then male-dominated realm of African American letters. West shows how developments in American social and literary life changed the climate for Hurston's reception, first leading to her eclipse under the rise of protest literature and the Black Arts movement and then to her resurrection as feminism, the rise of black studies, and new approaches to folk culture created a new audience.

Gay Wilentz situates Hurston in a more political context, considering the writer's radical strategies that seem to displace "race" men and women of the time but also critique color-struck black figures who seem embarrassed by folk culture. Focusing on that culture, and its rise to prominence in the latter "muck" portion of the novel, Wilentz shows us how to concentrate on the "they" implicit in the book's title.

On a related note, Carla Cappetti looks at how the timeless, rural, and often mythic qualities of *Their Eyes* can lead us away from considerations of history and society. She seeks to adjust that drift by making a case for the novel as both historical and proletarian.

John Lowe draws attention to the central role humor plays in the novel and asserts that Hurston uses comedy—especially that derived from a creative folk culture—in infinitely varied, often quite serious ways. Humor provides a ground for intimacy, both between characters and between author and reader, while functioning as the glue that holds the community together. Conversely, it can function in sharply critical ways—as communal correction of individuals, as subversive critique of white domination, and as a vehicle for rage against fate and even against God himself. Lowe also demonstrates the key role humor plays in each of Janie's marriages, particularly in the rituals of courtship and in the intimacies of daily life.

Trudier Harris considers the implications of the text for courses on feminist or women's or womanist literature and culture, reading *Their Eyes* through a rethinking of Janie's marital history. Harris makes us reconsider many of the platitudes that have been raised about the novel and especially the ways in which it has often been presented in courses devoted to women's literature and feminist theory. It also stirs up a new discourse about Hurston herself. Was she a feminist? What was her attitude toward the women in her works? Harris concludes by folding this line of questions into larger issues about the process of literary reputation and by depicting a devilish portrait of Hurston in heaven jiving Saint Peter.

James C. Hall thinks about the situation in the undergraduate classroom, particularly about how Hurston inevitably is forced to rub shoulders with other African American writers, both in anthologies and on syllabi. A chief irony here is that many of us teach her, cheek by jowl, with Richard Wright, her literary nemesis. Each dissed the other in print, and their feud has been made the apparatus for fashioning a symbolic polarity that frames African American literary production of the time. Hall demonstrates how teaching *Their Eyes* alongside *Uncle Tom's Children* (they were published at almost the same moment during the 1930s) can reap handsome dividends. He rehearses the original quarrel, charts its emergence as a key issue in literary scholarship, and shows us what to do with it in the classroom, where a "he said, she said" presentation can spark real interest and opportunity.

Dana Williams suggests an approach that would work in either a class on the Harlem Renaissance or a critical theory course. By linking Hurston's masterwork to others from that period, Williams uncovers various claims that have been made for the movement's dominant aesthetic and shows that *Their Eyes* can be read as a demonstration of the instability of the supposed aesthetic. Janie and the other characters, read through the lens of deconstruction, must be encountered in terms of who they are rather than in terms of who they are not, which Williams situates as characteristic of the Harlem Renaissance writers so often linked with Hurston. The essay points the way toward a classroom presentation of the novel's meaning as varied and even indeterminate.

The second set of essays takes up the value and complexity of Hurston's other major works. John Lowe concentrates on avatars of black masculinity—in particular the forms available to the black preacher—in his approach to teaching Hurston's first novel, *Jonah's Gourd Vine*. He provides historical background for the traditions of the "man of words" in African American culture and shows how John Pearson's rise in the novel stems precisely from his development of male performative styles, while his decline originates in his inability to separate his sexual appetite from his aspirations for communal and spiritual greatness. Lowe suggests thematic approaches that will engage students as well as cause them to extend the questions Hurston uncovers to areas beyond the story proper.

It has been argued that *Moses, Man of the Mountain* is Hurston's second masterwork, and Carolyn M. Jones makes us understand how such a statement can stand scrutiny. Her essay proceeds from Jones's training in religious studies and offers assistance to instructors of literature and religion courses, in particular, but also to teachers in a wide range of classes who seek to motivate students with religious backgrounds. Jones suggests a fourfold classroom focus: the state of the world in 1939, when Moses appeared; Moses as hero; Moses and Miriam as contrasts to Moses and as exemplars of the slave experience; and the overarching thematic of the book, the quest for freedom. Jones provides a useful set of commentaries on Moses that will aid all readers in linking theology with fictional narrative.

Hurston's controversial last novel, *Seraph on the Suwanee*, receives a helpful reading from Deborah G. Plant, who suggests the novel's grouping of mostly white characters enables Hurston to explore a new approach to race, class, and gender through overtly individualistic perspectives and thereby permits a demonstration of the self-defeating politics of dualism. Plant sees Arvay, who moves tortuously but successfully toward a united self-image, as the epitomy of the ills of American society and the solution to those ills.

Hurston's anthropological works have always been considered classic examples of African American and black diasporan folklore. Her first collection, *Mules and Men*, is now taught by scholars in several disciplines and has correctly been understood as a text that gives voice to a people. Accordingly, Kimberly J. Banks and Cheryl A. Wall here provide a way of using the text's polyvocality and sense of performance as a way of generating dynamic classroom presentation. They also separate the text into its constituent components—Eatonville, Polk County, and New Orleans—and provide useful historical background for all three communities. They suggest modes of relating to the many stories, focusing on deities, animals, names, and the varieties of voices, which vary widely in each community. The essay concludes by making useful links between Hurston's approach here and those of Claude McKay and Jean Toomer in their respective novels, *Banana Bottom* and *Cane*. This essay can work well for students in folklore, anthropology, and Harlem Renaissance courses.

Tell My Horse, Hurston's study of the folklore of the Caribbean, finds a perceptive reader in Annette Trefzer, who relates the book to the new discourse on both postmodernism and new applications of postcolonial theory to African American diasporan texts. Trefzer suggests a novel and productive way of presenting the controversial hoodoo and voodoo sections of the book, which she, like Hurston, situates against the backdrop of African retentions and the histories of slavery and hemispheric colonialism. She shows the advantages of a focus on Hurston's decision to inscribe herself as a performer in the text and relates this focus to the earlier presentation of Hurston's postmodernist aesthetics.

The remaining book-length Hurston text, *Dust Tracks on a Road*, has often been criticized as a very unsatisfactory life narrative. Kimberly D. Blockett and Nellie Y. McKay consider the various critiques the book has received and argue that readers have missed the central aim and achievement of the book—namely, the map it provides of Hurston as writer and as a conscious scholar of and participant in African American oral and literary traditions.

Hurston wrote a number of excellent short stories, and most anthologies choose "The Gilded Six-Bits" to represent her. Like *Jonah*, *Their Eyes*, and *Seraph*, the tale concerns a troubled marriage and the partners' efforts to find each other again after a seemingly insurmountable rupture in their relationship. Margaret D. Bauer suggests we can help students through the moral tangles of the tale by relating it to the myth of Adam and Eve in Eden. She also shows how the story may easily be related to other classic American tales, such as Nathaniel Hawthorne's "The Maypole of Merry Mount" and "Young Goodman Brown," often taught alongside Hurston's domestic narrative in American literature surveys and short fiction courses.

Hurston's role as playwright has increasingly received attention, particularly since several plays were discovered at the Library of Congress. The playwright and critic Elizabeth Brown-Guillory helps us understand Hurston's dramatic production by demonstrating methods she uses to teach three of the Floridian's early plays, *The First One*, *Color Struck*, and her three-act collaboration with Langston Hughes, *Mule Bone*. As Brown-Guillory notes, plays often require special attention from literature teachers, since drama rarely gets taught in English departments. She concentrates on stage directions and suggests that students be encouraged to act out key scenes. Like many teachers, Brown-Guillory admires Hurston's essay "Characteristics of Negro Expression," which is unusually suited to a reading of the plays. She also suggests a comparison with other plays written during the Harlem Renaissance, since Hurston's notions about theater were surely shaped by her contemporaries, as well as by the conventions of the contemporary New York stage, which was vitally interested in black-cast productions at this time. Finally, Brown-Guillory suggests themes and issues in the three plays, invariably intriguing to students, that concentrate on Africanisms in the plays, color prejudice within the race, and specifics of African American southern identity during the period graphed by Hurston.

Since these essays were commissioned and written, Hurston has enjoyed a second flowering of critical responses, many of them generated by the new interest in her politics, especially her stance in her international writing. The explosion of interest in transnational and postcolonial writing has made *Tell My Horse* perhaps the most discussed Hurston text after *Their Eyes*; she is now being situated in many new discussions of postcolonial theory, diasporan studies, and Caribbean studies. Ifeoma Nwankwo, Barbara Ladd, and Leigh Anne Duck ("'Rebirth'"), for instance, have lately considered Hurston's complex stance toward Haiti, Jamaica, and the Bahamas. Hurston's work as an anthropologist and folklorist has been interrogated by several scholars. Her plays have also drawn more scrutiny, particularly by David Krasner, who has placed her prominently in his study of African American theater.

Hurston's autobiography, *Dust Tracks on a Road*, has received several new readings, most extensively by Lesley Feracho, who considers the text alongside other key works by women writers across the Americas. It seems clear that Hurston continues to speak to a variety of audiences and issues as times and critical approaches wax and wane, surely a sign of her stature as a classic writer.

Another Hurston novel that has finally attracted significant attention is her last, *Seraph on the Suwanee*. No longer dismissed as a failed novel in which Hurston simply painted her black characters white, the book has elicited a variety of critical responses, including Chuck Jackson's fascinating application of racial eugenics and Delia Konzett's carefully nuanced consideration of the performance of gender, interracial relationships, and the portrayal of marital struggle in the novel.

Hazel Carby's much discussed critique of Hurston's alleged romanticization of the black folk has led to spirited responses, on both sides of the issue ("Politics"). Hurston's essays have also drawn attention lately, particularly by literary theorists interested in "Characteristics of Negro Expression" and "How It Feels to Be Colored Me." Cheryl A. Wall has examined "Art and Such" as part of a special issue of *Scholar and Feminist Online* on Hurston.

Teaching *Their Eyes Were Watching God* and the Process of Canon Formation

Genevieve West

My approach to teaching Hurston's *Their Eyes Were Watching God* grows out of two related pedagogical beliefs. First—to paraphrase bell hooks in *Teaching to Transgress*—one of my responsibilities as a teacher is to encourage students to ask questions about their educations. For me that responsibility includes pushing students to ask why they read one text instead of another. Second, students need an improved sense of literary tradition and of canon formation as a process. I share with them the cultural critic Cornel West's suggestion that "cultural" crisis "prompts, guides, and regulates" canonization (193). My approach to teaching *Their Eyes*, then, uses book reviews to trace the ways in which cultural changes have influenced responses to the novel and Hurston's place in the canon. Richard Wright ("Between Laughter") and Alain Locke ("Jingo"), for example, condemned the novel and Hurston. Yet since her death in 1960, she and *Their Eyes* have ridden a wave of scholarly and popular interest to become central to American, African American, and women's literary traditions. The questions for students become, How and why does a single text elicit such markedly different responses in fewer than fifty years? How and why did the novel—and Hurston—move from the margins to the center? Might both once again become marginalized?

The answers to such complex questions are difficult, sometimes elusive. I encourage students to ask questions and explore possible answers instead of offering or accepting precise answers. This approach requires that I provide overviews of Hurston's *Jonah's Gourd Vine* and *Mules and Men*, and it requires students to extend themselves. They read about books they haven't read and read reviews as ideologically embedded texts. I begin with these earlier texts because perceptions of Hurston before 1937 had a profound impact on responses to *Their Eyes* (see G. West's *Zora Neale Hurston and American Literary Culture*). Criticisms of Hurston increased over time as concerns about her literary agenda accrued. In the reviews of *Jonah's Gourd Vine*, *Mules and Men*, and *Their Eyes Were Watching God* students can follow Hurston's career as she becomes increasingly at odds with the literary establishment.

I first provide students with a brief overview of Hurston's early career, recounting accepted facts from biographies by Robert Hemenway (*Zora*), Lillie Howard (*Zora*), and Valerie Boyd. I talk about Hurston's awards from the periodical *Opportunity* for short fiction and *Color Struck*, her participation in the production of *Fire!!* with Langston Hughes and Wallace Thurman. I give them enough information on her early career and the Harlem Renaissance to establish Hurston as an up-and-comer, one to be watched. From 1933, I fast forward to 1960—the year Hurston died. I recount the tale of Hurston's death in a welfare home, her burial in an unmarked grave in a segregated cemetery, and the unavailability of her work (all out of print by then). Alice Walker's well-known essay "Looking for Zora," which records her search for Hurston's grave, provides additional depth for students. Students then face the disjunction between Hurston's early rise to prominence and her death as a marginal figure. In class we focus on four years, 1934 to 1937.

Many of the reviews I use are readily available in a single volume, Henry Louis Gates, Jr., and K. A. Appiah's *Zora Neale Hurston: Critical Perspectives Past and Present*. Most often, I make copies of selected reviews available. It is possible, however (depending on the quality of library holdings), to have students locate and bring the reviews to class. (Most students have no idea how to find book reviews, and digging around in old periodicals can capture their imaginations.) Once students have read the reviews, splitting into small groups permits each to focus on a single set of responses. Students can begin the work in class and continue afterward. The idea is to analyze the reviews: What are the sources of praise? What are the criticisms? What tone do the reviewers use? Students should note similarities and differences and which periodicals printed the reviews.

Generally, students observe that the reviews of *Jonah's Gourd Vine* by Martha Gruening and Margaret Wallace from periodicals targeting primarily white readers are enthusiastic, particularly about Hurston's use of language. Other positive and easily accessible reviews include those by Josephine Pinckney in the *New York Herald Tribune* and by John Chamberlin in the *New York Times*. Reviews appearing in periodicals targeting black readers, the *Crisis* and *Opportunity*, are more critical. Estelle Felton, for example, claims that Hurston's characters are "caricatures" and draws an unflattering comparison with Langston Hughes's first novel, *Not without Laughter* (5). In Andrew Burris's review for the *Crisis* is the first implication that Hurston's work is opportunistic. Although Burris does not openly accuse Hurston (as others will), he suggests that Hurston has "merely . . . jump[ed] on the bandwagon of the New Negro movement" (6).

In reviews of *Mules and Men* the divide between reviewers becomes still clearer, and some for the first time accuse Hurston of exploiting black culture for white readers. Evaluations by Henry Lee Moon, Lewis Gannett, and H. I. Brock in white periodicals provide only one perspective. Worth noting are positive responses, comparisons with Joel Chandler Harris's Uncle Remus tales (which is both a compliment and a criticism—depending on the source), language that (despite praise) suggests racial bias and condescension, and a sense of white outsiders looking into the quaint world of black folks.[1] Gannett notes, for example, that Hurston's informants "all lied, as only a black man can lie" (11). And what does his use of the adjective "rich" to describe the volume suggest (13)? What are the connotations, positive and negative? Brock suggests, "At the end [of *Mules and Men*] you have a very fair idea of how the other color enjoys life as well as an amazing round-up of that color's very best stories" (14). A short excerpt from or overview of *Mules and Men* easily demonstrates that Hurston's laborers do not represent "the other color" as a whole. Brock's word choice sets up an us-versus-them dichotomy, revealing his assumption that his *New York Times* readers are as white as Brock is.

Still more complex are reviews (not found in Gates and Appiah's volume) by Sterling A. Brown, Alain Locke, and Harold Preece. These reviews, in the words of Hemenway, initiate the earnest debate about "the nature and value" of Hurston's work (*Zora* 218). Locke, once one of Hurston's greatest advocates, complains about the "lack of social perspective and philosophy" ("Deep River" 9). Considering the hardships wrought by the Depression, Locke feels it his "duty to point out" that "this peasant Arcady" is "so extinct that our only possible approach to it is the idyllic and retrospective" (9). Brown reaches similar conclusions. The collection, in his words, is "incomplete; missing were the exploitation, the terrorism, the misery." He rejects Hurston's characters as "socially unconscious" (qtd. in Hemenway, *Zora* 219). Two years later he says, succinctly, "The picture is too pastoral" (*Negro* 160).

Preece's commentary takes the criticism of Hurston and her work to the next level, openly accusing her of exploitation for personal gain: "When a Negro author describes her race with such servile terms as 'Mules and Men,' critical members of the race must necessarily evaluate the author as a literary climber" (374). The difference between these two sets of reviews should be clear, and students should be aware that the most direct criticisms issue from Hurston's fellow black writer-critics Locke and Brown and from the white writer Preece in the pages of the *Crisis*, while the heartiest praise comes from white publications. This difference can initiate a discussion of the postmodern-feminist concept of positionality—that is, the importance of acknowledging the ways in which our identities and personal values shape interpretations of what we read. How, then, students should ask, are responses to Hurston's work influenced by issues related to race, class, gender, and political or social agendas?

At this point students are poised to tackle reviews of *Their Eyes*. Again, reviews from Gates and Appiah's volume should be sufficient, since it presents a range of responses, including praise in white periodicals and Richard Wright's famous response to the novel. The differences between the praise in Lucy Tompkins's and Sheila Hibben's reviews and the criticism in Locke's and Wright's reviews are stark. While Hibben in the *New York Herald Tribune* tells readers the book is "lovely," full of "Nature and salt" (21), Locke tells readers of *Opportunity* that Hurston's characters are "pseudo-primitives" ("Jingo" 18). Tompkins tells her *New York Times* readers that the novel "is beautiful" and "irresistible," while Wright in *New Masses* argues that "the novel carries no theme, no message, no purpose" ("Between Laughter" 17). Obviously these critics measure literary success with different yardsticks, but Wright and Locke also seem to be engaged in a dialogue with Tompkins and other white reviewers who praised Hurston's work. Wright's most stinging criticism highlights concerns about white America's responses to her work:

> Miss Hurston *voluntarily* continues in her novel . . . the minstrel technique that makes the "white folks" laugh. Her characters eat and laugh and cry and work and kill; they swing like a pendulum eternally in that safe and narrow orbit in which America likes to see the Negro live: between laughter and tears. (17)

To help students grapple with Wright's criticisms, Hurston's essays "What White Publishers Won't Print" and "Art and Such" can provide an important look at her literary agenda. Hurston argued against propagandistic fiction on aesthetic grounds, saying that the "groove of Race champions . . . is the line of least resistance and least originality" ("Art" 908). She wanted (white) readers to understand "that the minorities do think, and think about something other than the race problem" ("What" 952). From the perspective of her critics, Hurston's treatment of working-class, southern, black folk characters permitted racist white readers to continue in their limited (and limiting) pastoral thinking. From Hurston's perspective, however, her literary treatments of everyday life among the folk made political and social statements of their own, suggesting a vibrant, intact black culture thriving despite racist oppression. Students need to grapple with propaganda and protest as concepts crucial to understanding the values shaping Hurston's work and responses to it.

Students may want to engage in a discussion of who is right about the novel and about protest literature, but it is more productive for teachers to channel students' responses into looking at the values each review or essay advocates. For Wright and Locke, clearly the Great Depression and America's literary move toward protest literature demand a different kind of work than that advocated by Hibben and Tompkins. Teachers should encourage students to interrogate the notion of "good" literature. Who decides what is good, and how are such decisions made? What responsibilities does a minority author have to promote or protect members of his or her own group? Students can also engage gender as an issue (women reviewers tended to be more positive about the novel) and place *Their Eyes* in the social and literary context of 1937—the year Margaret Mitchell's *Gone with the Wind* won the Pulitzer Prize. The peak of the protest tradition would follow with the publication of Wright's *Uncle Tom's Children* (1938), John Steinbeck's *Grapes of Wrath* (1939), Pietro Di Donato's *Christ in Concrete* (1939), and Wright's *Native Son* (1940). In the context of increasing concerns about Hurston's literary agenda, the social crisis of the Great Depression, and the move toward social protest literature, Wright's criticisms begin to make sense. Students can see how Hurston's work and readers' responses to it push her to the margins.

I follow our discussions of Hurston's marginalization with an overview of Hurston's recovery in the 1970s and 1980s. We talk about the emphasis on oral traditions in the Black Arts movement and the emergence of second-wave feminism. Madhu Dubey's *Black Women Novelists and the Nationalist Aesthetic* has helped me come to terms with how the two movements coincided to facilitate Hurston's recovery. Elliot Butler-Evans's *Race, Gender, and Desire* might also be useful.

In the past I have lectured more on Hurston's recovery than on her marginalization, in part because students seem more familiar with more recent social history. Two valuable essays on Hurston's recovery remain Walker's "Zora Neale Hurston: A Cautionary Tale and Partisan View," which recounts her discovery of Hurston's work, and Mary Helen Washington's foreword to the 1990 Harper edition of the novel, which records the growing academic interest in Hurston in the 1960s and 1970s. Classic essays from the Black Arts movement I have successfully used with other classes include Larry Neal's "The Black Arts Movement," Hoyt W. Fuller's "Towards a Black Aesthetic," and Addison Gayle, Jr.'s "Cultural Strangulation: Black Literature and the White Aesthetic."

I argue that the Black Arts movement, feminism, and changes in American education (including an increasingly diverse student population and professoriat and the creation of black studies programs) converged to make *Their Eyes* a timely text for readers interested in black folk culture and oral traditions and a meaningful text for women, particularly black women, trying to find their own voices and trying to balance the demands of relationships with men with their own desires and needs. Walker has said of the novel, "*There is no book more important to me than this one*" ("Zora" 86).

With more advanced students, it might be possible to take class discussion in the direction of what Ann duCille has termed "Hurstonism" in critical discourse (*Coupling Convention* 69). Hurston has become such a common name in the field that in the 1990s critics used her to represent all black women writers, sometimes to the point of excluding those who do not write about the South or folk characters. Hazel Carby has been more direct in her criticisms of interest in Hurston's writings, linking it to attempts to avoid "the contemporary crisis of black urban America" ("Politics" 73). Further complicating the canonization of black women writers like Hurston, duCille points out, is that black women—for so long ignored in the academy—have become popular objects of currency, with the attendant advantages and disadvantages ("Occult"). Such difficult issues provide fertile ground for exploring the roles of teachers and critics.

In the shorter and easier version of the above approach, teachers provide students with excerpts from reviews of *Their Eyes*. Students are generally surprised at the diversity of opinion, which can prompt some of the same discussions about positionality and cultural shifts affecting canonization that arise from the more extensive approach. The big difference, however, is that, while less time-consuming, this condensed approach makes students more passive learners by placing all the responsibility on the teacher to fill in the background that can help make sense of the different responses.

Taking students through so much literary history may appear daunting, and challenging the notion of a timeless canon can unsettle students. And yet, this approach provides much-needed perspective from which students can see not only Hurston but also the concept of a canon and their education. In a good semester, students begin to ask *why* I assigned Hurston and the other authors on their syllabi. As with any approach, some students resist, but in my experience those readers who work through *Their Eyes* and its reception come to appreciate the novel better and come to understand that selecting reading material—for themselves, for their children, for their students, or for study—is an inherently political act.

NOTE

[1] For a discussion of Harris from Hurston's time, see A. Fauset.

False Gods and "Caucasian Characteristics for All": Hurston's Radical Vision in *Their Eyes Were Watching God*

Gay Wilentz

In teaching *Their Eyes Were Watching God*, I have found the most common question from students concerns Hurston's evocative title. The novel, apparently a woman's search for self-development, might be more clearly called *Janie's Story*, but the title begins by referring to the pronoun *they*. This formulation challenges the individualist conceptions and bourgeois construct of the novel. Zora Neale Hurston has been identified as a foremother to the black feminist movement but also as a precursor to the Black Arts movement and its emphasis on cultural identity and internal slavery.[1] By critiquing the mulatto "race uplifters" and privileging the folk (a tenet of the Harlem Renaissance), Hurston exposes the effects of prejudice and cultural hegemony by the larger society within the black community.[2]

Although the novel, despite its 1937 publication date, has been described as contemporary because of Janie's search for self, *Their Eyes Were Watching God* also presents a present-day ethos in its ethnic awareness and acknowledgment of heritage. Here I explore a lesser-examined theme in the novel—intraracial prejudice within all-black towns and migrant communities—exposing the underlying radical content of the novel. I focus in particular on the presentation in the last third of the novel of the dichotomy between Eatonville, an assimilated community, and the culturally rich, fertile world of the muck. Furthermore, I interrogate the character of Mrs. Turner and her worship of "Caucasian characteristics" (145), linking this topic to a discussion of the evocative title, referred to during the hurricane. In this way, the students and I explore the complexities of the move toward assimilation and its attendant color-based, intraracial prejudice, as well as Hurston's vision for a black community that is both independent of and connected to its rich, African-based cultural heritage.

Many contemporary critics of Hurston have referred to Richard Wright's condemnation of Hurston's novel in his review "Between Laughter and Tears." Wright dismisses *Their Eyes*, commenting, "In the main, her novel is not addressed to the Negro, but to a white audience whose chauvinistic tastes she knows how to satisfy" (25). In the essay "Liberation and Domination: *Their Eyes Were Watching God* and the Evolution of Capitalism," Todd McGowan notes:

> It is the contention of contemporary poststructuralist criticism, however, that a novel is politically subversive not merely because of its content, but because of a form which dismantles hierarchies and deconstructs the binary oppositions of rational thought. (109)

In this regard, McGowan follows in the footsteps of John Lowe, examining the playfulness and form of the novel as deconstructive resistance to the dominant culture, a technique Wright misses altogether. The novel's radical politics, however, expands beyond Janie's rejection of the hierarchies of patriarchy and materialism of her all-black town of Eatonville; Hurston presents a contemporary cultural critique, making a stand against both white cultural hegemony and the mulatto elite, predating the Black Arts view of internal slavery. The irony of Wright's comment is that, instead of satisfying the "chauvinistic tastes" of white society, Hurston joins Wright in exposing the effects of the dominant culture on her characters.[3] The difference is that the hegemony of white dominant culture is inscribed in the behavior and thoughts of these African American communities, even when no white people are around.

Hurston's validation of the voice of the black woman and the African-based cultural traditions of the "folk" is the embodiment of the aims of the Harlem Renaissance's "New Negroes," exemplifying Alain Locke's prediction and judgment that these writers stood for a "renewed race spirit that consciously and proudly sets itself apart" (qtd. in J. Anderson 202). Hurston reflects the most progressive artistic and cultural outlook of the Harlem Renaissance, perceiving her African heritage within the rich cultural context of her rural Floridian community rather than in the confused questioning lament "What is Africa to me?" of Countee Cullen's poem "Heritage" (250). Moreover, the novel challenges this sense of loss linked to conflicted notions of self, exposed by the values of the mulatto elite, and it stands as a precursor to a black consciousness that Hurston did not live to see (which is perhaps why this novel is now one of the most taught books on a college campus). Alice Walker, who grew up in the Black Arts time period and was instrumental in bringing Hurston's work back into print, notes in the foreword to Robert Hemenway's Hurston biography that Hurston was a little *too* close to her roots for many of her contemporaries:

> With her easy laughter and her southern drawl, her belief in doing cullud dances *authentically*, Zora seemed—among these genteel "New Negroes" of the Harlem Renaissance—*black*. . . . Though almost everyone agreed she was a delight, not everyone agreed such audacious black delight was permissible, or, indeed, quite the proper image for the race. (xv)

Of course this image of being black and connecting to her African cultural traditions makes Hurston, in our historical moment, a spiritual foremother to current concepts of the cultural self, a writer rejecting the Anglo-Saxonizing elements encoded in the works of many of her contemporaries.

Hurston's claim in *Dust Tracks on the Road*, as well as in her critical works, that she was sick of writing about the "Race Problem" (151) does not necessarily indicate that she did not feel a commitment to writing about the rich cultural traditions that she saw all around her. Angela Albright uses this famous quotation from *Dust Tracks on a Road* to identify *Their Eyes* as a "blueprint for Negro writing." Albright states that the novel is "clearly a story about a woman's coming to self-knowledge and gaining independence and less a story of race, though race is certainly at issue as well" (2). The most explicit theme of the novel, and one that students pick up on, is Janie's self-determination as a woman. If we return to *Dust Tracks* later in the same chapter, however, Hurston once again flips her earlier statement on the race problem in her tricksterlike style. She goes on to mention some of the other statements of the time, from "Race Prejudice" to "Race Consciousness." In her comments on race consciousness, Hurston notes that "no Negro in America is apt to forget his race." She adds, while discussing the intraracial (including class) conflicts, "The upper-class Negroes admit it in their own phrases. The lower-class Negroes say it with a *tale*" (159; emphasis added). In contemporary concepts of the intersections of race, sex, class, and culture, we can witness how Janie's story is a tale indelibly connected to the communal "they" referenced in the title. The novel explicitly explores Janie's search for her self as a woman as well as her self as part of a discredited but alternative African cultural base that Hurston felt gave life to her community.

By linking her creative fiction with the orature that inspired her, Hurston weaves a larger folktale of the white dominant culture as a false god that must eventually be discredited. Aspects of the novel's cultural resistance to this imposition appear throughout the work, examples being Janie's search for values in relation to the privileging of her light skin and "good" hair and the materialism identified in perceiving Jody initially as Mr. Washborn, a white man. The final third of the novel explicitly links the jealousy, quest for values, and intraracial prejudice. Janie's move to the muck with Tea Cake after the death of Jody brings together these conflicts within Janie's world and Hurston's aims in creating a culturally healthy self and community.

For Janie, life on the muck is very different from life in Eatonville. The white imagery in the Eatonville section is striking. Jody builds a "gloaty, sparkly white" house in the tradition of the old plantations and a large white porch for Janie to sit on (47). Jody, like the black bourgeoisie, who, according to E. Franklin Frazier, strove "to make itself over in the image of the white man" (131), desired to change his community into one that would be comparable with the white town up the road. Within his conceptualization of material success, Jody cannot understand Janie's disillusionment with their relationship because he did what he promised—made a "big woman" out of her (46). Yet Janie happily leaves her privilege and comfortable white house to find her own values in the rich, black soil of the muck, in its stories and folktales, and in the warm feeling of friendship shared there. Although she does not give up all her security—she keeps the house—through the rejection of the trapping of those values associated with the dominant culture, Janie becomes self-determining:

> Sometimes Janie would think of the old days in the big white house and the store and laugh to herself. What if Eatonville could see her now in her blue denim overalls and heavy shoes? The crowd of people around her

> and a dice game on her floor! She was sorry for her friends back there and scornful of the others. The men held arguments here like they used to do on the store porch. Only here, she could listen and laugh and even talk some herself if she wanted to. (134)

Through her love and spiritual partnership with Tea Cake as well as her active involvement in the storytelling, Janie finds an alternative to the impositions of white dominant culture that is not only hostile and unattainable but also sterile and confining. Tea Cake and Janie are not like the mulatto Mrs. Turner; they make no distinctions concerning the folks. They bring the West Indians into their group of friends, and their house is a center of activity. Unlike the big white house in Eatonville, which became a center by power and fear, Tea Cake and Janie's place on the muck is a center fashioned by her African diaspora community.

For Hurston, the muck represents a repository of African cultural traditions and a linking of the Afro-Caribbeans and the African Americans. Moreover, instead of dealing with the conflicted sense of one's African heritage externally, as we see in Cullen's poem, Hurston looks within the culture to validate those traditions. In her desire to be part of the storytelling traditions, Janie is not just reflecting a woman's desire for articulating her voice, as many critics have pointed out, but also emulating the role of African women to pass on the traditions in their communities.[4] Akua Duku Anokye comments in an essay on Hurston's letters that "[t]he ability of a person to use an active and variegated verbal performance to achieve recognition within the group is widespread in the African-American community, having its roots in African verbal art" (151). This view is clearly reflected in the novel as Janie becomes part of this African-based community. And if we might have missed the connections through a lack of knowledge of African cultural traditions in the United States, Hurston emphasizes the stronger Caribbean links to their African heritage as well as the legend of the Flying Africans. As their Bahaman friend 'Lias leaves the 'Glades before the hurricane, he tells them, "If Ah never see you no mo' on earth, Ah'll meet you in Africa" (156). Even as the storm threatens to break up this close-knit community, Janie and Tea Cake retain allegiance to the folk culture and the black world.

Yet even in the muck, which is rich and black and big and free, Janie must deal with the white hegemony, seen through the eyes of Mrs. Turner. For Hurston, Mrs. Turner is not a tragic mulatto, a trope identified in nineteenth- and early twentieth-century literature, but a ridiculous one.[5] Mrs. Turner is a caricature of African Americans who wish to reject their African heritage and try to assimilate into a hostile culture. She exemplifies the most extreme form of white identification—idol worship—demonstrating how warped a person can become when she chooses the white features as her god. Janie's "Caucasian" features, which are incidental to her, become paramount to Mrs. Turner. She separates Janie and herself from dark members of the community like Tea Cake. Janie, whose sense of identity is more grounded in her culture, does not understand why this distinction is necessary. In answer to Mrs. Turner's suggestion that they "class off," Janie replies, "Us can't *do* it. We'se uh mingled people and all of us got black kinfolks as well as yaller kinfolks" (141). Mrs. Turner is horrified that Janie lets her whiteness be subjected to "defilement" by Tea Cake's blackness (145), for Mrs. Turner has deified white features and is prepared to worship them and anyone who fits this description:

> Anyone who looked more white folkish than herself was better than she was in her criteria, therefore it was right that they should be cruel to her at times, just as she was cruel to those more negroid than herself in direct ratio to their negroness. . . . Once having set up her idols and built altars to them it was inevitable that she would worship there. It was inevitable that she should accept any inconsistency and cruelty from her deity as all good worshippers do from theirs. . . .
>
> Mrs. Turner, like all other believers had built an altar to the unattainable—Caucasian characteristics for all. Her god would smite her, would hurl her from pinnacles and lose her in deserts, but she would not forsake his altars. (144–45)

It is evident to those living on the muck, as well as to the readers, that Mrs. Turner's views are distorted. Overcome by the hegemonic impulses of the dominant culture, Mrs. Turner expresses views that alienate her from the others in her community to her own disadvantage while bringing her no closer to white people or the white features she worships. As we discuss in class, Tea Cake states humorously that Mrs. Turner lives in a fantasy of looking "white," since her hair is "jus' as close tuh her head as ninety-nine is tuh uh hundred" (143). Still, her view cannot be totally ignored, since it is referred to throughout this last section, linking Tea Cake's behavior to the events of the hurricane.

While Mrs. Turner ostensibly has little effect on Janie, that is not true for Tea Cake. Although Hurston writes that Mrs. Turner's views "didn't affect Tea Cake and Janie too much" (145), it is Mrs. Turner's light-skinned brother who is the object of Tea Cake's jealousy and leads to Tea Cake's beating of Janie. This incident, often disturbing to readers and students, appears out of character for Tea Cake, who is portrayed in the novel as a wonderful and equal partner to Janie. And often the scene in which Tea Cake beats Janie after Mrs. Turner's brother comes to the muck is interpreted solely on gender lines. Regarding the hegemonic structures of white dominant culture in all-black communities, however, we can witness an earlier version of Amiri Baraka's notions of internal slavery affecting Tea Cake through his discomfort with his dark skin. In some ways, Tea Cake's jealousy mirrors the behavior of Logan and Jody, and it is clear that Tea Cake beats Janie to send a message to Mrs. Turner and the community at large. Still, the discussion between Tea Cake and Sop de Bottom after the beating clearly emulates the convoluted concepts of linking skin color to earlier views of the plantation mistress versus the "African" female slave.[6] After declaring to Tea Cake, "you sho is a lucky man," Sop de Bottom makes his telling comment:

> Uh person can see every place you hit her. Ah bet she never raised her hand tuh hit yuh back, neither. Take some uh dese ol' rusty black women and dey would fight yuh all night long and next day nobody couldn't tell you ever hit 'em. (147)

These men in the muck, in this case both African American and Caribbean, reinforce the opposition between the tough dark-skinned women and the supposedly weak, privileged, light-skinned ones. Furthermore, they disparage the strength of what they see as a more Africanized woman and glorify an outdated notion of Victorian womanhood, reflected in the plantation mistress, what Ama Ata Aidoo calls the "dolls of the colonisers" (*Our Sister* 117).[7]

This scene is situated just after the section about Mrs. Turner's worshipping of Caucasian characteristics and right before the hurricane. During the hurricane section, there are references to the title as well as to the folkloric concepts of God as slave master. Hurston's understanding of the role of both God and the devil in African American folklore is identified in the glossary to her *Mules and Men* collection:

> The devil is not the terror that he is in European folk-lore. He is a powerful trickster who often competes successfully with God. There is a strong suspicion that the devil is an extension of the story-makers while God is the supposedly impregnable white masters, who are nevertheless defeated by the Negroes. (248)

The piecing together of this folkloric concept of the false god of white dominant practice encoded in the novel comes from what might be conceived as various subplots, isolated incidents, and plot devices. Discussion of the hurricane has been identified as a plot device to reflect the historical circumstances at the time and to move forward Janie's development, since it is clearly linked to Tea Cake's demise.

In "'The Monstropolous Beast': The Hurricane in Zora Neale Hurston's *Their Eyes Were Watching God*," Anna Lillios discusses Hurston's use of anthropological research and her own experiences in both Caribbean and Floridian hurricanes. Lillios then links Hurston's characters with the victims Hurston interviewed:

> Like the real-life victims of this natural catastrophe, Janie comes in touch with God as the creator of earthly disturbances and maker of destinies. Yet, Hurston drops the notion of God in the rest of the book and does not elucidate Janie's spiritual development. (91)

Although Lillios gives us good background to the hurricane and clearly establishes that people do pray when fearful, she misses the political implications of this section. By linking up issues of the valuing of white dominant culture with Mrs. Turner's worship of white features, Hurston gives us a secondary reading of God that indicates a reference not only to a supreme deity but also to the power of white hegemony.

Despite the problematic incidents identified here, Janie and Tea Cake's life on the muck appears idyllic until the hurricane comes. They have set up an African diaspora community and live in peace with the "Indians in their long, narrow dug-outs calmly winning their living in the trackless ways of the 'Glades" (130)—although this description offers a romanticized view of their life. Nevertheless, when the hurricane approaches, Tea Cake does not follow the Indians or listen to the voice of his Caribbean friend, even though he and Janie are relatively new to the muck. In a portentous conversation, Tea Cake and 'Lias discuss whether to leave the area or not. 'Lias comments to Tea Cake, "De Indians gahn east, man. It's dangerous." Tea Cake responds, "Dey don't always know. Indians don't know much uh nothin', tuh tell de truth. Else dey'd own dis country still. De white folks ain't gone nowhere. Dey oughta know if it's dangerous. You better stay heah, man." 'Lias answers, "[Y]ou gointuh wish you follow crow," and then leaves, saying, as cited earlier, that if he sees them no more on earth, he'll meet them back in Africa (156). As we discuss in class (especially living in eastern North Carolina, an area prone to hurricanes and floods), 'Lias's presentiments prove correct. But what we focus on is the fact that, rather than listen to the Native Americans, who have historically demonstrated a closer relation to nature, Tea Cake and the others follow the white folks, who live in more secure houses and on higher ground. So the question is, Why? Tea Cake's response to 'Lias is a perfect example of the effects of hegemony, where people act against their own best interests to support dominant practice.

At this point we return to the novel's title, to which there are numerous references. As the group that has remained in Tea Cake's house "huddle[s]" together and wonders about the wisdom of their choice to stay, the voice of the narrator returns to Tea Cake's comments to 'Lias: "The time was past for asking the white folks what to look for through that door. Six eyes were questioning *God*" (159). Just a few paragraphs after this reference to looking to the "white folks" for answers to the storm comes an exact reference to the title: "They seemed to be staring at the dark, but their eyes were watching God" (160). Returning to the glossary's view of God as the slave master and the devil as the trickster slave, we see that this section reinforces the folkloric context of the novel. During this scene, there are numerous references made to God as "bossman" and "Ole Massa." The God they are watching appears as a capricious slave master whose whims and dangerous acts are uncontrollable. Throughout the hurricane section, Hurston keeps us constantly aware of the duality of the Christian God with the God of the slave owners. This God of the white man takes on a sinister role in contradistinction to the savior God of the community's church. Therefore, the title and the word *God* incorporate a double yet contradictory meaning: There is the God to whom we look for answers and pray for help, and there is the other god, the cruel, false god whom we need to watch with a wary eye.

In an essay written in the 1970s, Roger Rosenblatt notes that Tea Cake and Janie "flourish" only when they "avoid the white world" (90). This novel exposes, however, that it is not so easy to avoid the white worldview, even when physically separated from that world. The Palm Beach incident, which has often been viewed as the only explicit example of racial injustice in the novel, appears in the light of this analysis to be a concrete representation of what has been happening all along: the imposition of the dominant culture on an oppressed group, whether the oppression be physical or psychological. When Janie and Tea Cake are pushed off the bridge in the storm to make room for the white people, and later in Palm Beach when Tea Cake is forced to throw the black corpses in a pit while he buries the white ones, spending precious time separating the bloated bodies, we see how Janie and Tea Cake are oppressed by the white world. Yet equally destructive to their sense of well-being are the Mrs. Turners and the internal oppression imposed on their community.

The glossary's notion of God as the slave master is once again alluded to in Janie's thoughts about help from God when Tea Cake is dying. Janie realizes that Tea Cake, bitten by a rabid dog while trying to save her from drowning, will "die for loving her." Questioning their fate, Janie looks up into the "blue ether" of the sky and waits for a sign. Like the cold, blue eyes of the slave master, "[t]he sky stayed hard looking and quiet so she went inside the house. God would do less than He had in His heart" (178). Janie sees no recourse in the God of the white man or in the dominant culture. Certainly the white doctor who tells her how dangerous Tea Cake is never sends the medicine to make Tea Cake's dying easier for him and less threatening to Janie. After Janie is forced to kill the rabid Tea Cake in self-defense, she "thank[s] him wordlessly for giving her the chance for loving service" (184). Janie realizes that she need not look to external sources to save Tea Cake, since love is stronger than death: "If you kin see de light at daybreak, you don't keer if you die at dusk" (159).

When Janie returns to Eatonville after Tea Cake's death, without him and without the fancy clothes she left with, she feels no need to justify herself to the community. The community of Eatonville educated her on the denial of one's cultural self and identity, but by becoming part of her rich cultural traditions, she found herself. Janie's advice to the town is that they better stop watching the false god and find out what their own lives are about before they go to God: "Two things everybody's got tuh do fuh theyselves. They got tuh go tuh God, and they got tuh find out about livin' fuh theyselves" (192). Janie does just that. She finds her humanity against all odds, despite the price she must pay for losing Tea Cake. The ending of the novel has been identified in feminist readings as an example of an African American woman who emerges whole: "Here was peace. She pulled in her horizon like a great fish-net. Pulled it from around the waist of the world and draped it over her shoulder. So much of life in its meshes! She called in her soul to come and see" (193). Yet Hurston's radical vision also clearly identifies this novel as one of cultural resistance. The novel is not negative, but it details Janie's fight for self-determination by negating the values imposed by white dominant culture during a period of change for African Americans. And although Janie's own values are not concretely articulated in the novel, they are real and fluid creations of a gendered and cultural self. Janie's resistance to the dominant culture is in itself a positive step, a life-affirming process that has evolved from the folk culture—a culture that has sought to keep its humanity in a hostile and life-opposing world.

In the introduction to *The Black Aesthetic*, Addison Gayle, Jr., notes that the black aesthetic "is a corrective—a means of helping black people out of the polluted mainstream of Americanism" (xxiii). He goes on to say that there are many approaches to this act of literary resistance, but few "would disagree with the idea that unique experiences produce unique cultural artifacts, and that art is a product of such cultural experiences" (xxiv). Although the language that Hurston uses to create her production of cultural experience is very different from Gayle's, it is clear that *Their Eyes* is a precursor to the acts of cultural resistance that the Black Arts movement calls for. In this context, we can comprehend *Their Eyes Were Watching God* as a broader type of folktale or folk novel similar to the dilemma tales of West Africa. Hurston's moral is that one can be proud of one's cultural heritage and should not look solely to the false gods of the white world. This interpretation does not deny other readings of the novel, but it certainly rejects the criticism of this novel as one filled with "facile sensuality that has dogged Negro expression" (Wright, "Between Laughter" 25). In "Private Thoughts, Public Voices: Letters from Zora Neale Hurston," Anokye questions why Hurston's voice needs to be restricted to only one voice, commenting, "It is precisely because she possessed a folk voice, a political voice, a racial voice, even a trickster voice, that we find her so intriguing" (150). All these voices come through in her multilayered novel. For Hurston herself seems to have taken on the role of the folk trickster: she tricked those early critics who perceived her as apolitical with her positive resistance—her ability to negate the values of the dominant culture in this novel without once saying it outright.

NOTES

1 For a full discussion of the tenets of the Black Arts movement, see the seminal study *The Black Aesthetic*, edited by Addison Gayle, Jr.

2 See Raymond Williams's discussion of totality and "the *selective tradition*" in his essay "Base and Superstructure in Marxist Cultural Theory" for further deliberation on my usage of hegemony and its effects on oppressed groups (39).

3 One irony of Wright's treatment of Hurston's novel and the aims of the Black Arts movement is that Hurston's novel reflects an aspect of this movement that Wright does not deal with. Hurston's validation of an African cultural base in her writings and her

resistance to the imposition of the dominant culture clearly predate and are easily identified with Black Arts works such as Paul Carter Harrison's *Kuntu Drama: Plays of the African Continuum.*

[4] See Gay Wilentz's introduction to her *Binding Cultures: Black Women Writers in Africa and the Diaspora* and "Toward a Diaspora Literature" for the role of women of African descent passing on cultural traditions.

[5] The trope of the tragic mulatto runs throughout the nineteenth and early twentieth centuries. See, for example, nineteenth-century novels like William Wells Brown's *Clotel*, Frances Ellen Watkins Harper's *Iola Leroy*, and Pauline Hopkins's *Contending Forces*, as well as *Quicksand* by Nella Larsen, another Harlem Renaissance writer.

[6] The binary opposition of the white plantation mistress and the African slave woman (especially one brought over on the slave ship) is, on the one hand, a stereotype that has plagued African American women in terms of gender and color prejudice. On the other hand, this stereotype is both flipped and dislodged if we examine the Eurocentric values that go into this view (see note 7).

[7] In her novel *Our Sister Killjoy; or, Reflections from a Black-Eyed Squint*, Aidoo comments that African men influenced by "hashed-up Victorian notions" of womanhood have forgotten the significant role of the West African woman in non-Westernized settings (117). In her more recent essay "Literature, Feminism, and the African Woman Today," Aidoo further examines the role of precolonial and postcolonial African women, stating that "in West Africa, she had been far better off than women of so many other societies" (30). For a further reading of Aidoo's critical and creative vision, see Wilentz, "Reading the Critical Writer."

History, Mythology, and the Proletarian in *Their Eyes Were Watching God*

Carla Cappetti

"Who owns Zora Neale Hurston?" Michele Wallace skeptically asked in 1990, as scholarly conferences, critical collections, and handsome editions of Hurston's work multiplied. "[L]ike groupies descending on Elvis Presley's estate," Wallace writes, "critics are engaged in a mostly ill-mannered rush to have some memento of the black woman" (174). The generally stately pace of the critics had become a stampede, starting with the canon wars of the 1980s. Since then, and with the assistance of three new biographies (Hemenway, *Zora*; Howard, *Zora*; Plant, *Zora*), the Hurston cottage industry has grown into a large-scale mainstream and academic industry. As a result, Zora Neale Hurston (1891–1960) has probably received more critical attention since the early 1980s than most twentieth-century American authors.[1]

Hurston, as Wallace points out, was fetishized as a symbolic ancestor, who is by definition beyond history. Hurston's removal from history made her politics and her worldview negligible. In the role of sentimental heroine and self-made woman, Hurston was cast as a southern peasant who triumphed over circumstances to become a famous novelist and anthropologist.[2] This role has reinforced the fetish. Hurston was, in fact, "one among the well-educated, well-read Black women authors of her era." She had lived and studied at the centers of intellectual and artistic power of the black bourgeoisie and of the United States (Foreman 659).

The earliest rediscovery was prompted by Hurston's death. "The Hurston revival," according to Adele Newson, "began, ironically, with a sympathetic obituary written in 1960, the year of her death" and the early dawn of the civil rights and the feminist movements (27; see also Hemenway, *Zora*). As these movements flooded the streets and spilled into academia, students and scholars asked why African American authors, male and female, and female authors, black and white, were absent from teachers' syllabi and scholars' research. A tangible and overdue outcome has been the visibility of African American literature in high school and college literature courses. In addition, Zora Neale Hurston has become the African American author of choice in literary humanities and United States literature surveys, and *Their Eyes Were Watching God* is now the African American novel that students are most likely to have read. This shift could not have happened without a large investment of intellectual resources in Hurston studies.

Starting in the 1980s, the rise of political conservatism has accompanied the popularity of *Their Eyes Were Watching God* at the expense of more explicitly urban and sociological authors like Richard Wright, Ann Petry, Ralph Ellison, and James Baldwin, who are now more likely to be read in specialized courses on African American literature than in literary surveys. The differences between *Their Eyes* and *Native Son*, the novel that has suffered most from Hurston's fame, exemplifies this conservative shift. *Their Eyes* can be read as a story outside time and place; *Native Son* cannot. Eatonville and the Everglades are less scary and more exotic than the Chicago black belt. Janie can be everyman or everywoman. Bigger Thomas cannot. Janie is escaping conformity and alienation—tormentors of many times, places, and people—while Bigger Thomas is escaping the police and possible lynching, not quite as universal an experience. The porch sessions of Eatonville and the Everglades and Janie's yearning for fulfillment have a timeless quality that lulls the reader away from reality and history. One can more easily ignore history and society in *Their Eyes* than in *Native Son*, a novel that only with difficulty lends itself to mythical or universal readings.

Their Eyes Were Watching God is a modernist novel, a historical novel, and a novel of manners. As such it fits nicely in many college courses. *Their Eyes* is also an ambivalent and recalcitrant proletarian novel of the red decade.[3] Because this genre is not valued—just as the literature of African Americans, women, and immigrants was not valued—the conflicted proletarian aesthetic and antiproletarian politics of the novel remain invisible. My argument here is threefold. First, as a proletarian novel of the 1930s, *Their Eyes* displays the precarious status that gender and ethnicity occupy in the proletarian novel, which was predominantly northern, urban, industrial, white, and male. Second, when we place *Their Eyes* in the dominant literary genre of the red decade, we can see its antiproletarian poetics and better understand its meaning. Third, reading *Their Eyes* as a proletarian novel gives us access to a more complicated, interesting, and accurate Hurston than a fetish or a myth allows.[4]

I first examine Janie's bourgeois romantic adventures as an escape from bondage and a quest for freedom through love and property, marriage and wealth. Janie's early matrimonial adventures—I suggest—celebrate the African American quest for empowerment through property and capital, in the good old-fashioned American way of the self-made man. Her adventures also expose the failure of that economic success, which leaves the African American woman still unfree and disempowered.

I then consider Janie's proletarian adventures in the work camps of southern Florida as an escape from history and a descent into nature.[5] Janie's proletarian romance with Tea Cake, her encounter with the soul of the proletarian black folk, and her escape from the bestial ferocity of nature capture the artistic quest for identity among the rural and urban proletariat of the Harlem Renaissance and of the 1930s. Janie's experience in the Everglades also highlights Hurston's uncomfortable embrace of the proletarian and primitivist aesthetic of the red decade.[6]

The novel opens with a narrative frame that captures the protagonist's homecoming, alienation, and exile.[7] The outer frame locates Janie and Eatonville in the narrative present and places the reader at the side of Pheoby, the faithful friend, sympathetic listener, and alter ego for the audience. The framed retrospective narrative recounts Janie's adventures, her life, and her becoming the grown woman who, Odysseus-like, has just come home.

Janie's return is the final destination of a journey that began long ago, a journey that is lyrical and epic, personal and historical, mythical and political. The narrative follows Janie's movements from the "white folks' back-yard" of her first childhood (9), to an independent cabin acquired by her grandmother "so you wouldn't have to stay in de white folks' yard and tuck yo' head befo' other chillun at school" (19), to the isolated sixty-acres farm of Logan Killicks, to the all-black town of Eatonville with Joe Starks, to the all-black and all-poor "muck" in the Everglades with Tea Cake, and, finally, back to Eatonville and the back porch, where the novel begins and ends.

Janie's life journey, the framed narrative, is composed of three movements. Janie's romantic yearnings and unromantic marriages, in the first part of the novel, recapitulate key moments of African American history before and after the Civil War. Janie's captivity in two conventional marriages highlights the black bourgeoisie's economic success, cultural dependence, and domination over women. Janie escapes south from Eatonville—in the second part—to the world of wild nature, the black proletariat, and folk culture. In the third and final part, Janie returns to Eatonville, to the world of modern bourgeois society, while the narrative returns to the outer frame and brings the story to its bittersweet ending.

The social world and experiences that make up the first part of Janie's life journey belong to what Umberto Eco calls "the world as it is": "the official order of the universe" and its "social contradictions."[8] The "world as it is" of Janie's adolescence and young womanhood is the world of arranged marriages, not romantic love. It is also the world of the African American experience in the nineteenth and early twentieth centuries as represented by the ex-slave Nanny, the farmer Killicks, and the entrepreneur-cum-politician Starks.

To convince Janie to marry Logan Killicks, Nanny tells her life story to Janie. Modeled on the slave narrative tradition, the life story creates a bridge between Janie's predicament and Nanny's under and after slavery—"Ah was born back due in slavery" (16). On the basis of those experiences, Nanny explains to Janie that the system was and remains fundamentally sexist and racist—with or without slavery. "Honey, de white man is de ruler of everything as fur as Ah been able tuh find out" (14). Decades before modern feminism found the language for articulating this condition, Nanny teaches Janie that the black woman is victim of multiple forms of oppression:

> [D]e white man throw down de load and tell de nigger man tuh pick it up. He pick it up because he have to, but he don't tote it. He hand it to his womenfolks. De nigger woman is de mule uh de world so fur as Ah can see. Ah been prayin' fuh it tuh be different wid you. Lawd, Lawd, Lawd! (14)

Nanny's lesson to Janie, and Hurston's to her readers, is that the black woman is still the slave of a slave.

To protect Janie against double slavery, Nanny insists that she marry Logan Killicks, an older man of respectable means and property. That he is old and inspires in Janie no romantic love does not factor into Nanny's plans. Nanny wishes to die knowing that Janie will not suffer the sexual exploitation suffered by her mother and grandmother:

> 'Tain't Logan Killicks Ah wants you to have, baby, it's protection. Ah ain't gittin' ole, honey. Ah'm *done* ole. . . . Ah ast de Lawd when you was uh infant in mah arms to let me stay here till you got grown . . . till Ah see you safe in life. (15)

At first Janie resists Nanny's persuasive sermon, but she eventually acquiesces only to recognize, too late, the errors of Nanny's reasoning. When a few weeks into her first marriage, she complains that marriage has not produced the promised love, Nanny scolds her without pity:

> You come heah wid yo' mouf full uh foolishness on uh busy day . . . and you come worryin' me 'bout love. . . .
>
> . . . Heah you is wid de onliest organ in town, amongst colored folks, in yo' parlor. Got a house bought and paid for and sixty acres uh land right on de big road and . . . Lawd have mussy! Dat's de very prong all us black women gits hung on. Dis love! (23; 3rd ellipsis in orig.)

Janie, however, grows to despise the sixty acres of land—"Ah could throw ten acres of it over de fence every day and never look back to see where it fell" (23–24)—and to hate her aged and unattractive husband, who loves only his property, not his wife. Like other literary heroines, Janie eventually reclaims her right to romantic love, to the free choice of her partner, to a marriage of love and not just work, thrift, and convenience: "Ah wants things sweet wid mah marriage lak when you sit under a pear tree and think" (43).[9]

Janie and Nanny's dialogue about protection and love is the dialogue of two generations with incompatible histories and ideals. Nanny is determined to protect Janie from the sexual exploitation and physical violence that she suffered under slavery and that Janie's mother suffered in freedom: "Ah didn't want to be used for a work-ox and a brood-sow and Ah didn't want mah daughter used dat way neither. . . . And Ah can't die easy thinkin' maybe de menfolks white or black is makin' a spit cup outa you" (16–20). Nanny's ideal is modeled on the white women of the Old South that she served. Sitting on the white rocking chairs, on the white porches, in front of the white houses, these women are for Nanny the epitome of femininity and protection, even in the absence of love or autonomy: "Ah been waitin' a long time, Janie, but nothin' Ah been through ain't too much if you just take a stand on high ground lak Ah dreamed" (16).

Nanny's historical wisdom, however, is imposed onto a new generation that is twice removed from the antebellum South and that inhabits the world of racism and sexism under modern capitalism, not under slavery.[10]

Just as Nanny brings into the novel the history of slavery, Logan Killicks and Joe Starks, their striking diversity notwithstanding, evoke the times of Reconstruction and post-Reconstruction. Readers tend to focus on the sexism of the two men and neglect the heroism of their wealth—which Hurston unequivocally celebrates. Readers also neglect the racism that makes the men's capitalism heroic.[11]

W. E. B. DuBois had acknowledged this heroism. In *The Souls of Black Folk*, DuBois captures the dream of Reconstruction and the cruelty of its demise in words that highlight the historical identity of Killicks and Starks:

> [T]he vision of *"forty acres and a mule"*—the righteous and reasonable ambition to become a landholder, which the nation had all but categorically promised the freedmen—was destined in most cases to bitter disappointment. And those men of marvelous hindsight who are today seeking to preach the Negro back to the present peonage of the soil know well, or ought to know, that the opportunity of binding the Negro peasant willingly to the soil was lost on that day when the Commissioner of the Freedmen's Bureau had to go to South Carolina and tell the weeping freedmen, after their years of toil, that their land was not theirs, that there was a mistake—somewhere. If by 1874 the Georgia Negro alone owned three hundred acres of land, it was by grace of his thrift rather than by bounty of the government. (71; my emphasis)

The triumph of Starks and Killicks shines when observed through DuBois's analysis of African Americans in the South, and his chagrin at the "small amount of accumulated capital" in their hands by the late nineteenth century (181):

> And yet these fifteen thousand acres are a creditable showing,—a proof of no little weight of the worth and ability of the Negro people. If they had been given an economic start at Emancipation, if they had been in an enlightened and rich community, which really desired their best good, then we might perhaps call such a result small or even insignificant. But for a few thousand poor ignorant field hands, in the face of poverty, a falling market, and social stress, to save and capitalize two hundred thousand dollars in a generation has meant a tremendous effort. . . . Out of the hard economic conditions of this portion of the Black Belt, *only six per cent of the population have succeeded in emerging into peasant proprietorship*; and these are not all firmly fixed, but grow and shrink in number with the wavering of the cotton-market. Fully ninety-four per cent have struggled for land and failed, and half of them sit in hopeless serfdom.
> (185; my emphasis)

DuBois is generally associated with the concept of the "Talented Tenth" and with the northern urban intellectuals who were to produce the leaders of the black folk. Killicks and Starks represent the "Talented Tenth" of the South. They belong to an exceptional minority of southern blacks who became landowners, as DuBois bitterly notes, "by grace of [their] thrift rather than by bounty of the government," and who are heroic because their wealth was accumulated in the face of the greatest odds.

Killicks and Starks also evoke the political debates of post-Reconstruction over self-improvement. Logan Killicks is the quintessential self-made man, in its African American, southern, and rural incarnation. In contrast to Joe Starks, Killicks represents a traditional model of capital accumulation that is built on thrift, saving, hard work, and land ownership. He embodies the rural African American petit bourgeoisie of the late nineteenth century that found in Booker T. Washington its political voice and in his self-help ethic a model of social advancement independent of political and civil rights.

By contrast, Joe Starks represents a newer type of wealth, and, appropriately, his marriage with Janie brings romantic and economic free enterprise together. Starks's power is built on free enterprise: capital accumulation, commerce, and speculation. He personifies the urban entrepreneurial black bourgeoisie of the early twentieth century that found a voice in the nationalist leader Marcus Garvey (Zagato 44). Garvey was the modern and urban interpreter of Washington, and his presence can be detected in the values, rhetoric, and style that Starks generously delivers to the Eatonville inhabitants:

> Joe Starks was the name, yeah Joe Starks from in and through Georgy. . . . [W]hen he heard all about 'em makin' a town all outa colored folks, he knowed dat was de place he wanted to be. He had always wanted to be a big voice, but de white folks had all de sayso where he come from and everywhere else, exceptin' dis place dat colored folks was buildin' theirselves. Dat was right too. De man dat built things oughta boss it. Let colored folks build things too if dey wants to crow over somethin'. He was glad he had his money all saved up. He meant to git dere whilst de town wuz yet a baby. He meant to buy in big. It had always been his wish and desire to be a big voice and he had to live nearly thirty years to find a chance. (28)

Starks's arrival in Eatonville produces a total revolution. In the first place, he "ups and buys two hundred acres uh land at one whack and pays cash for it" (38). This mesmerizes a town that, in his estimation, needs a leader and a dose of energy: "God, they call this a town? Why, 'tain't nothing but a raw place in de woods. . . . A whole heap uh talk and nobody doin' nothin'. I god, where's de Mayor? . . . Ah want tuh speak wid de Mayor" (34). Starks builds the streets, puts in streetlights, opens a store, brings a post office, and leads the political founding of the town. In short, he becomes the leader of the community and the interpreter of its ambition to become independent.

Entrepreneur, speculator, mayor, petit capitalist, and shop owner, Joe Starks represents a new South that is modeled after the entrepreneurial bourgeoisie of the North. Ironically, Starks chooses symbols of power that evoke the southern slaveholding aristocracy. The large white house that he builds, the white columns, the brass spittoon, the light skin and flowing hair of his wife, his demand that Janie take on the role of the white women of the Old South, even the liberation and the mock funeral of the mule—all bespeak a political autonomy that remains culturally and ideologically in a colonized and subaltern position.

Janie comes to hate Joe Starks as she realizes that this marriage, even though freely chosen for love, for a bigger horizon, for a handsome and eloquent man, has become yet again a relationship of alienation, not love.[12] On the death of Starks, and not one minute before, Janie realizes that Nanny's worldview and the marriages it has produced, both the arranged marriage with Killicks and the love marriage with Starks, have failed to deliver the pear tree. The interior monologue that expresses this painful insight takes shape after Joe's lavish funeral:

> She *hated* her grandmother and had hidden it from herself all these years under a cloak of pity. . . . Nanny had taken the biggest thing God ever made, the horizon—for no matter how far a person can go the horizon is still way beyond you—and pinched it in to such a little bit of a thing that she could tie it about her granddaughter's neck tight enough to choke her. *She hated the old woman* who had twisted her so in the name of love.
> (89; my emphases)

And then once more, in a dialogue with Pheoby that precedes her departure from Eatonville with Tea Cake, Janie defies her grandmother and the worldview she represents:

> Ah done lived Grandma's way, now Ah means tuh live mine. . . .
> She was borned in slavery time when folks, dat is black folks, didn't sit down anytime dey felt lak it. So sittin' on porches lak de white madam looked lak uh mighty fine thing tuh her. Dat's whut she wanted for me—don't keer whut it cost. Git up on uh high chair and sit dere. She didn't have time tuh think whut tuh do after you got up on de stool uh do nothin'. De object wuz tuh git dere. So Ah got up on de high stool lak she told me, but Pheoby, Ah done nearly languished tuh death up dere. Ah felt like de world wuz cryin' extry and Ah ain't read de common news yet. (114)

In harsh and angry language, Janie denounces the failure of the past and signals her determination to be free.[13] Her defiance echoes that of the young African American women who, in the early twentieth century, fought against the Victorian ideology of black womanhood. Through Janie, Hurston was likewise declaring her independence from the forms, the styles, and the ideals of the nineteenth century and of the black bourgeoisie, with which the Harlem Renaissance artists and intellectuals no longer identified.

The romance of Janie and Tea Cake—recounted in the central part of the narrative—is set in the Everglades. This world is the upside-down image of the conformist Eatonville society. The bourgeois marriages with Killicks and Starks are the antithesis of the romantic love with the proletarian Tea Cake; the domestic, landowning, and entrepreneurial strata of Eatonville are the antithesis of the poor African American, Bahamian, and West Indian rural proletariat of the muck; literary realism gives way to literary ethnography and surreal events.[14] Janie's new experiences represent a fall from history into nature, from civil society into the state of nature, from man and woman imprisoned by tradition, convention, and material objects into the primitive and free world of the "good savage."

The Everglades, or the muck, exists outside historical time in the universe of primitive, even primordial, nature, the nature of hurricanes, floods, and rabid dogs.[15] As an artist figure, Janie finds in the Everglades what the British Romantics sought in the sunny Mediterranean countries—escape from an alienating and utilitarian society. Janie finds a new sense of belonging in the Deep South, among the poorest proletariat, amid the generosity of nature and the folk.[16] Surrounded by a bountiful nature, she breaks free of the taboos of bourgeois society and becomes a new person. Janie, who has light skin and money and is a widow, marries a man who is poor, dark-skinned, and young. She learns to play checkers, to shoot, to work in the fields, and to participate in the popular culture that had been off-limits for the first lady of Eatonville.

The muck revives the harmony with nature of the pear tree and of Janie's adolescence. The organic harmony had been rudely violated by her grandmother, for whom nature was synonymous with slavery and sexual violence; it had been broken by Logan Killicks, for whom nature was synonymous with land to be owned and women or mules to be used; and it had been desecrated by Starks, for whom nature and wife were both trophies of wealth and power.

By contrast, nature in the Everglades is large, generous, bountiful, and free. As the narrator reports, in a style that echoes the documentary and reportage writings of the 1930s:

> Everything in the Everglades was big and new. Big Lake Okechobee, big beans, big cane, big weeds, big everything. . . . Ground so rich that everything went wild. . . . Dirt roads so rich and black that a half mile of it would have fertilized a Kansas wheat field.[17] (129)

On the muck, human nature as well is rich and free. In the raucous words of the narrator, "People wild too" (129). The "people" of the Everglades are seasonal itinerant laborers who are culturally rich, sexually free, and economically dispossessed.

> Day by day now, the hordes of workers poured in. Some came limping in with their shoes and sore feet from walking. . . . Permanent transients with no attachments and tired looking men with their families and dogs in flivvers. All night, all day, hurrying in to pick beans. Skillets, beds, patched up spare inner tubes all hanging and dangling from the ancient cars on the outside and hopeful humanity, herded and hovered on the inside, chugging on the muck. People ugly from ignorance and broken from being poor. (131)

Through these ethnographic descriptions—striking for their detachment, exoticism, and sensuality—readers become voyeurs and participant-observers in the novel's primitivist tableaux.[18]

The reader, along with Janie, encounters an independent African American folk culture whose proletarian author—unlike Nanny, Killicks, and Starks—is free of the hegemonic bourgeois culture, black or white. As the narrator observes:

> All night now the jooks clanged and clamored. Pianos living three lifetimes in one. Blues made and used right on the spot. Dancing, fighting, singing, crying, laughing, winning and losing love every hour. Work all day for money, fight all night for love. The rich black earth clinging to bodies and biting the skin like ants. (131)

In the state of nature of the muck, Rousseau's noble savage has the face of the itinerant worker, just as in the urban speakeasies it has the face of the gambler and petty criminal.[19]

The culture of the rural black proletariat, or, more precisely, of the mobile, marginal, and unstable part of the proletariat that the novel represents, enables Hurston to critique the colonized subjectivity of Nanny, Killicks, and Starks. Hurston's proletariat is conceived—in romantic and pre-1930s terms—not as a modern class but as a premodern folk admired not for its political culture but for its folk culture. Accordingly, its consciousness and subjectivity take the forms of songs, dance, music, idioms, tales, and sexuality rather than organized collective action and politics typically found in the proletarian novels of the 1930s (Paris).

If Janie's adventures and rebirth in the Everglades brought the novel to a close, one could say that Janie has found happiness in her communion with nature, love with Tea Cake, and encounter with the black folk. We could agree that the novel has a happy ending and that Janie has found herself. Hurston, however, does not end the novel here. While Janie did find nourishment for the soul in the Everglades, the metamorphosis of nature and the proletarian into wild and menacing monsters rudely breaks the spell.[20] The shift from nurturing to menacing nature is announced by a procession of Indians, rabbits, snakes, deer, and panthers that are leaving the muck to reach higher grounds in the expectation of a hurricane.[21] These fugitives seem to understand the power of nature. Tea Cake and his friends, by contrast, ignore the warnings of nature and its creatures and place their trust in the "white bossman":

> The folks let the people do the thinking. If the castles thought themselves secure, the cabins needn't worry. Their decision was already made as always. Chink up your cracks, shiver in your wet beds and wait on the mercy of the Lord. The bossman might have the thing stopped before morning anyway. (158)

In the Everglades, it now appears, autonomy and freedom only go so far.

The vivid scenes of the hurricane and the flood profoundly alter the style, imagery, and mood of the narrative:

> A huge barrier of the makings of the dike to which the cabins had been added was rolling and tumbling forward. Ten feet higher and as far as they could see the muttering wall advanced before the braced-up waters like a road crusher on a cosmic scale. The monstropolous beast had left his bed. The two hundred miles an hour wind had loosed his chains. He seized hold of his dikes and ran forward until he met the quarters; uprooted them like grass and rushed on after his supposed-to-be conquerors, rolling the dikes, rolling the houses, rolling the people in the houses along with other timbers. The sea was walking the earth with a heavy heel. (161–62)

The once fertile, nurturing, and passive nature, awoken from its slumber, is now a savage and primordial monster. The metamorphosis of nature is especially striking in the grotesque creations of the hurricane: "They passed a dead man in a sitting position on a hummock, entirely surrounded by wild animals and snakes. . . . Another man clung to a cypress tree on a tiny island" (164). As nature turns into a monster that hunts the people, the people become helpless primitives peering in the dark: "The time was past for asking the white folks what to look for through that door. Six eyes were questioning *God*. . . . They seemed to be staring at the dark, but their eyes were watching God" (159–60). As an anthropologist, Hurston uses the hurricane—"first nature"—to expose less the smallness of mankind than the smallness of whiteness—"second nature"—and of the mind-set that turns whiteness into a god (Lukács).[22] Here, as in Greek mythology, supernature functions as antidote for a person's fear of nature and the unknown. For Hurston, white fetishism is a false and deadly antidote. When Tea Cake and friends decide to do what the white people are doing, they stare at the horizon—just as the Eatonville male chorus does in the opening scene of the novel. Mrs. Turner's fetishism of whiteness and the violent riot it unleashed just before the hurricane—the novel's one example of collective action—exemplifies the same mind-set. As the ethnographic narrator comments: "All gods who receive homage are cruel. All gods dispense suffering without reason. Otherwise they would not be worshipped" (145).[23] Mrs. Turner is the epitome of self-hatred and white idolatry:

> Like the pecking-order in a chicken yard. Insensate cruelty to those you can whip, and groveling submission to those you can't. Once having set up her idols and built her altars to them it was inevitable that she would worship there. . . .
>
> . . . [B]ut she would not forsake his altars. Behind her crude words was a belief that somehow she and others through worship could attain her paradise—a haven of straighthaired, thin-lipped, high-nose boned white seraphs. The physical impossibilities in no way injured faith. That was the mystery and mysteries are the chores of gods. (144–45)

Amid the devastation of the hurricane and the racism it exposes and exacerbates, Hurston urges the reader to turn white idolatry back into history and society—"second nature"—lest we become the deadly victims of monstrous riots and deadly hurricanes, against which idols are helpless and even dangerous.

The transformation of the Everglades from pastoral arcadia into surreal nightmare reflects Hurston's uncritical association of wild nature with wild proletarian subjectivity. This conventional association underlies both the first attack by the rabid dog against Tea Cake and the second attack by the rabid Tea Cake against Janie. In the most dramatic scene of the hurricane, Janie is mortally threatened by a rabid dog standing on a large, floating cow:

> "Tea Cake!" He heard her and sprang up. Janie was trying to swim but fighting water too hard. He saw a cow swimming slowly towards the fill in an oblique line. A massive built dog was sitting on her shoulders and shivering and growling. The cow was approaching Janie. A few strokes would bring her there.
>
> "Make it tuh de cow and grab hold of her tail! Don't use yo' feet. Jus' yo' hands is enough. Dat's right, come on!"
>
> Janie achieved the tail of the cow and lifted her head up along the cow's rump, as far as she could above water. The cow sunk a little with the added load and thrashed a moment in terror. Thought she was being pulled down by a gator. Then she continued on. The dog stood up and growled like a lion, stiff-standing hackles, stiff muscles, teeth uncovered as he lashed up his fury for the charge. Tea Cake split the water like an otter, opening his knife as he dived. The dog raced down the back-bone of the cow to the attack and Janie screamed and slipped far back on the tail of the cow, just out of reach of the dog's angry jaws. . . . But he was a powerful dog and Tea Cake was over-tired. . . . They fought

> and somehow he managed to bite Tea Cake high up on his cheek-bone once. Then Tea Cake finished him and sent him to the bottom to stay there. (165–66)

The proletarian symbolism of the scene is intense. Janie escaped the world of bourgeois society and history for the world of nature and the proletariat. She is now holding on for dear life to a cow—a domestic animal and a representation of domesticated nature—while she is threatened by a rabid dog—a once domestic animal that has reverted to primitive and savage nature.

Having contracted rabies from the dog, Tea Cake eventually undergoes an analogous degeneration that the reader, even before Janie, recognizes: "She saw him coming from the outhouse with a queer loping gait, swinging his head from side to side and his jaws clenched in a funny way" (182–83). Like a mythical frontier heroine, Janie must face the violent beast at the point of a rifle:

> [She] saw the ferocious look in his eyes and went mad with fear as she had done *in the water that time*. She threw up the barrel of the rifle in frenzied hope and fear. Hope that he'd see it and run, desperate fear for her life. But if Tea Cake could have counted costs he would not have been there with the pistol in his hands. . . . The fiend in him must kill and Janie was the only thing living he saw.
>
> The pistol and the rifle rang out almost together. . . . Janie saw the look on his face and leaped forward as he crashed forward in her arms. She was trying to hover him as he closed his teeth in the flesh of her forearm. They came down heavily like that. Janie struggled to a sitting position and *pried the dead Tea Cake's teeth from her arm*. (184; my emphases)

The earlier scene is replayed with Tea Cake in the role of the rabid dog. His vampiric bite is a telling detail because it points to the kinship of gothic monsters and wild beasts and to their respective roles in the European and the American novel as personifications of historical guilt and social fear.

Infected with rabies from the monstrous dog and with jealousy that is rooted in Janie's high class and light skin, the proletarian "good savage" becomes the wild savage. Contrary to fables and fairy tales, the handsome deerlike Tea Cake changes not into a prince but into a ferocious beast.

Janie's trial for murder technically still belongs to the world of the Everglades. In reality we are back in the civil society of segregated institutions in the Jim Crow era. The courtroom scene mirrors the Eatonville porch in the opening and closing scenes. In each case Janie is alone. She is alienated from and misunderstood by the black audience at the trial as she is by the Eatonville inhabitants on the porch. Janie is found guilty of murder by the disenfranchised black audience. She is also found guilty for her unconventional behavior by the porch people of Eatonville. Appropriately, they are "sitting in judgment" all the while that Janie is telling her adventures to Pheoby, her last and only link to society.[24]

The narrative closes on a solitary woman who has returned to her house but has not found a home in her community and among her people and whose final silence has a ghostly and haunted sound:

> Soon everything around downstairs was shut and fastened. Janie mounted the stairs with her lamp. The light in her hand was like a spark of sun-stuff washing her face in fire. Her shadow behind fell black and headlong down the stairs. . . .
>
> . . . Then Tea Cake came prancing around her where she was and the song of the sigh flew out of the window and lit in the top of the pine trees. Tea Cake, with the sun for a shawl. Of course he wasn't dead. He could never be dead until she herself had finished feeling and thinking. The kiss of his memory made pictures of love and light against the wall. *Here was peace.* She pulled in her horizon like a great fish-net. Pulled it from around the waist of the world and draped it over her shoulders. So much of life in its meshes! She called in her soul to come and see.
>
> (192–93; my emphasis)

Readers like to see Janie, at the end of her ordeal, as a woman who has achieved identity, happiness, synthesis, and autonomy. They like to celebrate her return as the happy ending of the story. My reading suggests otherwise.

At the end of her journey, the beautiful and privileged African American fugitive from bourgeois society has become a fugitive from nature and the proletarian folk. With the hieratical gestures of a priestess, Janie buries herself metaphorically in her tomblike house.[25] The priestly figure of Janie securing the windows and enshrouding herself with the memory of Tea Cake speaks of alienation, not belonging. Like other modernist artists and intellectuals of the 1920s, Janie chooses exile from both the alienation of bourgeois society, racism, and sexism and the irrationality and subjectivity traditionally attributed to nature and the proletariat.[26] Here, as in the philosophical underpinnings of the novel, *Their Eyes* is representative of early-twentieth-century modernism and Janie of its lonely artist figure who curses at society from a literal or symbolic underground.

The sombrous lyricism of the close—celebrated as the style of black and female self-consciousness—expresses to me death rather than rebirth. While homecoming in fable and myth signifies hope, Janie's is too colored by loss and the quietude of death to signify new life.[27]

For Hurston, as for Joseph Conrad, the romantic impulse to abandon society and seek renewal in the folk culture of the muck, or in primitive Africa, leads to degeneration and despair. For women and for African American people, who have always been cast in the role of primitive nature, exotic primitivism is more deadly than bourgeois conventions. This message is also conveyed by Nella Larsen's *Quicksand*—an earlier novel of the Harlem Renaissance of a woman's escape from bourgeois society by way of the Deep South.[28]

Published in 1937, *Their Eyes Were Watching God* was out of sync with the literature of the 1930s, which is full of heroic gestures of collective agency by idealized but not primitive proletarians. Hurston as well was out of sync with the 1930s, when artists and intellectuals identified with and joined the radical mass movements of the decade.[29] These movements dispelled the conventional image of the proletariat as monstrous nature that Hurston reproduces, just as they drove away the dark mood of the postwar period.

Their Eyes Were Watching God gives us finally the paradox of a culturally radical and politically conservative Zora Neale Hurston. Her radicalism informs the novel's sharp critique of sexism and racism. Her conservatism produces both the cliché proletarian primitive and the heroic black capitalist.

Whether we share her view of the world—of society, of men and women, of race and class—if we intend to own Hurston as an artist and not as a fetish, then we cannot afford to disregard her worldview. By the same token, we cannot build the importance of *Their Eyes* on a mythical universalism that erases Hurston's complicated politics and poetics.

Their Eyes Were Watching God deserves to be read as a conflicted proletarian novel of the 1930s. Likewise, Hurston deserves to be owned in all her complexity, as a politically conservative, African American, highly educated southern woman who lived in the North, who was surrounded by radical intellectuals, who was financially supported by liberal white patrons and institutions, and who was a pioneer artist and ethnographer of the Harlem Renaissance. We will then discover that Hurston's radical black feminism and conservative politics alienated her from the proletarian radicalism of the 1930s, found a welcome embrace within the feminist movement of the 1980s, and was at home within the political conservatism of the late twentieth century.

NOTES

An earlier version of this essay was published as "Zora Neale Hurston: La mitologia e la storia" (*ACOMA: Rivista Internazionale di Studi Nordamericani* 4 [1995]: 76–83). My thanks to Bruno Cartosio, Sandro Portelli, and the anonymous peer reviewers for their suggestions. I have found Hazel Carby's comments very helpful ("Politics of Fiction"; *Reconstructing Womanhood*).

1 The main bibliography of Hurston literary criticism is Rose Parkman Davis's *Zora Neale Hurston: An Annotated Bibliography and Reference Guide*. See also "Materials" in this volume.

2 "What is amazing," Alice Walker writes, "is that Zora, who became an orphan at nine, a runaway at fourteen, a maid and a manicurist . . . before she was twenty, with one dress, managed to become Zora Neale Hurston, author and anthropologist at all" (qtd.

in Newson 33). Likewise, Mary Helen Washington asks, "How did this poor, unschooled girl from a peasant background in the all-black town of Eatonville, Florida, manage, in the early 1900s, to get to Howard University, Barnard College, and Columbia University, and eventually become one of the shapers of the important black literary and cultural movement of the twenties, the Harlem Renaissance?" (*Invented Lives* 9). See also Gates, *Signifying Monkey*; Stepto.

[3] On the literature of the 1930s and the proletarian novel, see Mullen and Linkon; Denning; Wald; Foley; Rabinowitz; Nelson; Shulman.

[4] On Hurston's conservative politics, see Sollors, "Of Mules," as well as Sailer; McGowan; Thompson; Sorensen.

[5] On the theme of the journey to the underworld in African American literature, see Thornton.

[6] On the worker in American fiction, see Hapke; Wixson.

[7] The journey that, in the novel, takes Janie from Eatonville to the muck and back to Eatonville parallels the field trips that took the ethnographer Hurston from New York to various locations in the South and the Caribbean and back to New York. The fictional Eatonville therefore contains not only Eatonville, Hurston's hometown, but also New York, her adopted city. Janie's return to Eatonville, at the beginning of the novel, reflects both the challenge of Hurston's visits to her birthplace as an educated modern woman and the defiance of Hurston's return to New York as an ethnographer who has been "in the field" and who, like Margaret Mead, comes back with ideas that appear extremely unconventional to those who have stayed home.

[8] "In narrativa la rivoluzione si attua a livello di forme narrative 'altre', che prefigurano una diversa definizione del mondo, oppure, in ogni caso, affermano l'impossibilità di accettare il mondo cosi com'è. . . . Dostoevskij è rivoluzionario perchè il fallimento dei suoi eroi è una critica all'ordine ufficiale dell'universo. . . . Non potendo essere rivoluzionario perchè deve essere consolatorio, il romanzo popolare è costretto ad insegnare che, se esistono delle contraddizioni sociali, esistono forze che possono sanarle" (97–98; my trans.).

[9] On the theme of romantic love in American literature in relation to ethnic and class identity, see Sollors, *Beyond Ethnicity*; Ferraro; duCille, *Coupling Convention*.

[10] Nanny's ex-slave narrative includes the antebellum period and the Civil War, when the grandmother was a slave; according to Nanny, Janie's mother was born in 1865—"Freedom found me wid a baby daughter in mah arms" (16)—and Janie was born in 1883: "Dat school teacher had done hid her in de woods all night long, and he done raped mah baby and run off just before day. She was only seventeen, and somethin' lak dat to happen! Lawd a 'mussy! Look lak Ah kin see it all over agin. It was a long time before she was well, and by dat time we knowed you was on de way" (19). Her narrative includes as well the year 1899—a symbolic date on the border between centuries, when the sixteen-year-old Janie is married off to Killicks and childhood ends and womanhood begins.

[11] Hurston's claims about the underrepresentation of the southern black bourgeoisie are discussed by Gabrielle Foreman, who quotes two revealing passages where Hurston attacks publishers' lack of interest in African American protagonists who are not poor and uneducated. "There is," Hurston explains, "a large body of Negroes in the South who never get mentioned. They are wealthy, well-educated. . . . [T]he propagandists always talk about the share-croppers and the like, but never mention these people" (qtd. in Foreman 662).

12 For a perceptive discussion of this theme, see Jennifer Jordan.

13 This is the same alienation, expressed in similar language, that leads Cathy Earnshaw Linton, the Byronic protagonist of *Wuthering Heights*, to a premonitory dream: "If I were in heaven, Nelly, I should be extremely miserable. . . . I dreamt once that I was there. . . . [H]eaven did not seem to be my home, and I broke my heart with weeping to come back to earth" (Brontë 82). Both novels juxtapose arranged marriages based on material interests and social conventions, and romantic marriages based on passion and affinity; both stories are told to mother-servant figures, Pheoby and Nelly, who become the repository of the story.

14 Literary and qualitative anthropology were practiced in the early twentieth century, especially at Barnard and at Columbia—where Hurston studied—under the leadership of Franz Boas. See Sollors, "Modernization."

15 In this same way, historically, European culture has viewed non-European cultures, the bourgeoisie has represented the proletariat, and American culture has cast immigrants and African Americans. See Fabian; Paris.

16 Concerning the theme of "romantic pastoralism" and its underlying ideology, see Donald R. Marks's rich essay "Sex, Violence, and Organic Consciousness in Zora Neale Hurston's *Their Eyes Were Watching God*." Marks discusses the marriage paradigm in very perceptive terms. According to Marks, Janie's four relationships fall into two groups: those of "love"—Johnny Taylor and Tea Cake—which speak of "fertility and sexuality"; and those of materialism—Logan Killicks and Jody Starks—which speak the language of "deformity, decay, sterility and impotence." The two sets of relationships create a set of significant dichotomies: labor, material production, social status, accumulation, and wealth—in short materialist capitalist ideology as represented by Killicks and Starks; and free play, sexuality, gaming, fighting, gambling, carnival, spending, leisure, and festivity—that is, antiwork ethic, as represented by Johnny Taylor and Tea Cake. The result, Marks suggests, is a novel torn between the "organicist ideology of romantic pastoralism" and the "materialist ideology of bourgeois capitalism" (152).

17 Like Hurston and unlike Janie, the narrator sees the Everglades through the eyes of the urban, intellectual North; of Washington, D.C., and New York City; of Howard University and Columbia University; of modern literature and anthropology.

18 On the relationship between ethnography and the novel, see Delgarno; Cappetti.

19 Hurston's short story "Muttsy" is set in a Harlem speakeasy that resembles the social world of the muck. Both the muck and the Harlem speakeasy of the story are characterized by sexuality still free of bourgeois conventions and by a robust and highly expressive folk culture.

20 The theme of pastoralism and the proletarian novel is discussed in Klein; Empson. Of related and broader interest is Zuckert.

21 The stylistic register of the novel also moves away from Romanticism toward fin de siècle decadence. The concept and the literary traditions of decadence are discussed in Poggioli; Bongie.

22 In *The Theory of the Novel*, Georg Lukács writes: "Estrangement from nature (the first nature), the modern sentimental attitude to nature, is only a projection of man's experience of his self-made environment as a prison instead of as a parental home. When the structures made by man for man are really adequate to man, they are his necessary and native home; and he does not know the nostalgia that posits and experiences nature as the object of its own seeking and finding. The first nature, nature as a set of laws for

pure cognition, nature as the bringer of comfort to pure feeling, is nothing other than the historico-philosophical objectivation of man's alienation from his own constructs" (64).

23 On the theme of the "white bossman" and the "God-bossman," see Wilentz, "Defeating"; Pondrom.

24 Hurston was born, like other modernist writers, in small-town America. Located in central Florida, the Eatonville where Hurston grew up was unusual—it was a self-governing all-black town and, thus, if not free of perhaps less exposed to the violent racism that increasingly characterized larger urban communities after the end of Reconstruction. The importance of Eatonville as a "rich source of black cultural traditions" and, generally, as "a supportive and nourishing environment" has been emphasized (Hemenway, *Zora* 12). Judging by Hurston's novels, short stories, and autobiography, Eatonville was also typical of small-town America at the turn of the century: narrow-minded in its understanding of gender and class roles, intolerant of difference and change, and coercive in its use of gossip as a means of enforcing consensus and conformity. In reading *Their Eyes*, no less than in reading James Joyce or Sherwood Anderson, one must notice not only the supportive but also the coercive aspects of small-town life and of the relationship between the individual, specifically a female individual, and the community (i.e., the "sitters and talkers").

25 Ann duCille's discussion of Hurston in general and of *Their Eyes* in particular is outstanding. In her book *The Coupling Convention* she writes: "Remembering the bite of the rabid Tea Cake, however, we must wonder whether this fishnet is shawl or shroud" (123). My answer is that it is unequivocally a shroud. See duCille's *Coupling Convention* as well for her discussion of the novel of manners, the marriage plot, the sentimental novel, and romantic love in the novels of African American women writers.

26 By contrast, irrationality and savagery are characteristic of the dominant class in Wright's *Native Son* and in "The Man Who Lived Underground."

27 Following Lukács's analysis, we might say that Janie's quest for meaning and totality has failed because the world of conventions and "man-made structures" has become "second nature," and, "like nature (first nature)," it has become "incomprehensible, unknowable" (62).

28 The theme of primitivism and sexuality in Larsen and Hurston is discussed in Carby, "Quicksands"; Portelli 232–35; duCille, *Coupling Convention* 86–109.

29 See note 3.

Laughin' Up a World: Humor and Identity in *Their Eyes Were Watching God*

John Lowe

The world has finally rediscovered Zora Neale Hurston. Her books are back in print, a new wave of black women writers have claimed her as their literary ancestor, and today's generation is eagerly exploring Eatonville and its citizens in the nation's classroom. Her plays and plays based on her stories and life have been produced on Broadway and off-Broadway. Zora must be somewhere, ridin' high and having the last laugh over her critics, especially the ones—like Richard Wright—who consigned her to oblivion because her work didn't fit their program for social action. It smacked too much, as far as they were concerned, of embarrassing folk culture and minstrel humor. Although we now know better, thanks to a new cadre of Hurston scholars, our appreciation of her literary genius has thus far been largely (and understandably) confined to gender issues or to the convergence in her work of folk materials and literary imagination. Even in these realms, however, scholars have almost universally commented on the rich humor in her work, while ignoring its details or how it works. I would like to suggest that all readers of Hurston—but particularly teachers, who need to engage students with printed texts—can greatly profit by showing how central humor was to Hurston's imagination and to the folk culture that fired it. Using recent developments in social science approaches to humor, we can delineate the crucial role humor plays in the identity formation of Janie Crawford Killicks Starks Woods and understand how she in turn reflects the rich folk culture that engenders this elemental source of being.

This joyous personal humor found its way into all Hurston's novels, especially her masterwork, *Their Eyes Were Watching God*, one of American literature's greatest love stories but, more important, the story of a black woman's search for identity and voice. Humor functions as a buoyant liftoff for all Hurston's infectious narratives, but almost always, as frequently happens in great fiction, it simultaneously functions as the vehicle for serious themes.

Hurston learned how to achieve these ends in her first novel, *Jonah's Gourd Vine*, a largely autobiographical text based on Hurston's parents and their troubled marriage. Her father's fictional equivalent is John Pearson, a rural lad from "across the creek" (14). When he receives a call from God to preach, his mission is strengthened and sustained by his wife Lucy, a saintly but strong figure. Although this pair resembles Hurston's parents, significant differences are inserted, partly because *Jonah* was also influenced by the years Hurston spent gathering folklore as an anthropologist, work that ultimately resulted in the important collections *Mules and Men*, *Tell My Horse*, and *Every Tongue Got to Confess*. *Jonah* was Hurston's first opportunity to use humor as a vehicle and unifying device for an extended fictional narrative, something she had already done in nonfiction prose. The focus on the family enables her to work out complicated types of joking relationships, using kin and nonkin systems and patterns to create a vibrantly textured sense of community and communal wisdom, while forming a vehicle for the narrative and a mode of commentary on it. The book features verbal duels between the sexes, coined expressions, black on black humor, country versus city humor, courtship riddles and rituals, call and response, comic sayings, references to the dozens, a tirade against "book larnin'," and many other ingenious modes of humor. Perhaps the two most important comic devices used in the novel are folk proverbs (sometimes piled on rather too thickly and impeding the narrative) and signifying.

One of Hurston's objectives in *Jonah* was to show the world the glory of black folklore and language and their central role in sustaining the community, particularly in the rhetoric of the minister and in the metaphors of everyday games and verbal exchanges. It was meant to demonstrate what Hurston had challenged blacks in general to do in her December 1934 article in the *Washington Tribune*: recognize the fact that Afro-American folk expression had an integrity that was every bit as fine as that of Anglo-American culture ("Race"). Elsewhere, she declared:

> There is no such thing as a Negro tale which lacks point. Each tale brims over with humor. The Negro is determined to laugh even if he has to laugh at his own expense. By the same token, he spares nobody else. His world is dissolved in laughter. His "bossman," his woman, his preacher, his jailer, his God, and himself, all must be baptized in the stream of laughter. ("Folklore" [n.d.] 2)

The battle of the sexes in *Jonah* includes a declaration by John that becomes a central theme in Janie's story in *Their Eyes*:

> Jus' cause women folks ain't got no big muscled arm and fistes lak jugs, folks claims they's weak vessels, but dass uh lie. Dat piece uh red flannel she got hung 'tween her jaws is equal tuh all de fistes God ever made and man ever seen. Jes' take an ruin a man wid they tongue, and den dey kin hold it still and bruise 'im up jes' es bad. (158)

This assessment is confirmed in *Their Eyes*, where Janie achieves maturity, identity, and independence through the development of a voice, a voice that ultimately resonates with laughter. She uses this voice, however, in ways that both embrace and transcend the male-female relationships of *Jonah*.

Their Eyes, a book about a quest, ends with the heroine returning to the community for reintegration, whereby she is made whole again, while enriching society with her newfound wisdom. Most critics, however, have neglected the fact that Janie also excels as a narrator who entertains, indeed, mesmerizes, because of her considerable gifts as a humorist. In this respect she is providentially armed, for the community has an arsenal of scorn waiting for her: "Seeing the woman as she was made them remember the envy they had stored up and swallowed with relish. They made burning statements with questions, and killing tools out of laughs" (2), thereby returning us with a vengeance to Freud's concept of humor as an aggressive force. After Janie wordlessly enters her gate and slams it behind her, "Pearl Stone opened her mouth and laughed real hard because she didn't know what else to do" (2). Like Hester Prynne in the opening scaffold scene of *The Scarlet Letter*, Janie will be the victim of cruel, unthinking humor until she silences it, and, unlike Hester, she must cap the discussion by having the last laugh herself, as in the finale of the dozens.

Significantly, her friend and initial audience, Pheoby, represents Janie's case to the other women with a scornful humor: "De way you talkin' you'd think de folks in dis town didn't do nothin' in de bed 'cept praise de Lawd" (3). She greets Janie's arrival more positively: "'Gal, you sho looks *good*. You looks like youse yo' own daughter.' They both laughed" (4). The irony and therefore the doubling of the joke lies in the fact that Janie, in a metaphorical sense, *is* her own daughter, in that she has created a new persona out of the woman who left the town some time earlier with Tea Cake. Janie's exuberant appreciation of the dish Pheoby has brought her—"Gal, it's *too* good! you switches a mean fanny round in a kitchen" (5)—inaugurates her in the reader's mind as a woman versed in folk wisdom and humor and also demonstrates humor's power to quickly initiate intimacy and warmth.

The retrospective story of Janie's life begins when she remembers a joke that was played on her as a child. Raised with the white Washburn children, she doesn't know she is black until all the children view a group photograph. When she exclaims, "where is me?"—Janie's distinguishing question throughout the book—the assembled group laughs at her.

> Miss Nellie . . . said, "Dat's you, Alphabet [the comic, all-purpose nickname they have bestowed on her], don't you know yo' ownself?"
>
> . . . Ah said:
>
> "Aw, aw! Ah'm colored!"
>
> Den dey all laughed real hard. But before Ah seen de picture Ah thought ah wuz just like de rest. (9)

The frame story of the novel repeats this situation, for once again Janie's identity is at stake for a circle of questioning faces, but this time it is Janie herself who provides the answers, fighting the fire of cruel, aggressive laughter with narrative, uniting, communal laughter. Her voice, multiplied by those of the characters, does indeed become an alphabet at last, one that spells out the human comedy and condition.

As in Honoré de Balzac or William Faulkner, Hurston's human comedy is replete with tragedy as well, but virtually everyone in the book has some comic lines. Even Nanny, whose grim revelation of her own history is monumentally tragic, communicates in a dialect-driven, metaphor-drenched language. Fearing that Janie has been beaten by her new husband, Logan Killicks, Nanny erupts with comic invective, signifying and using a wrong but curiously right word: "Ah know dat grassgut, liver-lipted nigger ain't done took and beat mah baby already! Ah'll tak a stick and salivate 'im!" (22). Nanny also correctly reads Janie's sexual frustration, seen most prominently in the young bride's cry:

> Ah hates de way his head is so long one way and so flat on de sides and dat pone uh fat back uh his neck.
>
> . . . His belly is too big too, now, and his toe-nails look lak mule foots. And 'tain't nothin' in de way of him washin' his feet every evenin' before he comes tuh bed. (24)

This signifying speech affords a fine example of a technique we have seen before, where a character may speak in deadly earnest, even in pain, but Hurston sees to it that her speech is comically adorned for the reader's benefit and, indeed, seems to suggest throughout her work that comic expression of the most painful things somehow eases heavy psychic burdens, even if the characters speaking and listening do not necessarily seem amused at the utterance.

The drama of Jody's explosion onto the scene profits from his contrast with Logan, a figure notably lacking in humor. After Nanny's death, Logan decides to quit hauling wood and drawing water for Janie, as Nanny predicted; he even wants his wife to start plowing. This draws a comic tirade from Janie, a play on words that nevertheless sends a message: "'Scuse mah freezolity, Mist' Killicks, but Ah don't mean to chop de first chip" (26). Her "freezolity" combines a sense of iciness and frivolity, expressing both the way she feels and how she knows he will interpret her feeling. Soon she leaves Logan for the flashy but ambitious Jody Starks, even though he "did not represent sun-up and pollen and blooming trees, but he spoke for horizon. He spoke for change and chance" (29). Moreover, "It had always been his wish and desire to be a big voice," and he intended to develop it in Eatonville, an all-black town where a man can have a chance (28). His abundant humor makes Janie laugh: "You behind a plow! You ain't got no mo' business wid uh plow than uh hog is got wid uh holiday! . . . A pretty doll-baby lak you is made to sit on de front porch and rock and fan yo'self" (29). Over the next twenty years, however, this joke pales, for it is grimly prophetic. Jody, now mayor, soon banishes any sense of fun or joy from their marriage. He, even more than her first husband, wants a proverbial nice girl for public view, and nice girls don't joke in public.

There is humor aplenty, however, in the salty, gossipy tale-telling, or "lyin'," that happens on Jody's store porch, the town center, and the mayor's bully pulpit.

But he quickly silences Janie; at the meeting where he is elected, Janie is called on to make a speech, but Jody intervenes: "Thank yuh fuh yo' compliments, but mah wife don't know nothin' 'bout no speech makin'. Ah never married her for nothin' lak dat. She's uh woman and her place is in de home" (43). Janie forces herself to laugh in response—apparently that is what a decorative woman does—but she is inwardly disturbed. Appropriately, these pages of the book are relatively humorless, until the introduction of Matt Bonner's skinny yellow mule, the object of a whole series of jokes at Bonner's expense:

> "De womenfolks got yo' mule. When Ah come round de lake 'bout noontime mah wife and some others had 'im flat on the ground usin' his sides fuh uh wash board." . . .
>
> Janie loved the conversation and sometimes she thought up good stories on the mule, but Joe had forbidden her to indulge. He didn't want her talking after such trashy people. "You'se Mrs. Mayor Starks, Janie." (52–54)

Joe does, however, respect Janie's outrage over the physical torture of the old mule; he buys him and pastures the animal just outside the store, as a gesture of largesse. As the mule fattens, new stories are concocted. In one version, he sticks his head in the Pearsons' window while they eat; Mrs. Pearson mistakes him for Rev. Pearson and hands him a plate.

When the mule dies, the reader finds out that what originally won Janie—Jody's combination of a big voice and a sense of humor—is effective with the town as well; at the funeral, Jody leads off with a comic eulogy on "our departed citizen, our most distinguished citizen." The result? "It made him more solid than building the schoolhouse had done" (60). In a daring move, Hurston extends the scene into the realm of the surreal, by adding a parody of the parody: a group of vultures headed by their "Parson" descends on the carcass (61). "What killed this man?" is the first "call" from the "minister." The response:

> "Bare, bare fat."
> "Who'll stand his funeral?"
> "We!!!!!"
> "Well, all right now."
> So he picked out the eyes in the ceremonial way and the feast went on. (62)

When we remember, however, that Janie is telling the story to Pheoby, this becomes *her* added touch and revenge against Jody, who forbade her to attend the ceremony, much less speak of it. The mule's funeral offers a perfect example of what Mikhail Bakhtin calls a carnival pageant, and, indeed, in medieval Europe there was a mock "feast of the ass." The animal-inspired mock masses featured braying priests; laughter was the leading motivation, for, as Bakhtin notes, "The ass is one of the most ancient and lasting symbols of the material bodily lower stratum, which at the same time degrades and regenerates" (78). Since the mule has frequently been used as a metaphor for black people, the comic funeral represents the people's triumph over their fear of death. As Hurston says, "They mocked everything human in death" (60). Bakhtin would add, "The people play with terror and laugh at it; the awesome becomes a 'comic monster'" (91). Moreover, here, as in the festivals he describes, "[t]he basis of laughter which gives form to carnival rituals frees them completely from all religious and ecclesiastic dogmatism," and they are free to parody the church's forms. Another benefit: no distinction exists between actors and spectators in carnival: "Carnival is not a spectacle seen by the people; they live in it, and everyone participates because its very idea embraces all the people" (5–7). Jody understands this aspect of it, and another reason he attends may be that he fears the townspeople will seize the occasion to signify on *him* if he doesn't. Although his participation in this "mess uh commonness," as he describes it to Janie (60), has the potential to uncrown him, staying away might be worse.

Sam Watson's speculations about "mule-heaven" parody the folktales about blacks flying around heaven, using the absurd image of "mule-angels" in "miles of green corn and cool water, a pasture of pure bran with a river of molasses . . . and . . . *No* Matt Bonner. . . . [M]ule-angels would have people to ride on" (60–61). This particular image recalls folk tales about the trickster rabbit conniving the fox to ride him on his back and basic images of social inversion. One version posits Bonner / Ole Massa plowing under the devil's lash in hell.

Comic reversals such as these are ubiquitous in black folktales. Once again, we have a parody of a parody, and yet more, for the signification on "mule-heaven" may be Hurston's sly dig at the white folks' love of the white playwright Marc Connelly's Pulitzer Prize winner, *Green Pastures*, which Hurston hated for its stereotypical depiction of black angels in a fish-frying heaven.

In a revealing passage, Jody, who seemed to relish the mock funeral, takes on a smug "dicty" attitude of disapproval afterward. "Ah had tuh laugh at de people out dere in de woods dis mornin', Janie. You can't help but laugh at de capers they cuts. But all the same, Ah wish mah people would git mo' business in 'em and not spend so much time on foolishness." Janie's response is no doubt Hurston's as well, and we may be sure she is thinking of those critics in the Harlem Renaissance circles who accused her of "cuttin' the monkey" for the white folks. "Everybody can't be lak you, Jody. Somebody is bound tuh want tuh laugh and play" (62). Jody has to laugh, too, at the verbal duels of Sam Watson and Lige Moss, regulars on the store porch. Hurston gives them some choice lines from her Eatonville folklore collections, in tales of sheer hyperbole; "[t]he girls and everybody else help laugh" (67). Hurston the anthropologist thereby signals to us the ritualized nature of Eatonville humor and the value it has for the community.

Another funny episode in the book reprises "Mrs. Tony," the begging woman from Hurston's sketch, "The Eatonville Anthology." Mrs. Tony begs the store owner (Jody this time) for some meat—because "Tony don't fee-eed me!" Hurston adds some delicious details too:

> The salt pork box was in the back of the store and during the walk Mrs. Tony was so eager she sometimes stepped on Joe's heels, sometimes she was a little before him. Running a little, caressing a little and all the time making little urging-on cries. (73)

But when Jody cuts off a smaller piece than she wants,

> Mrs. Tony leaped away from the proffered cut of meat as it if were a rattlesnake.
>
> "Ah wuldn't tetch it! Dat lil eyeful uh bacon for me an all mah chillun!"
>
> . . .
>
> Starks made as if to throw the meat back in the box. . . . Mrs. Tony swooped like lightning and seized it, and started towards the door.
>
> "Some folks ain't got no heart in dey bosom." . . .
>
> She stepped from the store porch and marched off in high dudgeon! (74)

Some of the men laugh, but another says that if she were his wife, he'd kill her "cemetery dead," and Coker adds, "Ah could break her if she wuz mine. Ah'd break her or kill her. Makin' uh fool outa me in front of everybody" (74, 75).

Although Mrs. Tony's caricature is meant to be amusing, it touches on several levels of the plot and offers a fine example of the way Hurston uses humor to convey a serious meaning. Mrs. Tony plays to Joe's enjoyment in acting the "big man," one who is swaggeringly generous in public, as when he paid for the mule's "retirement" fund. Furthermore, the scene brings out his falsity (he charges Tony's account anyway) and comically underlines Jody's marital stinginess toward Janie—he doesn't "fee-eed" her spiritually or emotionally. Finally, the men's insistence on the propriety of using violence to "break a woman" and the shared assumption that it's Mr. Tony rather than his wife who is the ultimate butt of their humor lends male communal sanction to Jody's slapping of Janie for speaking out of place and prepares the reader for Janie's final public showdown with Jody.

When Jody's youth and good health begin to wane, he tries to draw attention away from himself by publicly ridiculing Janie. "I god almighty! A woman stay round uh store till she get old as Methusalem and still can't cut a little thing like a plug of tobacco! Don't stand dere rollin' yo' pop eyes at me wid yo' rump hangin' nearly to yo' knees" (78). Such a ritual insult directed at a male would possibly initiate a game of the dozens, or physical violence, but Jody, assuming Janie will know her place and not engage in a forbidden joking relationship, expects her silence. Instead, she accepts his challenge and powerfully concludes a spirited exchange:

> "You big-bellies round here and put out a lot of brag, but 'tain't nothin' to it but yo' big voice. Humph! Talkin' 'bout *me* lookin' old! When you pull down yo' britches, you look lak de change uh life."
>
> "Great God from Zion!" Sam Watson gasped. "Y'all really playin' de dozens tuhnight." (79)

Not only has Janie dared to play a male game, she has capped Joe forever with this ultimate insult and, in the eyes of the community, has effectively emasculated him. "They'd look with envy at the things and pity the man that owned them. . . . And the cruel deceit of Janie! Making all that show of humbleness and scorning him all the time! *Laughing at him*, and now putting the town up to do the same" (80; my emphasis).

These thoughts offer more than a sense of betrayal; Jody casts Janie in the diabolical role of trickster, that omnipresent menace of folktales who, like Brer Rabbit, strikes down his physical superiors, as David slew Goliath. Joe can't consciously give her this much typological credit, and so he compares Janie to Saul's scheming daughter.

In the framing device, when Janie later tells this story to Pheoby and, by extension, to the community, she is doing so from a somewhat privileged position, which she doesn't have earlier in the book. Although multiple restrictions exist against women expressing themselves humorously in public in most societies, these are frequently relaxed as women age. In many cultures, older women, especially after menopause, are permitted much more verbal freedom and eventually are allowed to compete with men, if they so choose. In this sense, Janie's challenge of Jody in the male territory of tall tales, verbal dueling, and, finally, ritual insults and capping isn't as outrageous to the community as it might be, for she is mature, experienced, and widely recognized as a relatively wealthy, independent woman who isn't vulnerable to sexual manipulation and appropriation.

At the time of Jody's death, however, some men in the community don't understand Janie's position. Janie learns to laugh again after the funeral, partly because of the hypocrisy of her abundant suitors: "Janie found out very soon that her widowhood and property was a great challenge in South Florida. . . . 'Uh woman by herself is uh pitiful thing,' she was told over and again" (90). Janie laughs, because the men know plenty of widows, but she has money.

Her relationship with her eventual third husband, Tea Cake, is central to the book's meaning, and it begins on a note of humor. He walks into the store on a slow day; most of the community is off at a ball game in Winter Park. " 'Good evenin', Mis' Starks,' he said with a sly grin as if they had a good joke together. She was in favor of the story that was making him laugh before she even heard it" (94), and so begins our association of Tea Cake with comic narrative. Their entire first interchange is a series of little jokes, and Janie's thrilled reaction to his invitation to play checkers could just as well apply to his subsequent willingness to admit she is his comic equal: "she found herself glowing inside. Somebody wanted her to play. Somebody thought it natural for her to play. That was even nice" (95–96). Tea Cake wants her to play in every sense of the word, thereby ending the long line of naysayers that stretches back to Nanny.

Their afternoon of joking and play continues when the townspeople begin trickling in, and it seems important to note that Tea Cake's courting is done both in private and in public. His second visit again involves a game of checkers, but this time in front of an audience. "Everybody was surprised at Janie playing checkers but they liked it. Three or four stood behind her and coached her moves and generally made merry with her in a restrained way" (101).

What Janie and the rest of the community like about Tea Cake is his spontaneity, creativity, and positive attitude toward life. In a moving scene, Hurston pinpoints these qualities and his teaching ability. Tea Cake combs Janie's hair and says, "Ah betcha you don't never go tuh de lookin' glass and enjoy yo' eyes yo'self. . . . You'se got de world in uh jug and make out you don't know it. But Ah'm glad tuh be de one tuh tell yuh" (104; see 1 Cor. 13.12 [*New American Bible*]). Tea Cake's gospel of laughter here becomes the New Testament revision of the black aesthetic; it is meant to replace the tragic, Old Testament litany of Nanny and others like her who still labor under the stubborn heritage of slavery. Nanny, we remember, believes that "folks is meant to cry 'bout somethin' or other" (24), and Tea Cake's creed reverses hers. His doctrine is profoundly American and hopeful, even though he too has been and will be the victim of white racism—indeed, one could argue his ultimate death is due to it—but that does not blind him to the glories of the world or the possibilities of the self. Like Ralph Waldo Emerson and Walt Whitman, he believes in living in the NOW, but his self-love and sheer joy in living comes out of a black heritage, and his admonishment to Janie is echoed in a traditional blues lyric: "Baby, Baby, what is the matter with you? / You've got the world in a jug / Ain't a thing that you can't do."

This sense of possibility functions importantly in the world of play. In *Their Eyes Were Watching God*, play is frequently conducted in social parameters, in communal games of checkers and cards and throughout the evenings with the people in the Everglades, but it often takes place on the periphery of convention or even outside it (the widow Janie and Tea Cake go fishing in the middle of the night). But the games Janie loves most are those that involve Tea Cake's imagination and creativity. Early on in their relationship he pretends to play on an imaginary guitar. Later, arriving in a battered car, he jumps out and makes the gesture of tying it to a tree.

The widow Starks's neighbors, however, are not amused; this gets expressed in a litany of play disapproval: Janie "sashaying off to a picnic in pink linen"; "[g]one off to Sanford in a car . . . dressed in blue!"; "gone hunting . . . gone fishing . . . to the movies . . . to a dance . . . playing Florida flip" (110). Janie *has* flipped the town's expectations; instead of mourning atop the pedestal Jody created for her, she has lost her "class" by gambling on Tea Cake and love. Janie's neighbors want her back as an icon of respectability, but that isn't what they say; Pheoby, their emissary, warns Janie, "[Y]ou'se takin' uh awful chance" (113), to which Janie, twice-married already, replies, "No mo' than Ah took befo' and no mo' than anybody else takes. . . . Dis ain't no business proposition, and no race after property and titles. Dis is uh love game," thereby setting the play element of their relationship out for the community (113–14).

Tea Cake's sense of the present moment and its possibilities helps him create a magical realm of joking and play. Johan Huizinga has proved play to be a basic human need that strongly relates to laughter; play is an instinctual impulse that must be satisfied. Janie, who said as much to Jody, wants no exception to this rule and relishes her third husband's playfulness and joking creativity. She learns as much as she can from him on this subject during their brief two years together. The verb "to laugh" crops up again and again in the chapters devoted to their marriage, especially in the scenes set in the Everglades, where their joyous, joking relationship offers a model to other couples in the community. This removal to south Florida to work on the muck with the common people completes Janie's transformation. There, folks "don't do nothin' . . . but make money and fun and foolishness" (128), and Janie grows there, like everything else: "Ground so rich that everything went wild. . . . People wild too" (129).

Tea Cake, with his guitar, his songs, and his infectious laughter, plays Orpheus for the folk. Janie's growing ability to joke and laugh soon makes her a favorite with the people too, especially after she starts working alongside Tea Cake in the fields. When she and Tea Cake carry on behind the boss's back, "[i]t got the whole field to playing off and on" (133), recalling the role humor played in relieving the drudgery of work in the fields during slave times. Soon, Janie joins Tea Cake in storytelling for the appreciative audience that gathers each night at their shack:

> The house was full of people every night. . . . Some were there to hear Tea Cake pick the box; some came to talk and tell stories, but most of them came to get into whatever game was going on or might go on. . . . [O]utside of the two jooks, everything on that job went on around those two. (133)

Janie learns to "woof," to "boogerboo," to play all the games, and through it all, "[n]o matter how rough it was, people seldom got mad, because everything was done for a laugh" (134). In this school and laboratory, Janie "marks" (imitates) the other storytellers and becomes an accomplished comedian herself.

In particular, life on the muck acquaints us with all sorts of card games and their comic lingo, as expertly played and "sayed" by folk comedians whose very names, such as Sop-de-Bottom, Bootyny, Stew Beef, and Motor Boat, cause a smile. Their lingo, emerging directly from black folk culture, is equally tinged with violent menace and outrageous, creative play, as when they raise stakes: "Ah'm gointuh shoot in de hearse, don't keer how sad de funeral be"; "You gointuh git caught in uh bullet storm if you don't watch out" (134). Black-on-black jokes play a role as well: "Move, from over me, Gabe! You too black. You draw heat" (134–35).

Opposed to this group is the near-white Mrs. Turner, who hates how black people behave:

> Always laughin'! Dey laughs too much and dey laughs too loud. Always singin' ol' nigger songs! Always cuttin' de monkey for white folks. If it wuzn't for so many black folks it wouldn't be no race problem. De white folks would take us in wid em. De black ones is holdin' us back. (141)

Mrs. Turner becomes Hurston's surrogate for critics who accused the author of "cuttin' the monkey for white folks," and we are reminded that although Janie is Hurston's double in the novel, so is Tea Cake, for here he becomes the polar and positive opposite, as an agent of the laughter Turner hates, and it is he who plots her banishment.

Hurston doesn't stop with Mrs. Turner, either; she exposes the similar racist and sexist views of some black men, whose repository of "black black women" jokes she despised. Sop-de-Bottom compliments Tea Cake on having a light-colored woman, whose skin reveals a man slapped her, who never fights back.

> Take some uh dese ol' rusty black women and dey would fight yuh all night long and next day nobody couldn't tell you ever hit 'em. . . . You can't make no mark on 'em at all. . . .
>
> . . . Mah woman would spread her lungs all over . . . let alone knock out mah jaw teeth. . . . She got ninety-nine rows uh jaw teeth and git her good and mad, she'll wade through solid rock up to her hip pockets. (148)

Yet after saying this, Sop-de-Bottom agrees that Mrs. Turner is "color-struck," and he helps run her off (149). Hurston's clever juxtaposition of these sentiments could hardly be more ironic or damning.

As the hurricane approaches, the people on the muck turn to the cheering resources of their culture; they first sit in Janie and Tea Cake's house and tell stories about Big John de Conquer and his feats and tricks. They also listen to Tea Cake's guitar and sing comic songs that come from the dozens, the male verbal dueling ritual. These comic, bawdy performances help them gird their loins against cosmic forces; John, a traditional and daring figure, frequently gambles with both God and the devil, and aspects of both alternately appear in the specter of the violently approaching storm (157).

Later, Tea Cake and Janie are amused when they find that Motor Boat, whom they left dozing in a house at the height of the storm, slept through it all and survived, even though the raging waters moved the house. They joke about it: "Heah we nelly kill our fool selves runnin' way from danger and him lay up dere and sleep and float on off!" (173). Weeks later, their amusement pales, for they realize that if they had stayed with Motor Boat, Tea Cake would never have been bitten by what they now know was a rabid dog.

In the aftermath of the hurricane, whites impress Tea Cake for a burial squad, and several other examples of racial oppression are raised. The situation becomes less oppressive through a terrible kind of levity, as in the hurricane scenes. The grim sequence of events that leads to Tea Cake's infection with rabies is chilling, but, looked at with a surrealist's detachment, getting bitten by a mad dog that is riding the back of a cow in a hurricane is wildly funny, a scene only a cosmic joker could write.

Mankind has its own absurdities, however; making the impressed men determine whether the bodies are white or black so as to bury them in segregated graves creates gallows humor with a vengeance. Only the whites get cheap pine coffins, causing Tea Cake to say, "They's mighty particular how dese dead folks goes tuh judgement. . . . Look lak dey think God don't know nothin' 'bout de Jim Crow law" (171).

Interracial humor permeates the penultimate scenes. Tea Cake bitterly remarks:

> [E]very white man think he know all de GOOD darkies already. . . . [A]ll dem he don't know oughta be tried and sentenced tuh six months behind de United States privy house at hard smellin'.
>
> . . . Old Uncle Sam always do have de biggest and de best uh everything. So de white man figger dat anything less than de Uncle Sam's consolidated water closet would be too easy. (172)

The bitter pun implicit in United States privy / United States privileges appropriately bristles. When Tea Cake comments further on the dangers of being "strange niggers wid white folks," Janie adds, "Dat sho is de truth. De ones de white man know is nice colored folks. De ones he don't know is bad niggers," which causes Tea Cake to laugh too, helping both of them bear an unbearable situation (172).

The wrong kind of humor enters the book at the end, when Tea Cake, near death, is treated by a white doctor, who greets his patient with some racist jocularity: "''Tain't a thing wrong that a quart of coon-dick wouldn't cure. You haven't been gettin' yo' right likker lately, eh?' He slapped Tea Cake lustily across his back and Tea Cake tried to smile as he was expected to do. But it was hard" (176). The biggest joker of all, however, seems to be God. Janie ponders, "Did He *mean* to do this thing to Tea Cake and her? . . . Maybe it was some big tease and when He saw it had gone far enough He'd give her a sign" (178). This idea of God as cosmic joker appears in the very first paragraph of the book:

> Ships at a distance have every man's wish on board. For some they come in with the tide. For others they sail forever on the horizon, never out of sight, never landing until the Watcher turns his eyes away in resignation, his dreams mocked to death by Time. That is the life of men. (1)

Thus we see right away the possibility of God the joker, an idea everywhere in Hurston's works; Time/God, Watcher/Man, and the promise of life itself are all subject to interpretation as a series of cosmic jokes, a race that must be run but never won. This somewhat ominous opening and its relation to Tea Cake's death should be borne in mind by those who only see the book as a simple and joyous tale.

After Tea Cake's death and the trial that follows, Janie's story is meant to function like his bundle of seeds, which Janie has brought with her; both are meant for planting in the community, which needs their laughing, loving example. This purpose is implicit in Pheoby's reaction: "Lawd! . . . Ah done growed ten feet higher from jus' listenin' tuh you, Janie. Ah ain't satisfied wid mahself no mo'. Ah means tuh make Sam take me fishin'. . . . Nobody better not criticize yuh in my hearin'" (192). But Janie has shown she has her own defense against the town's evil tongues and killing laughter. Their cruel aggressive laughter has a base in presumed dichotomies, always a rich source of mirth; the blue satin dress of her departure against the overalls of her return, the money left by Jody and the money now presumed squandered, the woman of forty with the loose hair of "some young gal," but most of all, the woman of forty alone, not the woman who left with "dat young lad of a boy." Janie, they hope, will turn out to be a comic script they know well and hope to use, for they intend their humor to uncrown Janie, to make her "fall to their level" (2).

Through her story, warmed by humor, and Pheoby's retelling of it, Janie will point the way to both personhood and community while showing that individual fulfillment finds its conjunction with others. As Mary Helen Washington wisely observes, "[T]he deepest and most lasting relationships occur among those black people who are most closely allied with and influenced by their own community" (Introduction xxx). Throughout the novel, Hurston indicates that to refuse one's heritage is cultural suicide, and the loss of laughter is an early symptom. In a unique way, Zora Neale Hurston recognized and harnessed humor's powerful resources; using its magical ability to bring people together, she established the intimacy of democratic communion.

Celebrating Bigamy and Other Outlaw Behaviors: Hurston, Reputation, and the Problems Inherent in Labeling Janie a Feminist

Trudier Harris

I taught Zora Neale Hurston's *Their Eyes Were Watching God* for the first time in 1973, when I was just out of graduate school. I used the Fawcett paperback edition, which had a drawing of Janie pumping water for Jody on the cover; it cost seventy-five cents. During that period, when most of Hurston's works were out of print, I was careful to keep as many copies available as I could. By the mid-1970s, I was buying back copies of the novel from my students so that I would have sufficient copies for the next time I taught it. Shortly thereafter, in part because of Robert Hemenway's 1977 biography of Hurston (*Zora*), I could begin to rely on the Illinois University Press 1978 edition of the novel to be a constant in my teaching. Over the next ten years, in a process of recovery and reclamation, Hurston became a literary phenomenon, and several editions of the novel were readily available.

As with any black writer so chosen, this favoring has been a blessing and a burden. It has been a blessing because Hurston rightfully deserved to be reclaimed from the dustbins of unknown and unnamed black writers, to be restored to the status of genius that wonderfully fits her. Yet in making Hurston an ancestor, a foremother, an often quoted, disembodied authority, a deity of sorts, we in academia have perhaps made her into something that she never intended to be, something that benefits our own pursuits more than it benefits anything in which she ever believed. As John Henrik Clarke asserted in his presentation at the opening session of the 1991 Zora Neale Hurston Festival in Eatonville, Florida, scholars studying Hurston now are "creating a Hurston who did not exist anywhere in fact or fiction."

In retrospect, we project onto Hurston much more agency than she had during her lifetime. We need only to contemplate her dependency on the largesse of the philanthropist Charlotte Osgood Mason and the letters Hurston wrote to her to know that Hurston was frequently without the necessities she needed in life, such as clothing and shoes. And we need only to contemplate her living situations to know that she was not always secure in those either. Still, we persist in our efforts to make her more powerful and more in control of her life than she actually was. Like Ralph Ellison's Rinehart in *Invisible Man*, some name her trickster, supreme manipulator, master of illusion, while others assert that her masks are so elastic that a discussion of substance is irrelevant. Hurston has become national communal property, and the community manipulates her image and reputation as best suits whatever purpose is immediately at hand.

Consider, for example, how often the famous or infamous passage about the black woman as the mule of the world has been quoted from Hurston's

Their Eyes Were Watching God (14). I figured, and rightfully so, that no conference on Hurston would go from beginning to end without a question or a comment about mules. The description of the black woman as the mule of the world might have been—and may be—apt for describing a specific type of black female character, but no serious-minded critic would assume it accurately describes the range of complexity of black female portrayal in African American literature. Yet the extensiveness of its quotation, combined with easy references to Hurston, allows that evocation to occur in any extensive discussion of African American female character. With its sense of finality, the description runs the risk of closing down discussion of black female representation instead of expanding it. It also encourages some readers to attempt to position Hurston as sufficient background to all black female writing before the 1960s. We need to be reminded that Hurston is in a long line of black women writers who are indeed *her* foremothers, writers such as Harriet Wilson, Frances Ellen Watkins Harper, Pauline Hopkins, Nella Larsen, and Jessie Fauset. Recently, there has been research on ties between Wilson, Hurston, and Gloria Naylor, which may yield a different set of results about influence and foremothering.

That Alice Walker claimed Hurston in the 1970s and that scholars like Hemenway explored ties between Hurston and Walker does not mean that the tradition begins and ends with these writers or that earlier African American women writers do not need more scholarly attention. Certainly, when writers of the 1970s picture black women who resemble Hurston's mules of the world, such as Ntozake Shange in *For Colored Girls Who Have Considered Suicide When the Rainbow Is Enuf*, that keeps associations with Hurston alive. Similarly, downtrodden, abused black women such as Walker's Celie in *The Color Purple* echo Hurston's sentiments about Janie, but they are not the whole of African American female literary representation.

In addition to trends to elevate Hurston in a claiming of self-sufficiency and to interpret black female characters as the mules of the world is progressive critical response to Janie. We keep labeling Janie feminist, even after keen-sighted critics such as Jennifer Jordan have shown rather convincingly that Janie is *not* a feminist heroine. We somehow feel that we have to ignore the fact that Hurston, the model on whom Janie is partially based, was thrice-married, liked men, and was never as self-determining as contemporary feminist models would suggest.[1] Certainly Hurston was unique in her relationships and in her place in the world, but why is it necessary that we label her and her characters feminist in order to appreciate her? Or at least why not redefine *feminist* (or prefeminist or womanist) in terms of the 1930s, which might prove much more fruitful, than in terms of the 1970s and 1980s? Why the insistence on readings of feminist subversions into her texts when such readings are as far-fetched as likening Eatonville to Barnard? No matter how much we would like to claim kinship for Hurston with feminists who advocate complete self-determination, it will not wash. We will always end up trying to force a round peg into a square hole. When all the dust clears away from *Dust Tracks on a Road* and any other Hurston biographical material, we find a woman who was frequently more at the mercy of the whims of fate and the kindness of strangers than she was in control of her life. When all the dust clears away from Hurston's first novel, *Jonah's Gourd Vine*, we are left with violated relationships and women who define themselves in terms of men. When we quit gushing about Janie and Tea Cake, we are still left with the fact that he "went upside her head." We are still left with the fact that Janie is more passive than active, more fairy-tale heroine than Joan of Arc. And we are still left with the fact that Janie could go traipsing off on a lark with Tea Cake because she had a healthy bank account; all she would have to do if Tea Cake does not work out is wire or write to her bank, and, as the Western Union commercials suggest, instant financial relief would be hers.

Feminist readings follow in the path of Walker's observations on Janie in her poem "Saving the Life That Is Your Own":

> I love the way Janie Crawford
> left her husbands
> the one who wanted to change her
> into a mule
> and the other who tried to interest her
> in being a queen.
> A woman, unless she submits,
> is neither a mule
> nor a queen
> though like a mule she may suffer
> and like a queen pace the floor. (7)

The word "left" in Walker's poem contains the agency that I assert is missing from most of Janie's actions, and the multiplicity in "husbands" is also problematic, for it is only Logan Killicks that Janie leaves. In a riff on Walker's poem, Mary Helen Washington uses "I Love the Way Janie Crawford Left Her Husbands" as part of the title of an essay in which she asserts that Janie is more passive than active throughout *Their Eyes*, even down to the language she uses. Janie also "submits" more than she does anything else in the relationship with Jody, which suggests a voluntary relinquishing of agency that erases Walker's qualifying "unless." The comparison to mules again highlights the analogy that Hurston gave inadvertently to readings of African American female character. It is the assumption of implicit agency, however, that deserves further examination.

Let's look more closely at some of the reasons that calling Janie a feminist is a superimposition on the part of readers that amounts to mere wish fulfillment. In the consideration of Janie as feminist, we seldom stop to ponder her relationship to Logan Killicks, her first husband. Students—especially undergraduates—and some scholars consistently either ignore Logan or feel that Janie is justified in leaving him. Ageism is the usual factor in denigrating Logan. How dare this old man, students seem to assert, think that Janie should be with him? He is not only old but also unromantic; in addition, his feet stink. When I ask students how old they think Logan is, they invariably place him in his late fifties or early sixties, implying that he should just die and be quiet. Their cultural backgrounds lead them to treat him almost as a child molester who deserves what he gets.

Few of them are willing to consider Janie *through* Logan's eyes. From that perspective, Janie is an ungrateful, immature little spoiled brat who cannot accept the consequences of her actions (while it is true that Nanny arranges the marriage, Janie nevertheless acquiesces in the decision—which ought to suggest something about the feminist quality of self-determination that readers like to apply to Janie). In the cultural context and historical moment from which Janie's character is drawn, African American women *did* work in the fields along with their husbands, fathers, and brothers; they plowed, sowed seed, and harvested. Yet we lock our sympathies consistently with Janie and simply dismiss Logan, which amounts to schizophrenia in our own readings. We want fulfillment for Janie, but we implicitly declare that it is inappropriate for Logan, that he has no desires that we should be inclined to respect.

What Janie wants in her first marriage is antithetical to feminist assertions that women should not be defined by or subordinated to men. Janie thus espouses the roles for women with which many traditional feminists would have trouble. Initially, Janie wants to be placed on a pedestal, pampered, and taken care of. In other words, she wants to continue in the same spoiled vein in which Nanny has raised her. That desire amounts to a questing after a kind of worship, which seems opposite to what feminists who espouse self-fulfillment would applaud. Inherent in Janie's complaints about Logan is the desire for romance, the tangible, superficial kind of romance with which many movies end. Janie maintains that Logan "don't even never mention nothin' pretty" and that she "wants things sweet wid [her] marriage lak when you sit under a pear tree and think" (24). Again, that glitter without substance is something of which many feminists would disapprove. While there is nothing inherently wrong with romance, it is not one of the primary features for self-determining feminism. Romance locates the site of fulfillment outside the self, which is grossly antithetical to the presumed feminist tenets of self-fulfillment and self-determination.

Still, undergraduate and graduate students generally celebrate when Janie leaves Logan. Then I ask them, What, precisely, has Logan done to deserve Janie's behavior toward him? I maintain that he has loved her, ignored her disrespectful attitude toward him (not just as a husband but as a human being), and allowed her more of a leisured existence than perhaps any other married woman in her neighborhood. But, students retort, he is going to buy a mule for her, which means he expects her to work outdoors, in the fields. So? What exempts her from field work? What—except the attitudes by which she is surrounded and that are implicit in her sympathetic narrative positioning? By insisting that Logan do the work outside the home while she does domestic chores, Janie is opting for traditional gender roles, traditional places in which men and women should appropriately remain. Is this feminist? Significantly, for all Janie's denigration of him, Logan is the only one of Janie's three husbands who does not beat her (though he threatens her on one occasion).

Not only does Janie leave Logan, but she is also emotionally unfaithful to him with Jody for several days before she actually departs, which raises an interesting question. Is infidelity a feminist ideal? After Janie gives Jody Starks that life-changing glass of "sweeten' water" (28), she sneaks out to meet him during the "week or two" that he is resting in the area: "Every day after that they managed to meet in the scrub oaks across the road and talk about when he would be the big ruler of things with her reaping the benefits" (29). Since Janie just wants romance, obviously Jody is defining the conversation, which means that Janie will be—and she is—subsumed into his vision. Perhaps it would have been less detrimental for her to stay with Logan and learn how to plow.

The affair and departure with Jody raise another important issue in the consideration of Janie's so-called feminism.[2] If Jody had not happened to walk down the road past her house, would she ever have changed her status? Would she simply have been content to denigrate Logan and continue to reap the benefits of those sixty acres that she claims she could toss over the fence acre by acre? The basic issue here is self-determination. How much gumption does Janie have to decide what her future will be—without the aid of her grandmother and some man? (But then, if she hadn't gone down the road, we would not have had the novel to discuss.) Although she holds back for a while in deciding to go with Jody, she nonetheless makes up her mind in that "week or two" that he is resting in the area. Thus she has to be persuaded—by a man—to change her life; in this instance (but *only* in this instance), Jody could be perceived as more feminist than Janie.

In terms of Janie leaving with Jody, another question arises. Is feminism a philosophy that espouses desertion and bigamy? Should we simply excuse Janie for trampling on Logan's heart? If she has treated him this way on her path to finding romance, then why should any of her lovers treat her any differently? Readers who celebrate Janie's leaving with Jody are comparable to those who sympathize with Goldilocks over the three bears. Janie and Goldilocks are the violators, not Logan Killicks and the bears. Janie treads on Logan's heart, and we ignore his pain. Yet we sympathize with her when her heart is torn to shreds as a result of Tea Cake's death. How do we justify the shifting morality that enables these dramatically different responses? (Of course, *whose* pain is dramatized in the text certainly guides our sympathies, but the troubling morality is nonetheless an issue.)

Janie's marriage to Jody, which has been much more written about than her relationship to Logan, is equally troubling from the perspective of applying a feminist reading to the novel. Janie stays with Jody for the better part of twenty years—until he dies—primarily because no man comes along to rescue her. It might reasonably be argued, therefore, that if Jody hadn't come along while Janie was married to Logan, she would have remained with Logan until he died.

In other words, Janie lacks the ability to determine her own fate. She is primarily passive, which is also anathema to feminist philosophy. Feminism is about women finding ways to determine their own fates, to change their lives for their own spiritual, emotional, and financial well-being. While Janie maintains that Jody has problematic values and acts in problematic ways, she is nonetheless reaping the financial and social benefits of being "Mrs. Mayor." She is thus either a hypocrite or totally incapable of thinking for herself and making decisions that would change her life.

Let's also contemplate the matter of Jody's slapping Janie; after she prepares an almost inedible meal, "he slapped Janie until she had a ringing sound in her ears" (72). What does she do? She simply takes it and remains in the same place in relation to Jody. While the spirit of the marriage may leave the bedroom and reside in the parlor (71), it still reflects a union; Janie is nonetheless still married to Jody. Of course, students might reasonably ask, What options were available to her? There are characters without partners in the text (remember Logan?), although it is not clear that divorce is an accepted or common practice. Nonetheless, if Hurston had allowed Janie to be truly embarked on a feminist quest, truly about the business of determining her own life, then options available to her might have been represented differently in the text. That Janie accepts Jody's emotional and physical violence for almost twenty years evokes comparison with her first marriage. Is Logan any uglier in behavior than Jody? Would Janie have ever made a change if Jody had not died? How feminist is passivity? How feminist is the fairy-tale "waiting for my hero to come" mode into which Janie seems to be locked for most of her life?[3] Men and death rescue Janie; she does not rescue herself.

Janie's final strategy in dealing with her marriage to Jody is to "sav[e] up feelings for some man she had never seen" (72). She is still passive and still in the mode of locating self-fulfillment in an exterior source. Jody slaps Janie at the seven-year mark in their marriage. She thus puts herself on hold for almost thirteen years, until Jody dies. Nanny did not want Janie to have mere "breath-and-britches" with Johnny Taylor; instead, she gets "breath-and-britches" with money with Jody Starks. He is neither "a higher bush" nor "a sweeter berry" (13).

And lest we forget, consider that Jody slaps Janie a second time (that Hurston records; given Jody's increasing displeasure with Janie, there might have been additional occurrences as well). When Janie asserts that Jody looks like "de change uh life" when he pulls down his "britches," Jody is shocked beyond words (79). Shamed beyond reclamation before the men on the porch to whom he considers himself infinitely superior and turned into a perennial object of laughter, Jody does not envision a way ever to regain his swaggering status. Therefore, he "struck Janie with all his might and drove her from the store" (80). Years of silence and "taking low" lead Janie to a verbal explosion that might have been prevented if she had developed the habit of voicing her criticisms of Jody on a regular basis. Certainly readers can point to Janie's trying to speak up against Jody on a couple of occasions (71) and even "thrust[ing]" herself into a conversation once (75), but she is basically long-suffering until the scene in which she unmasks Jody's manhood and that much discussed deathbed scene (85–87) in which she confronts and perhaps liberates herself from Jody. Well, it's about time. Still, it is harsh and perhaps, as Darwin T. Turner suggests, even cruel. Janie can only fully talk back to Jody for an extended period when she knows that he is no longer in control of her life; he has been leveled by illness and his imminent demise. Is it feminist, then, to triumph over the weak and dying, to make someone's exit into eternity as uncomforting as Janie makes Jody's? Is this a model of feminist human interaction? Again, our sympathies are so drawn toward Janie that we seldom contemplate the consequences of that authorial manipulation.

Perhaps the most ticklish part of considering Janie in a feminist mode is the beating she receives from Tea Cake and her response to it. It is described as "[n]o brutal beating at all. He just slapped her around a bit to show he was boss," and Janie responds lovingly to his "pett[ing]" and "pamper[ing]" of her in the fields the next day (147). A whupping is a whupping, no matter who delivers it and no matter how lovingly it is delivered or received. One of my favorite awful passages is the one in which the other men compliment Tea Cake on his beating of Janie:

> "Tea Cake, you sho is a lucky man," Sop-de-Bottom told him. "Uh person can see every place you hit her. Ah bet she never raised her hand tuh hit yuh back, neither. Take some uh dese ol' rusty black women and dey would fight yuh all night long and next day nobody couldn't tell you ever hit 'em. Dat's de reason Ah done quit beatin' mah woman. You can't make no mark on 'em at all. Lawd! wouldn't Ah love tuh whip uh tender woman lak Janie! Ah bet she don't even holler. She jus' cries, eh Tea Cake?"
>
> "Dat's right."
>
> "See dat! Mah woman would spread her lungs all over Palm Beach County, let alone knock out mah jaw teeth. You don't know dat woman uh mine. She got ninety-nine rows uh jaw teeth and git her good and mad, she'll wade through solid rock up to her hip pockets." (147–48)

The pride Tea Cake exhibits in response to their flattering observations is basically sick. And he is clear about why he considered the beating necessary; it revolves around his ownership or possession of Janie: "Ah didn't whup Janie 'cause *she* done nothin'. Ah beat her tuh show dem Turners who is boss" (148). Since whipping Janie is a message that Tea Cake sends to the Turners, it makes Janie as much of a pawn in male competition as some other of Hurston's female characters. It is almost impossible, therefore, to build a feminist perspective on top of this set of circumstances—women are beaten (and accept those beatings) for the sake of male pride; passivity during the beating is considered a golden trait. If these are the tenets of romance that Janie so desperately desired from Logan, then it is an inherently flawed romanticism that informs her very being.

That romanticism informs the language of the text. Language can smooth over objectionable actions from an acceptable character and linger unflatteringly on unpleasant words from an objectionable character. Consider the linguistic differences that surround Logan Killicks and Tea Cake Woods. Logan certainly says ugly things when he threatens to beat Janie, yet we are led to believe that his words are even more violent than the actual beatings that Janie receives from Jody and Tea Cake. Tea Cake does and says ugly things to Janie (he takes her money, beats her, and accuses her of infidelity when he is ill), but we are encouraged to forgive his transgressions, smooth over those things, because he is surrounded by the aura of romance that Janie has been seeking throughout the text. In Tea Cake, during the time that he and Janie share good years, the form of language and the substance of language become one. Thus Hurston draws on our socialized visions of romantic relationships to make Logan unacceptable and to encourage acceptance of Tea Cake no matter what he does before he is bitten by the dog. The romantic conceptualizations that we bring to the text make Logan seem violent without his actually committing violence and excuse Tea Cake even when he executes violence.

When that romanticism ends with Tea Cake's death, the readers who claim a feminist reading posit that Janie's shooting of Tea Cake is her ultimate act of self-determination; she chooses life instead of sacrificing herself for or to Tea Cake. I can see this interpretation, though it is kind of late in the novel for Janie to finally take a dramatic action. Still, at least she acts. What will happen *beyond* the ending of the novel, however, after she has freed herself, cannot be retrospectively applied to the novel that is just concluding.

It is important to focus for a moment or two on Tea Cake's death and the violence that brings it about. Again, through authorial manipulation, we are not allowed to contemplate the gaping surprise, the gush of blood overly long. Quickly, Tea Cake's death is relegated to the background as we are directed to Janie's grief and to her developing a defense for the white judge and jury. Tea Cake's loss is thus made small by comparison. That this man loses his life is less important than the grand funeral Janie gives for him. The symbolic love surrounding his funeral comes to mean more in the text than the fact that Tea Cake is no longer breathing and that it is Janie's shot that has stopped his breathing. Another question arises: If Tea Cake hadn't been bitten by the dog and killed by Janie, would Janie have ever been inclined—or forced—to locate self-fulfillment in some source other than men?

Yet, despite all these problematic areas, many readers—students and scholars—persist in their desire to make Janie a feminist. Even the way the narrative is told, they argue, illustrates Janie's self-determination.[4] It is her story, they insist, and she shapes it as she desires. I have difficulty with that. Certainly Janie begins the narration, but Hurston takes over and never relinquishes those narrative reins to Janie (despite all those critical discussions about free indirect discourse and other creative methods for trying to put Janie in charge of something in the text).

Where the cracks in a feminist reading of the text widen into major breaks, or where there is no feminism at all, some scholars try to insert womanism, the concept articulated by Walker (*In Search*). Carol P. Marsh-Lockett identifies Hurston as an African American writer who incorporates a womanist perspective into her works. However, Marsh-Lockett identifies a couple of features of womanism that appear to be inapplicable to Janie. Womanists, Marsh-Lockett asserts, are concerned about the greater good of the African American people. Janie seems to be locked into an individualistic focus that does not imply the "for the greater good" imperative of womanism. Womanism also seems to exempt Janie in its emphasis on sisterhood. She certainly does not develop any healthy sisterhood with Mrs. Turner (and that is to her credit), and the strong friendship she has with Pheoby seems totally apolitical. Issues of race, gender, and class that are inherent in womanism might surface briefly in the text, but overall perhaps womanism applies more to Hurston's other works than specifically to *Their Eyes Were Watching God*.

When all is said and done, there is no question that *Their Eyes Were Watching God* is a fascinating text, one that has engaged its readers from its date of publication—and it will undoubtedly continue to do so. Yet attempts to persist in reading it as a feminist text and Janie as a feminist heroine lift the novel out of Hurston's body of work, make it an aberration in comparison with her other texts. Why should Hurston have discovered feminism all of a sudden in *Their Eyes Were Watching God* when there is little evidence of it anywhere else? Female characters in her short stories are at the mercy of and are defined by men, and few of them have the prospect of heroes coming to rescue them. Delia in "Sweat" literally sweats her life away. Missie May in "The Gilded-Six Bits" commits an (undramatized) infidelity that places her permanently at the mercy of her husband's will. Lena in "Spunk" is simply a prize for any man who is brave enough to claim her; she shares kinship with Daisy in *Mule Bone*.

When we boil *Mule Bone* down to its essence, Daisy is a pawn in the hands of black males. Despite her final dismissal of both her suitors, she is still, like Lena, the object of contest, not the initiator of it. Like females in African American trickster tales, Daisy is a prize in a contest and has value only as the award. Like Toni Morrison's Sweet in *Song of Solomon*, the woman's sexuality is not hers to dispense outside the approval or disapproval of the male community. And consider Arvay in *Seraph on the Suwanee*. Hurston is equally unable, with a white woman protagonist, to affect a feminist philosophy of representation. Arvay's husband, Jim, rapes Arvay on their wedding day (*before* the ceremony) just to show her whose property she is; she does not deviate substantially from that placement during the course of the text.

In the end, women are more often than not detached from their very bodies in Hurston's works. Babies arrive without sex, menses seldom occur, and there is little to distinguish femaleness from maleness except at the abstract emotional level. It is striking that children never appear in Hurston's fictional texts, though a baby is born in "The Gilded Six-Bits" (Hurston does include children playing games and telling stories in *Mules and Men*, her collection of folklore). The daughter in Hurston's play *Color Struck* is an adult when we first see her. This absence could be an argument in favor of feminism (women without children trying to find themselves first), but the pattern reflects more Hurston's own desire to be free from maternal obligations; her characters are merely the beneficiaries of her desire. Still, the critical insistence on feminist intent in Hurston's works goes on.

Why, then, has Hurston been chosen? Aside from the intrinsic moral rightness of the selection, if we want to graft morality onto such choices, Hurston has been a safe choice. She has become the literary flag, the symbol around which diverse critical elements in the national scholarly community could raise their arms in salute. From her transgressions to her successes, her political quirkiness to her disappearing acts, she provides an inviting complexity. Previously resistant nonblack scholars and teachers can show their liberalism by embracing Hurston, a wronged woman who has earned posthumously the extensive cross-racial respect and affection she never garnered while alive. Romanticization, too, holds sway in giving Hurston this widespread acceptance. Practically speaking, the fickleness of the publishing industry has also enabled her popularity. More of her books are available, and so more of her devotees teach the works, and budding devotees join them in extending the body of criticism available about the works. Understandably, the cycle—thus far—has perpetuated itself. The Hurston phenomenon, therefore, offers much to a diverse group of advocates.

For those black activists or nationalists who looked down the long corridors of history to find a tradition, Hurston has served as an ancestor of quality. She was one of the writers who bore the burden of legitimizing the literature at a crucial point in the history of its reclamation. There, we pointed out to all who would heed us, perched just there on a mountain top of her own creation, stands Hurston. Is she not wonderful in the depiction of African American life and culture? Is she not a fitting example of literary history? Ah yes, we responded, we shall set her up on a rock and worship her from afar. So we applaud Hurston because she fits so well into our need for a cultural, literary, spiritual identity.

It was also easy for us to choose Hurston because she was a victim, and it is in the great American tradition that we sympathize with the weak against the strong. Hurston was downtrodden by black male writers, like Richard Wright and Sterling Brown—who were also sometimes her reviewers[5]—as well as by the publishing establishment. In his belief that politics in art could be manifested in only one form, Wright decried what he did not recognize as Hurston's equally political bid to claim black culture for the annals of cultural creativity. Her folk were just too folksy for him. So here was this lone image of woman, this mythologizing goes, who stood against the hoards of male disapproval. How utterly victimized by authoritarian voices she was, we maintain, in the account of the male-owned and -operated press that treated her so despicably in that sexual abuse case. Poor woman, we moan. She deserved so much better than was her lot in life. And so we now turn to stand by her side and, through our positive rereadings of her works, catapult her to the pedestal we think history was remiss in denying her. This status especially offered an opening for feminists. They could cry out against male publishing power as well as against the predominantly male newspaper industry. They sentimentally flock to Hurston's defense and repay her posthumously for all the rewards she did not receive during her lifetime.

We profess love for Hurston and have chosen her because of her ties to the masses of humanity. She was just folksy enough for us to feel camaraderie and equality if not superiority toward her. She thereby represents, in this reading, the best of an American democratic ideal. Her absence of class snobbery, her social position in the society makes it easy for us to claim sympathy and understanding toward if not downright biological kinship with her.

We also like Hurston because she was a sinner. In this case we become the great black Baptist church congregation listening through the pages of history to the repentant's testimony of her sins. We extend our largesse to her by forgiving her of her sins, by explaining away her plagiarism, by blaming her husbands for the demise of their marriages, and by claiming that Langston Hughes and Louise Thompson were just mean-spirited in the events surrounding the composing and aborted production of *Mule Bone.* We even forgive Hurston for the lying Henry Louis Gates, Jr., documented so carefully and extensively in his keynote presentation at the 1991 Zora Neale Hurston Festival. Our critical efforts on her behalf are mostly couched in this discourse of forgiveness, of recognition of her intrinsic humanity, even as we deify her.

Not only was Hurston a sinner, but she was also a clown, another dimension that showed her humanity. She was always clowning, however, with a purpose. Clarke portrays Hurston as a confidence woman in the schemes she transmitted to her fellow suffering blacks under the heading "How to Get Money from White People When You Hit Rock Bottom." Her clowning with a purpose is equally measurable in what Clarke refers to as Hurston's "bring me some damn furniture party." Of course, we have heard or read the stories of her bad typing, her antics of measuring people's heads on the streets of Harlem, or her borrowing money and conveniently forgetting the correct amount to return. From Hughes's description of Hurston as "a perfect book of entertainment in herself" (239) to Mrs. Winifred Hurston Clark's accounts of Hurston's public masquerades in fancy pajamas, we have come to see Hurston as a person who honed style and laughter to her personal gain, whether the gain was tangible (money) or intangible (prestige). The pictures all portray an iconoclast, a woman whose morality was flexible but whose trickster status always emphasizes what is missing from our own straightjacketed existences.

We further choose Hurston because she makes black people (most of them, anyway) feel good about black folk speech; that speech also allows whites an unintimidating entrée into African American culture. As Clarke has indicated, perhaps Hurston's "greatest achievement" is that she "restored our speech to the literary arena"; he asserts that "Zora Neale Hurston gave us back our language." We identify vicariously with a scholar-collector-writer who is secure enough in her own black cultural identity to say "ain't," "y'all," and "monstropolous," without apology, in front of white folks as well as in front of saddity black folks. "Sock it to 'em, *Zora*," we cry. "Whip 'em with those words like Amiri Baraka urged us to do in the 1960s." But obviously the words are not merely political brickbats; they are cultural affirmations and confirmations.

And, my goodness, we certainly choose Hurston because she was poor. It again gives us a sense of the largesse of our humanity that we can reach out and embrace a woman who, despite the glorious accomplishments of her life, died penniless in a Florida hut. In our great bourgeois safety, we can elevate Hurston and sanctify her posthumously. Our efforts become a communal rite of expiation for what did not happen in her lifetime. As keepers of history, we think we can thereby right the wrongs of the past, and somehow it will matter less that Hurston could not quickly get sanitary napkins or pain pills when she needed them.

We choose Hurston especially for her philosophy. She believed in black folk and their culture, in women, in writing, in as much self-determination as her circumstances allowed. Her traveling adventures evoke admiration from us sedentary types. She believed in the earth, the soil, in exploring all she could in the United States, the West Indies, and South America. At home and abroad, she was a good patriot. We remember how, in a time of war, she offered "High John De Conquer," her culture's spirit of laughter, to the nation as a whole. And from this vantage point, we realize that her opposition to the integration of schools in this country was not all sounding brass and tinkling cymbal, for we have seen the detrimental effects of integrated schools on the minds of black children who have been babysat instead of challenged.

It has been easy to choose Hurston, for literary, social, political, and moral reasons. Therefore we, like James Weldon Johnson's narrator in *The Autobiography of an Ex-Colored Man*, have eagerly gone about the business of elevating what was intrinsically of value to what we perceive as a superior level of value. Recall that Johnson's unnamed narrator, after traveling with his patron in Europe, wanted to return to the United States to collect black folk songs and "classicize" them. In our critical endeavors, we may similarly have decided to try to make Hurston better than she was—more sophisticated, more intellectual, more topical, more philosophical, more complex, more feminist, more contemporary with the issues that concern us now.

But there is an interesting contradiction here. Not only have we been in a process of elevation, but we have also engaged in a process of leveling. How are we responding to Hurston when we adopt her into our families with the affectionate appellation "Zora"? Are we being disrespectful? reductionist? Consider this. We never refer to Shakespeare as William or Bill. We never call Faulkner

Billy. Most of us say Hughes, not Langston; Wright, not Rich or Richard or Dick. We say Morrison, not Toni. But we casually say Zora in an all-embracing claiming that gives us the illusion of closeness to her, as if we have her in our hip pockets and can whip her out to sit around and chat at the family dinner table any time we want her to.

There is a distinctive breakdown of the distance between scholar-critic and author. What does that mean in our attitudes toward Hurston or in the scholarship we complete on her? As we progress to being really generous, we elevate her from Zora or Zora Neale to Miss Hurston, which means we are still seeing her in a limited, gendered way that presumes familiarity and ownership—our ability to presume familiarity, to use her however we wish. What is it that makes us feel we have such license? Perhaps each of us, in our individual ways, needs to answer that question as we conduct our research and writing on Hurston.

Zora Neale Hurston probably comes close to being a true Renaissance woman. That status has its own complexities. Do we need to make her more? When we finally peer through the clouded mirror of the Hurston mirage, way past our own mixed motivations, what do we see, what can we finally grab onto as something more solid than a magician's slight of hand? And does it matter? Certainly it does to me. I am tired of the gushing critics, tired of the scholars who impose the theory-laden, culturally void, pseudosophisticated analyses on Hurston's works in feeble attempts to legitimate them. So I content myself with believing that Hurston indeed is having the last laugh. As creator, artist, instigator, and manipulator of all the works, illusions, and legends with which we have grappled, she is the author of the sermon around which we have all tried to wrap our lips and bring the congregation to shouting. We are acting out roles that the texts of Hurston's works and the patterns of verbal exchange in the culture she studied have defined for us. Even as we choose her, we are caught in the trap of already having been prescribed and chosen by her.

I content myself, therefore, with the elusive, nonscholarly explanation. And, as the congregation never says a mumbling word despite all we do, I imagine Hurston in a little exchange with Saint Peter. He yells out down the heavenly corridors, "Hey, Zora" (he can call her that), "Zora Hurston. There's a conference going on down in Eatonville on you and your works. You wanna check this out on the heavenly video? No . . . wait. It's a collection of essays this time. Some folks are putting one together on you. You wanna check this out?" And Hurston yells back, "Naw, Pete, I don't think so. I'm still trying to teach these ten-year-olds how to sing in the heavenly choir." "You mean," says Saint Peter, "that you ain't interested in what they saying about you?" "Ah, Pete," says Hurston, "I took care of that a long time ago. Like I said, you always set something outside your mind for these kind of folks to play with. They'll never figure the thing out." "OK," says Saint Peter, "if that's the way you want it. But I always like to let the inhabitants know what's coming across the airways. Watcha doing later? Me and Mrs. Peter thought we might have a few folks in to celebrate her nineteen hundredth birthday. You wanna come?" "Sorry, Pete," says Hurston, "but I got a full schedule. This afternoon I promised to teach some angels how to play Florida flip. And tonight. Well, tonight's real special. Mr. and Mrs. Nora are giving a toe-party. How could I possibly miss that?"

NOTES

[1] There has been speculation that Hurston could have been married as many as five times.

[2] I label Janie's affair with Jody emotional infidelity because it is always difficult in Hurston's texts to determine if sexual activity has occurred.

[3] For a discussion of this phenomenon, see Lieberman.

[4] See, for example, Gates, "Zora Neale Hurston."

[5] For their reviews of *Their Eyes Were Watching God*, see S. Brown, "Luck"; Wright, "Between Laughter."

Vehicles for Their Talents: Hurston and Wright in Conflict in the Undergraduate Literature Classroom

James C. Hall

I have consistently taught Zora Neale Hurston's *Their Eyes Were Watching God* in dialogue with Richard Wright's *Uncle Tom's Children* for as long as I have taught either book. I do it not without some trepidation. Wright's dismissive review in the *New Masses* of *Their Eyes* ("Between Laughter") and Hurston's caustic *Saturday Review* response essay taking apart *Uncle Tom's Children* ("Stories") certainly lend themselves to a kind of tabloid pedagogy. The "he says / she says" approach is good, recognizable fun for undergraduate nonmajors hungry for any sign that the reading matters. On the one hand, the dangers are evident enough and abundant. The limited time available in the average undergraduate survey course requires a reduction of historical complexity encouraging a rush to judgment and crowning of a canonical or critical victor where arguably there is really little cause for celebration, which seems a tad grotesque. On the other hand, given that a version of that game has been de rigueur in scholarly and popular literary circles for the past seventy years, it hardly seems fair to deny our students whatever pleasures remain available either on the surface or within some denser nexus of history, ideology, and textuality. If Hurston's attack on both the idea and performance of *Uncle Tom's Children* was a brief and acerbic intervention in the overdetermined field of 1930s literary politics, it was certainly reperformed or revisited with striking regularity for the next forty years or more. In many ways, Hurston's outrage foreshadowed related attacks from Ralph Ellison and James Baldwin in the decades to come. And while contemporary literary and cultural critics are somewhat more restrained and nuanced, if one pushes hard one can usually find some remnant of the conflict just beneath the surface of even the most erudite essay.

And why not? There is more than a little truth to the assertion that the conflict between the two writers seemed to reveal (or pleasantly provide) a structure for the nascent literary tradition. The affirmation/negation dialectic does indeed shape our sense of the possibilities of twentieth-century African American creative expression and is a neat pedagogical device that foregrounds the possibility of more sophisticated questioning for new and experienced students alike. The key is sorting out how to communicate to students that while the binary helps us shape the story of African American literature, it remains crude and at least partially distorting and cries out for dismantling. I think that the call made by Hazel Carby (among others) in the late 1980s to introduce more nuance to our understanding of an ideology of the folk that undergirds much (but not all) of the debate between the two writers has revitalized the dialectic and given us a more sophisticated classroom tool ("Ideologies"). William J. Maxwell's response to Carby's call in his essay "Black Belt / Black Folk: The End(s) of the Richard Wright–Zora Neale Hurston Debate" is especially effective at taking apart the notion of Hurston and Wright as polar opposites. Maxwell suggests that Wright as much as Hurston is invested in an ideology of the folk, and I suggest below other significant repetitions and overlaps.[1] All teachers of African American literature are in a better position today than in the past to reveal for students the complex ideological (and methodological) commitments that foreground the two writers' pointed confrontation. The most basic cultural accomplishments of each can continue to be recounted confidently, but now teachers have better access to basic archival data and better contextual narratives. This line of inquiry suggests that the project of recovering Hurston is complete and that we can pursue more critical and total readings of her place and influence. (Interestingly, what may remain incomplete is a full feminist account of Wright's oeuvre, method, and ideology.) The conflict between Wright and Hurston, then, has rich pedagogical possibility as long as one recognizes the possibilities for sensationalism.

But if the revisionary left narrative is now in ascendance, I remain disinclined to subsequently shape a pedagogy that looks to choose between Wright and Hurston. It is possible in most mainstream curricular formats—the survey of modern American literature or most any configuration of African American literary tradition—to imagine making either Hurston or Wright the hegemonic voice and the other the weak conversation partner: compelling, idiosyncratic, yet ultimately a kind of historical runner-up. Again, the appropriate arrival of an anti-anticommunist revisionary narrative in the post–cold war era is certainly cause for some reshuffling of the curricular deck. But, at least in the context of shaping the first (and often last) culture critical reading experience of American undergraduates, I tend to insist that each of these writers is major. We need to continue to confront the perspective of each because they each give evidence of having wrestled in a deep and sustaining way with the American cultural, social, and political landscape.

June Jordan's encouragement to leave behind "choose-between" games when it comes to Hurston and Wright still seems sound advice. Jordan initially wrote out of a black feminist urge to challenge Wright's status as unquestionably canonical, a status that seemed to come at the cost of other (especially female) voices not receiving full consideration. Part of her effort is participation in the monumental process of recovering Hurston from the margins, but Jordan also rightly illuminated and defended literary diversity as a value in interracial and intercultural educational environments. Famously, Jordan described one tradition of affirmation and a second, equally vital, of confrontation, even hate, that together were suggestive of the most psychically whole response to the experience of alienation: "We should equally value and equally emulate Black Protest and Black Affirmation, for we require both; one without the other is dangerous, and will leave us vulnerable to extinction of the body or the spirit" (89). Written to temper some of the more extreme responses in the widely dramatized gender wars in African American cultural circles in the late 1970s, Jordan's work offers up solid pedagogical advice too.

While I'm attracted to Jordan's high humanist defense of cultural affirmation and rigorous self-assertion, this consideration—like the feminist and left revisionary projects—at least partially overshoots my sense of the appropriate pedagogical mark. While my undergraduate students respond warmly to the idea of Hurston and Wright representing a kind of total human continuum, and sometimes to the urgency of the ideological critiques, usually they are looking for the more straightforward anchoring that interpersonal entanglement—a story outside the story—can provide. I do not avoid the opportunities to introduce students to the culture of American literary studies or the peculiarities of twentieth-century cultural politics, but what seems most propitious is the reinforcement of theme, the delineation of available cultural choices and their magnitude, and an extended introduction to the character of (African American) authorship. The entanglement of Hurston and Wright, then, is a matter not just of singular difference but also of vital repetition.

The "Debate": A Recap

"Debate" earns the qualifying quotation marks because the actual intellectual and social contact between the two writers was slim. Neither Hurston nor Wright's primary biographers record significant formal interaction between the two. By debate, then, we mean two relatively brief book reviews in contrary cultural settings and the kinds of ways in which scholars and teachers have figuratively elevated understood or perceived positions. As Hurston was recovered over the course of the 1970s, her version of and commitment to an authentic and affirming African American vernacular culture was seen as a lost primary component of constructions of the Harlem Renaissance. She is (especially in her role as anthropologist) the avatar of cultural health and articulates a vision of a community with rich psychic and representational resources that can be used to combat the destructive forces of racism. Slightly later, reconstructions of African American literature's close relation with cultures of the American left similarly led to urgent articulations of Wright as sociologist and activist and exemplar of a belated Chicago renaissance. If Hurston sees health, so the story goes, Wright documents and describes a dense web of pathology and alienation. Community is certainly present—and in some ways Wright's *Twelve Million Black Voices* can be read as an interesting conversation partner to Hurston's *Mules and Men*—but for Wright that community must be relentlessly qualified with attention to the detrimental effects of capitalism and modernity.

On 6 October 1937, *New Masses*, the primary cultural organ of American communism, published Wright's review of two novels: Waters Turpin's *These Low Grounds* and Hurston's *Their Eyes Were Watching God*. The essay was a coming-out of sorts, an important marker of Wright's arrival in New York from

Chicago. Hurston, Wright incorrectly observes, "seems to have no desire whatever to move in the direction of serious fiction." As does Hurston in her later review, he acknowledges writerly skill but complains that her "dialogue manages to catch the psychological movements of the Negro folk-mind in their pure simplicity, but that's as far as it goes." (We might be inclined to ask, Why isn't that far enough?) He insists that hers is a minstrel vision that places black life "in that safe and narrow orbit in which America likes to see the Negro live: between laughter and tears." This interesting remark illuminates the complexity (rather than transparency) of some scenes in the novel that continue to give readers trouble. Wright's concluding remarks, however, seem petulant and perverse: "The sensory sweep of her novel carries no theme, no message, no thought" ("Between Laughter" 25). As an experienced teacher of *Their Eyes* knows, a more troubling pedagogical situation is the bluntness with which Hurston insists on her thematic material. While Wright may mean that there is significant artistic purpose in the novel outside its "sensory sweep"—in plotting, say, or in character—the impact of his dismissal as closing remark is devastating and total.

Hurston's opportunity for an answer came on 2 April 1938, in the *Saturday Review*, where Hurston responded to Wright's series of novellas *Uncle Tom's Children*. It's a brief review, fewer than 750 words, but she takes full advantage of the opportunity to continue to advance her important reconstruction of black life and, we suspect, return the favor of a demoralizing negative review. After acknowledging Wright's literary skill, she moves to her perception of his great failure. "With his facility," she writes, "one wonders what he would have done had he dealt with plots that touched the broader and more fundamental phases of Negro life instead of confining himself to the spectacular" ("Stories"). Wright's fixation on corrupting and redemptive violence is—not without some cause—dismissed with the assertion that it is the product of an obsessive black male gaze. If Wright's hyperbole is to assert an absence of authorial control, Hurston's is a somewhat overstated insistence that Wright has gravitated toward political authoritarianism: "Mr. Wright's author's solution, [sic] is the solution of the PARTY—state responsibility for everything and individual responsibility for nothing, not even feeding one's self. And march!"

I would suggest that the most substantive parts of each writer's review of the other is in the insistence that the other is lacking in a sufficiently rich vision of African American life. Wright is not "broader and . . . fundamental" while Hurston is trapped in a "narrow orbit." This territory is good for students to confront and investigate. What makes for a rich vision of African American life? Explanatory power? A sense of the sublime? Aesthetic density or complexity? Or a more synergistic relationship to the culture represented? I rarely have undergraduates who find either review especially compelling or convincing literary criticism. While students readily gravitate toward the ideological vision of one book or the other—harboring a sympathy for Hurston's impatience with the violence at the center of Wright's book or suspecting that Wright is correct to perceive some shadowed minstrel performance in Hurston's literary landscape—they are generally quick to defend both books from the shortsightedness of the assessment. This brief literary dispute offers the chance for relatively inexperienced readers to add depth to a crude but not unimportant encounter. Students also see the fallibility of canonical writers.

Thematic Reinforcement

Before beginning such work, however, it is important and worthwhile for teachers to return to a straight comparative study of *Uncle Tom's Children* and *Their Eyes Were Watching God*.[2] If *Their Eyes Were Watching God* is my central text—and I give it chronological primacy, if nothing else—I use Wright's *Uncle Tom's Children* (and each writer's review) to build for students some sense of shared thematic materials and, perhaps, shared challenges with regard to method, audience, and tone. I discuss each primary text and then introduce the polemical reviews and often take up ground already covered. Sometimes I prepare students by telling them ahead of time about the pointed and public conflict, and other times I introduce the conflict cold after their reading and discussion. Both methods work and seem to produce different kinds of anticipation and energy. The dialogue invites the broadest of context-building questions: Why would these urbanized, modern, cosmopolitan writers choose to set their initial creative efforts in an almost wholly rural South? How does each writer handle regional and class-based speech patterns? Are both black and white communities portrayed as internally diverse? How are the communities—as cultural traditions—distinct or similar? How does each text portray racism? moral failing? social pathology? Any of these large questions can be productively handled (and more effectively and effusively handled than with either writer on their own), but I want to focus briefly on two questions that might be pursued from a comparative perspective, by paying close attention to the prompts provided by the review essays. (*Uncle Tom's Children* can be excerpted to generate from student readers a more profound focus on one of the questions.)

Hurston's review of *Uncle Tom's Children* is especially urgent on the question of gunplay, to the point of suggesting that the book itself is an act of violence. But if Hurston objects to Wright's fascination with violence, her complaint can draw attention to the seeming randomness of real and symbolic violence in *Their Eyes*. Students themselves are often worn thin by the relentlessness of acts of ritual assault and retribution in Wright's book, and so it is not difficult to generate conversation on the subject. By taking up Hurston's complaint, however, there is opportunity to investigate whether her Florida is as utopian as some readers have made it out to be. While Wright's use of climactic violence leaves a lasting impression, for me the random violence of *Their Eyes* is equally if not more upsetting. Nanny's tale of casual rape, the informal social violence associated with folk speech, the ritual killing of a mule, Tea Cake's beating of

Janie, a hurricane and flood of Old Testament proportions, forced gang labor, the dog attack on Tea Cake, and the infamous shooting of Tea Cake do more than suggest a troubled landscape. In the context of a conversation about the meaning of violence in both books, the charge that Hurston has created a utopian or sentimental setting (made by Wright and other male critics of the day) seems especially thin. More troubling now is how to associate clear purpose and meaning with Hurston's violence. When I have taught *Their Eyes* on its own, I have found that the question of violence has taken a backseat to a discussion of voice, whereas I believe that the partnership of Hurston and Wright brings it more effectively to the forefront.

Since I often teach these works in the context of reflection on the frame of modern America, I also like using the dialogue between the two books (and writers) to introduce for students the question about the basic conditions of modernity. This question is important for Hurston because of her investment in the anthropological project of preservation. She makes clear her sense that something is disappearing, but she expresses it with an optimism about the emergence of new and hybrid forms. Wright has adopted to some extent the perspective that black peasants in the South constitute a repressed class—the black belt as nation—and this view must be revisited as a question about the future of African American community. While post–cold war students are perhaps less likely to share Hurston's revulsion at Wright's "solution of the PARTY," they do not have any basic investment in a perspective suggestive of a necessary reordering of a society in the face of modernity or postmodernity. Maxwell is once again very helpful in delineating the ways in which it may be too easy to contrast quickly a gentle, nurturing Hurston with a stoic, political, and hostile Wright. Describing a nascent rural nostalgia beneath the surface of the Chicago sociological traditions Wright loved (in addition to Joseph Stalin's theories of ethnically defined nations), Maxwell notes significant resonance with Hurston's academic training in Boasian anthropology and foregrounds a good conversation about the role of rural nostalgia in both books (161). This comparison suggests to me the importance of some discussion about the likely impact of writing the books after each writer has left the South and gained a variety of informal and formal education.

Some attempt must be made to describe this intellectual landscape for students, but, again, there is some danger of pedagogical overkill. Much more basic for undergraduate students is coming to terms with ideas about massive shifts in basic social, intellectual, and economic commitments. One good starting point is to take up the question of the measurement of time in each novel. This measure of modernity is usually recognizable by most students with a basic sense of the impact of standardization and Fordism. The plotting of *Their Eyes* points to some sense that Hurston is, in fact, trying on various models of modern existence through Janie's love affairs. Logan (traditional rural), Joe (emergent modern), and Tea Cake (liminal) can be presented to students as potential modes of existence in a changing rural landscape. But Wright provides a sharper point of entry, perhaps, in the novella "Long Black Song," from *Uncle Tom's Children*, which uses a nonfunctioning clock in a sharecropper's shack as a primary repeating figure. Wright's protagonist, Sarah, is accosted in a rape-seduction scene by a white salesman from the North. Of all Wright's women characters, Sarah seems most like Hurston's Janie in that she is caught between the forces of modernity and a black man, her husband, Silas, who is about to be washed away by his inability to correctly read the changes.[3] Hurston's complaint that Wright's people and stories "are so grim that the Dismal Swamp of race hatred must be where they live" ("Stories") can be used to initiate an extended conversation about Janie and Sarah toward sorting out the particular contours of each writer's vision of change. Each survives the death of her man but is left to an uncertain future.

Cultural and Political Choices and the Nature of (African American) Authorship

If one can encourage enough patience in the classroom, the entangled issues of violence, sentimentality, and racial reconciliation are made more accessible—and more resonant—through careful consideration of the conflict between the two writers. Patience is the key since for many students these issues are quickly resolved. Violence is an unfortunate necessity, or violence is the ultimate taboo; familial, romantic constructions are necessary to imagine new racial possibilities, or real racial reconciliation requires a head-on confrontation with difference; utopian dreams are necessary, or utopian dreams have been revealed as a cruel fantasy. Maxwell and others provide contemporary classroom teachers with more than adequate resources to avoid either/or games.

The hostility that remains, however, at the center of each writer's review can be used to communicate to students the real stakes involved. This approach requires revisiting a historical moment at which political choices seemed more vital and were arguably richer in range and possibility (and danger) than they are today. While I have had little luck in convincing students to be excited about revisiting the politics of the Popular Front for their own sake, I do find that this small cultural conflict is effective at communicating to students that literature can matter. This dispute is not about mere aesthetic preference but about a more basic and fundamental vision of how the world might and should be organized. Whether students determine that representation matters as nascent allegory for real world politics or as testimony or even as slipperier symbolic capital is not important to me. I continue to find that patient, measured, and sustained attention to this debate often energizes students who previously found little to engage with in the English studies classroom.

I return, too, to the subject of my own discomfort in using the pedagogical strategy of pairing these accomplished fictional works and combative reviews. One important opportunity this event provides if it is transparently and energetically taken up is an encounter with the fraught character of African American authorship. Transparency and energy are key, however; anything less risks leaving each writer locked in an undignified embrace. Why would either writer feel the need to go at the other so vigorously at such an early stage in their careers? Could their objections, concerns, and anger have been dealt with differently? If they were kinder and gentler, would we have cared as much? In reading such a conflict, how can we ensure the dignity of each writer? Most important, is there some unique African American component to this kind of public conflict about representation? (My students are inevitably more storied than myself in recent and ongoing hip-hop battles and usually have a ready supply of parallel tales.) If so, what is the cost? And what is gained?

NOTES

[1] Other important rereadings of this nexus include Duck, "'*Go* There'"; Kadlec; Levy; and Nicholls, "Migrant Labor."

[2] I focus here on the most likely comparative study for introductory-level undergraduates, but there are certainly other opportunities: *Dust Tracks on a Road* and *Black Boy*; *Mules and Men* and *Twelve Million Black Voices*; *Seraph on the Suwanee* and *Savage Holiday*, in addition to shared Works Progress Administration work, travel writing, and later accounts of the two writers' encounters with American communism.

[3] This resemblance comes as no surprise to Maxwell, who makes a strong case that Hurston's story "The Gilded Six-Bits" is a source for Wright's story; Hurston's story might be introduced into the mix to expand this comparison.

The Seams Must Show: *Their Eyes Were Watching God* as an Introduction to Deconstruction

Dana A. Williams

One approach to teaching Zora Neale Hurston's *Their Eyes Were Watching God* is to examine the novel in the context of the Harlem Renaissance. Though the height of the Renaissance had long ended by 1937, when Hurston's novel was published, *Their Eyes* is still undeniably a product of the movement. This is not to say that the novel complies with the Harlem Renaissance's ideologies about literature. On the contrary, *Their Eyes* is unfairly critiqued because of its unwillingness to ignore black folk life for the sake of promoting antistereotypical images of black people, life, and culture. Richard Wright's now infamous review of the novel, for example, claims:

> Miss Hurston *voluntarily* continues in her novel the tradition which was *forced* upon the Negro in the theater, that is the minstrel technique that makes the "white folks" laugh. Her characters . . . swing like a pendulum eternally in that safe and narrow orbit in which America likes to see the Negro live: between laughter and tears. ("Between Laughter" 17)

While Alain Locke, unlike Wright, sees the value in Hurston's use of folklore in the novel and even acknowledges it as "an overdue replacement for so much faulty local color fiction about Negroes," he fails to see the complexity of Hurston's character development, particularly of Janie, one of the most effectively developed characters to emerge out of the movement. Instead, he suggests that Hurston's gift for folkore keeps her "flashing on the surface of her community and her characters and from diving down deep either to the inner psychology of characterization or to sharp analysis of the social background" ("Jingo" 18). A deconstructionist reading of the novel, however, reveals that both Wright's and Locke's failure to receive Hurston's novel positively has more to do with a desire for the stability of meaning as it relates to the Harlem Renaissance's dominant aesthetic of what constitutes good literature than with the aesthetic value of the novel as a work of art. Correspondingly, a deconstructionist reading of the novel encourages students to see the instability of a literary period's dominant aesthetic and, subsequently, to seek out and to value equally its counteraesthetic. And because Hurston's presentation of voice in *Their Eyes* is ambiguous at best, approaching the text through deconstruction highlights the novel's internal instability and encourages students to think critically, first about the question of Janie's achievement of a voice, then about the relation between voice and power, and finally about the effectiveness of attempting to read the novel as an early feminist text.

This essay assumes that the undergraduates studying this novel may or may not be English majors and that instructors will want to complement their examination of literary texts with useful but cursory introductions to literary theory and practice.[1] For that purpose, I have found especially helpful Charles E. Bressler's *Literary Criticism: An Introduction to Theory and Practice*. In his interpretation of Jacques Derrida's concept of deconstruction, Bressler avoids citing deconstruction as "a critical theory, a school of criticism, a mode or method of literary criticism, or a philosophy" (120). Instead, he adopts Derrida's approach and treats deconstruction as a reading strategy. Such a strategy must discover the binary operations that govern a text; comment on the values, concepts, and ideas beyond these operations; reverse these present binary operations; dismantle previously held worldviews; accept the possibility of various perspectives or levels of meaning in a text based on the new binary inversion; and allow meaning of the text to be undecidable. This approach is conducted in no particular order and seeks simply to show that the text can be (and should be) interpreted on several different levels, none of which can be adopted as the right interpretation.

When read in the context of the Harlem Renaissance, *Their Eyes* emerges as a text that seeks to highlight the instability of the movement's dominant aesthetic. Responding largely to stereotypes of black life and culture and to negative portrayals of black characters, early authors of the Harlem Renaissance who conformed to this aesthetic sought to use literature to prove that black Americans and white Americans were more alike than they were different. More often than not, this resulted in binary constructions of the black self. Instead of defining blackness on its own terms, Harlem Renaissance authors and aestheticians were trapped into creating images of blackness that largely proved what blackness was not. In an attempt to counter the stereotypes of the Negro that dominated American literature and culture for years, Harlem Renaissance authors set out to portray the New Negro. Emerging as a figure that would assert a black self, the New Negro was interested only in high culture and shunned most forms of folk art. For some authors, such a limiting portrayal could not offer a full representation of Negro life. But because publishing houses were largely controlled by aestheticians who adopted this position, it became the movement's dominant aesthetic. It looked less kindly to folk or so-called low representations of black life (even when these representations were authentic) than to portrayals of the Negro as socially acceptable. W. E. B. DuBois's response to Claude McKay's *Home to Harlem*—DuBois said he felt the need to bathe after reading the novel—is a telling example ("Two Novels").

While *Their Eyes* was better received than *Home to Harlem*, it similarly suffered from Hurston's indifference to the movement's dominant aesthetic and its corresponding concern about perpetuating stereotypes. This indifference allowed Hurston to portray characters in terms of who they are rather than who they are not. This counteraesthetic of *Their Eyes* uncovers the binary operations that governed both the Harlem Renaissance as a movement and Hurston's novel as a Harlem Renaissance text. A deconstructionist reading of the novel helps reverse these binary operations.

Set in an all-black narrative situation, *Their Eyes* is less concerned with race than are texts written by Hurston's contemporaries that take a similar theme of female self-actualization. In Jessie Fauset's *There Is Confusion* and *Plum Bun* and in Nella Larsen's *Quicksand* and *Passing*, for example, race is perhaps the most important factor in the lives of the female protagonists. This release from a highly racialized narrative situation helps enable Hurston to avoid an exclusively binary presentation of blackness, thus making *Their Eyes* more about affirmation than about response and protest. Hurston allows her characters simply to be, instead of trying to make sure that they cannot be used to justify racial segregation. They speak in dialect, they have limited education, and Janie privileges love over class. And even as the male characters tend to emulate white behavior, they do so on their own terms. The New Negro, in other words, is deconstructed both as the prototype for art and literature and as the prototype of good black living.

But a deconstructionist reading of the text helps students see that Hurston is careful not to try to replace the New Negro with the folk hero. Her intentions for the meaning of Janie's character are as unstable as the character types Janie decries. Though Janie has visions of grandeur for the love of her life, she settles for Logan Killicks because her grandmother insists that she marry him. She gathers enough strength to leave Killicks for Joe Starks, but she quickly realizes that Joe, too, has a set place for her, and she adapts to fit into it. After many years, she renders Joe powerless with her loud "back talk" about his manhood, and he dies. She then invites Tea Cake to be a part of her life until she is forced to kill him to protect herself. In each marriage, her personality changes. As Janie evolves as a woman and as a character, Hurston's meaning for her as a questing protagonist becomes less and less stable.

An exemplary way to investigate this instability is to analyze voice as Hurston projects it in the text. Among the critical essays that discuss the ambiguity of voice in *Their Eyes*, Mary Helen Washington's "'I Love the Way Janie Crawford Left Her Husbands': Emergent Female Hero" in particular can guide students' deconstructionist readings. Highlighting Janie's silence at critical moments in the text, Washington questions her characterization as a stable hero.[2] She argues:

> Part of Janie's dilemma in *Their Eyes* is that she is both subject and object—both hero and heroine. . . . As object in that text, Janie is often passive when she should be active, deprived of speech when she should be in command of language, made powerless by her three husbands and by Hurston's narrative strategies. (99)

Hurston's choice to have Janie assume roles as both hero, when the narrative focuses on her quest for self, and heroine, when she is viewed more in terms of her relationship to her husbands, renders any characterization of her as a feminist hero highly unstable. A deconstructionist reading of the novel further underscores this instability. Such a reading encourages students to see the binary system through which Hurston knowingly or unknowingly writes. The novel is undoubtedly about Janie's self-actualization, but Janie comes to this actualization and explains and interprets it almost exclusively through her relationship with an other. Thus *Their Eyes* is as easily about these other characters as it is definitively about Janie.

Having inverted the binary operations that govern the text, students will likely observe that the levels of meaning of the novel become more varied and less concrete. Instead of being a text that is rightfully excluded from the Harlem Renaissance canon because of its focus and content, *Their Eyes* becomes a valid representation of the very movement that made Hurston a writer. Instead of being read definitively as a feminist text, the novel forces astute readers to notice its ambiguities regarding its feminist undertakings.[3] After being introduced to deconstruction and after performing their deconstructionist readings of *Their Eyes*, students come to accept that the meaning of the novel is both varied and indeterminate. Ideally, they will allow this variability and indeterminacy to open them up to as many possibilities as readers, writers, and critical thinkers as there are possible ways to interpret the text.

NOTES

[1] Based on this assumption, I only engage deconstruction here as a reading strategy in its most elemental sense. Classes populated by more specialized students would, of course, need to engage detailed approaches to deconstruction and to expose students to deconstruction's specific terminology. My intent in this essay is not to perform a deconstructionist reading of the novel but to suggest ways that such a reading can be helpful and might be conducted.

[2] Washington's essay is in dialogue with key essays that focus on Hurston's use of voice in the novel. See B. Johnson; Stepto; Gates, "Zora." Washington also engages Rachel Blau DuPlessis's distinction between hero and heroine as detailed in *Writing beyond the Ending: Narrative Strategies of Twentieth-Century Women Writers*.

[3] See Jennifer Jordan's "Feminist Fantasies."

Modes of Black Masculinity in *Jonah's Gourd Vine*

John Lowe

Zora Neale Hurston's first novel, *Jonah's Gourd Vine*, offers a fictionally transformed but closely parallel account of her parents' troubled marriage. Hurston would continue her focus on marriage in two subsequent novels, *Their Eyes Were Watching God* and *Seraph on the Suwanee*. Marriage occurs but is not a subject of interest in her other novel, *Moses, Man of the Mountain*, which concerns itself more with racial and religious leadership. This subject, however, had already been addressed powerfully in *Jonah's Gourd Vine*, whose John Pearson, modeled on John Hurston, illustrates the conundrums of the preacher's dual role as communal and spiritual leader and generally charts the myriad models for male identity, expression, and struggle in the African American community. Hurston, an aspiring playwright, admirably demonstrates in this novel how black masculinity gets performed in the community, on various stages, and, most often, through oral presentation, including verbal dueling.

Before she wrote *Jonah's Gourd Vine*, Hurston had collected folklore for what ultimately became *Mules and Men*. The many jokes she gathered about preachers no doubt made her remember life as a preacher's daughter. One can easily trace, in fact, direct parallels between John's interactions with his parishioners outside the pulpit and the traditional tales about black ministers. Louisiana blacks had a verse that went, "I wouldn't trust a preacher out o' my sight, / Say I wouldn't trust a preacher out o' my sight, / 'Cause they believes in doin' too many things far in de night" (Levine 327). As Gerald Davis reminds us, "preacher" stories often "turn on his supposed gluttony, lust, avarice, and ironically, his malapropisms," even though this figure operates centrally in the formulation of African American cultural forms (xiv). Or as a parishioner in South Carolina stated in a more earthy way:

> Dey holler, "God, Jesus" an' "Lord," an' talk 'bout heaven an' Sunday atter dey done preach, an' you better pray or you'll burn in hell, den dey will eat up all de grub you kin put on you' tale, set down an' go to pickin' dey teet' an' lookin' at you' baby gal. Don't tell me 'bout no preachers.
>
> (Adams 259)

Accordingly, teachers might want to present some of the material dealing with preachers in *Mules and Men* to introduce both the novel and the subject of black male leadership. Hurston always thought of the Bible as a folk history, featuring the cantankerous Hebrew people engaged in pig-headed and glorious rebellion against the God who chose them. She began a large-scale investigation of the possibilities of these insights in her first novel, whose central character, a preacher, individualizes the constant struggle between a rebellious, sensual people and God. The writing of the book came about unexpectedly. Hurston was surprised when a publisher at Lippincott, impressed by her short story "The Gilded Six-Bits," asked if she had a novel for them. "Why, yes," she said, knowing she didn't (Boyd 246). Speedily manufacturing one from scratch meant going to the two sets of material she knew best: her family's history and the folklore in her then unpublished *Mules and Men*.

Students are interested to learn that there was a ready market for tales involving philandering ministers in the 1930s. Sinclair Lewis's 1927 *Elmer Gantry*, a serious satire of American religious hypocrisy featuring a womanizing minister, was a runaway best seller. Hurston claimed that Lewis was one of her favorite authors, and so she may have read the book (Kunitz and Haycraft). There was also Marc Connelly's 1930 Broadway sensation, *The Green Pastures*; its success demonstrated America's interest in black religion. In a matter of months, Hurston had written a book studied from life, which documented her father's rise from an "across the creek nigger" to his marriage with the talented and intelligent Lucy Potts to his further ascent under her guidance to minister and state Baptist official to his decline and fall, occasioned by constant adultery and philandering before, during, and after his marriages to Lucy, Hattie, and Sally. In many ways, this trajectory (at least in its ascent) echoes the classic Horatio Alger story of American masculine culture. But the mode of masculinity here is decidedly black. As the manuscript title page indicates, the novel was originally "Big Nigger." Hurston may have had second thoughts, however, after remembering the brouhaha that ensued over Carl Van Vechten's use of the word in his *Nigger Heaven*. "Big Nigger" would have signaled a double message to the black audience, who would realize that the term meant one thing to whites (someone uppity and to be feared) and another to blacks. Although the first meaning would refer to an upper-class member of the race (obviously the main reference Hurston had in mind), it is also very close in meaning to "bad nigger," which Daryl Dance tells us, from its beginning, has had positive connotations to certain black people and negative connotations to white people. "Big Nigger's" early meaning was a man who fought against the system, and sexual prowess was one of his signifiers. The "bad nigger," however, has been defined as a man working out his hostility to his mother, who raised him to suppress his masculinity in an effort to equip him with the mask he needs to confront white racist society (Dance 225). Moreover, many "bad niggers" confine their courage to dealings with black people (Brearly 583), as John largely does. John, as we see early on, loves his mother, seems virtually fearless, even before whites, and appears to love women, though he surely undervalues them in his overt focus on their bodies. On the other hand, his first wife, Lucy, becomes a mother figure for him, gives him detailed instructions about how to handle his ministry, and in her loving forgiveness of his sins simultaneously creates a never-ending source of guilt. His infidelity in some ways seems a rebellion against both her authority and her charity, which forms an analogue with that of the church he serves.

The title "Big Nigger" also resonates with the theme of envy. John's enemies in the book are always trying to "pull him down," "chop him down," and so on, out of the desire to punish pride, as with Jonah's gourd vine, but also out of jealousy. This theme of "big niggers" being cut down to size by the community would be addressed years later by Richard Wright in *The Long Dream*, when Professor Butler gives Fish advice through a folk rhyme on his setting out in the world:

> Big niggers have little niggers upon their back to bite 'em.
> And little niggers have lesser niggers, and so on *ad infinitum*.
> And the big niggers themselves, in turn, have bigger niggers to go on;
> While these again have bigger still, and bigger still, and so on.

Butler comments, "The white folks are on top of us, and our own folks are on top of our folks, and God help the black man at the bottom" (208).

One way to avoid being on the bottom, as Hurston's book demonstrates, was to mount the pulpit. Accordingly, *Jonah's Gourd Vine* begins Hurston's lifelong, intense examination of her inherited religion, a subject always centered on the male minister as performer. Hurston knew that the black preacher inspired both veneration and joking traditions in the black community. Black parishioners accept the fact that their leader functions as God's anointed in the pulpit and as an ordinary human being away from it. Hurston viewed black preaching as a folk art form and saw her father's story as metaphoric of a larger experience. In a letter to James Weldon Johnson, she wrote, "I see a preacher as a man outside of the pulpit and so far as I am concerned he should be free to follow his bent as other men. He becomes the voice of the spirit when he ascends the rostrum." And John indeed develops into a cosmic poet, saving himself several times from disgrace by mapping the heavens and the earth for his parishioners with his golden tongue. As a man who "talks that talk" without equal, he excels as a master of oral discourse. We see a remarkable parallel between the two halves of John's masculine identity: the sacred—serious, mystical, poetic, formal—and the secular—folkloric, comic, sensual, all too human and thus understandable. The preacher and the man that "talks that talk" must be able to speak spontaneously, to derive readings of sacred and secular texts from deeply personal re-creations of them. The Christian Bible, spirituals, gospel songs, and daily events that are employed in the black sermon find their secular counterparts in folktales, tall tales, work songs, toasts, marking, signifying, and the blues. We might usefully think of these two voices musically, as spirituals and blues. Moreover, both of John's roles overlap with those of the male African griot, who keeps the community's culture alive through narration and music. The black preacher was the master storyteller of African American culture, one who used personal experience, retellings of biblical stories, and jokes to make his points. The community expects the minister to be able to comfort the bereaved with a droll story about the deceased or to spice his remarks at weddings, baptisms, and public social events with jokes.

In many ways, Hurston used *Jonah's Gourd Vine* to come to terms with her affinities with her father, a process of discovery that continued in her autobiography. There, her mother becomes alarmed at Zora's tendency to wander, saying someone had sprinkled "travel dust" around the doorstep on the child's birthday. Hurston wonders why her mother never saw the connection to John Hurston, "who didn't have a thing on his mind but this town and the next one. That should have given her a sort of hint. Some children are just bound to take after their fathers in spite of women's prayers" (*Dust Tracks* 32). This connection would also empower Hurston as a female writer, permitting her to employ some of the sacrosanct traditions of the black male oral tradition in fiction, especially the figuration of serious issues in comic and coded discourse and the invitation to expand on a text of the black minister.

There are several ways to read the title of Hurston's first novel, which refers to God's using a worm to cut down the gourd vine that had provided his disobedient servant Jonah shade. The most obvious one pertains to John's sexuality (the worm) destroying Lucy, his career, and the spreading comfort his voice gives his parishioners (all versions of the gourd vine). This central trope expands in power through parallelism; very early in the book John sees a train for the first time and becomes transfixed by it. The figure of the train, in its power and thrust, develops into a symbol of both John's potent rhetoric and his sexuality, merging in the surge and roll of his magnificent train sermon. The locomotive therefore operates as one of the most important unifying symbols in the book; it signifies John just as the pear tree signifies Janie in *Their Eyes Were Watching God*. Hurston introduces this theme in an initiation scene, when John leaves his rural home to seek work on the Pearson plantation and spies a train for the first time in a hamlet railroad station. John instinctively responds to its threatening power: "The engine's very sides seemed to expand and contract like a fiery-lunged monster" (16), presenting rather overtly the sexual symbolism of the black train that will be identified with John throughout the book and that will kill him. Even before his death, however, the "engine" of his sexuality takes him down a tragic track; as Anthony Wilson notes, the train's refrain, "[w]olf coming, wolf coming" is proleptive of John's devouring sexuality (73). The phallic metaphor is expanded by Hurston's use of snake symbols, which students can easily identify and ponder. Hurston makes John's courtship of Lucy heroic by having him kill a huge moccasin that lives under the footbridge, a monster made mythical by Lucy's assertion that this "ole devil . . . been right dere skeerin' folks since befo' Ah wuz borned" (34). But they both know the snake's mate must be near; the victory could be momentary. And indeed, the parallel serpent under the high road symbolized here emerges in John's sexual philandering, the worm that cuts down this Jonah's gourd vine, as one of John's enemies dubs him.

If we extend the aptness of the train imagery for both John and the black pulpit in general, a markedly sexual quality often emerges in the structure of the black sermon, in that the minister and the people, striving together in call-and-response mode, aim toward a spiritual climax. The audience's shouts, comments, and general "getting happy" all work toward this moment. Rhythm and timing are especially important as the moment comes closer. As Joyce Marie Jackson notes, most preachers evoke this by using some form of intonation, "variously referred to as 'moaning,' 'hollering,' 'shouting,' 'chanting,' 'grunting' or any one of several other terms, especially in the inspirational climaxes of their sermons" (213). Grace Sims Holt adds that the rich language is calculated to raise the church sisters into a state of "fainting, sweating, groaning, and simulating a mass orgasm," and, indeed, "[t]he preacher's ability to arouse an erotic response is an index of his success and vitality" (327–28). Thus John's duality—his earthy sexuality and his spirit-filled voice—makes him a success in the pulpit.

Students may trace this pattern in John's delivery of his famous "dry bones" sermon, a response he gives to a rival preacher whom the congregation may install to replace John. The theme is second chances, how God can take dry bones and make them live. John's powerful sermon proves this capability, for his adulteries have made him "dry" too. The sermon also refers, of course, to a sinning people, who need the renewal offered by the restoration of the covenant. In many ways, John's wandering from Lucy and the church parallels that of the idol-craving Hebrews and thus combines the story of a sinning individual with that of a sinning people, both watched and judged by an angry God. Writing this novel not only recapitulated a sorrowful past for Hurston but also represented a powerful rehearsal for her *Moses, Man of the Mountain*, which traces a similar pattern of redemption and sin but emphasizes the society rather than the individual.

John's "dry bones" sermon seems to recharge him and his parishioners: "He brought his hearers to such a frenzy that it never subsided until two Deacons seized the preacher by the arms and reverently set him down"; Sister Hall gloats, "Dat's uh preachin' piece uh plunder" (158). Taking over the pulpit from John, his rival, the Reverend Felton Cozy, advertises himself as a "race man" and proceeds to examine black-white relationships. "After five minutes . . . Sister Boger whispered to Sister Pindar, 'Ah ain't heard whut de tex' wuz.' 'Me neither.'"

Cozy's litany of the accomplishments of black men, including the claim that Christ was black, gets interrupted by his revealing need to order the parishioners to say amen. "Don't let uh man preach hisself tuh death and y'll set dere lak uh bump on uh log and won't he'p 'im out. Say 'Amen'!!" (159). When Deacon Harris asks the sisters how they liked Cozy's sermon, Sister Boger makes "an indecent sound with her lips: 'dat wan't no sermon. Dat wuz uh lecture.' 'Dat's all whut it wuz,' Sister Watson agreed and switched on off" (159). These comically scornful physical gestures beautifully underline the difference between the merely intellectual and the sublimely spiritual, as well as the link between physical presence and effective male performance. As C. Eric Lincoln and Lawrence H. Mamiya show, failure to achieve spiritual ecstasy often results in polite compliments of "good talk" or "good lecture," not the ultimate "You *preached* today!" (6). In such scenes, Hurston suggests, the very thing that makes John a powerful servant of God causes his downfall, first in the personal realm but eventually in the church as well.

John Hurston, like his fictional counterpart John Pearson, grew up near Notasulga, Alabama, the early locale of this novel, which is in Macon County, about ten miles from Tuskegee. Tuskegee Institute would thus loom large in Hurston family legend. Moreover, Booker T. Washington's emphasis on washing, rebirth, cleanliness—most memorably when Washington has to clean a room completely to prove his worthiness to enter Hampton Institute—fits quite well in a story about John the Baptist in modern dress, for John serves a Baptist church, as did Hurston's father. To maintain pastoral control and piety, however, one must constantly publicly "wash" one's soul clean, as John attempts to do repeatedly in this story. Although later in the book Lucy claims that John can't wash himself clean from sin, like a cat with his tongue, the church's doctrine permits precisely that, forgiving John over and again after his movingly poetic and confessional sermons. Although as readers we too disapprove of John's many infidelities, we remember that time and time again women throw themselves at him, suggesting that Hurston wants us to recognize that women have sexual drives as well, that they too can choose to exercise choice and seek partners, and that men, just like women, may be viewed as sexual objects.

Where does John's verbal skill begin? Early in the novel, the oedipal struggle of John and Ned, his stepfather, comes to a physical and verbal climax, a deadly serious duel structured and punctuated by comic modes of speaking and maneuvering. The crux of the matter seems to be the illiterate Ned's displeasure over his hated stepson's acquiring power through language by learning to read and write. John's biological father, the white Alf Pearson, who never acknowledges his paternity, offers another reading of "gittin' biggety": he takes vicarious pride in John's sexual appeal and appetites, seeing a repetition of his own fondly remembered youthful womanizing and no doubt a contrast to his white son, who is studying in Paris. After warning John not to court Duke's wife, Exie, Alf seems hugely amused to learn that she in fact has been pursuing John. "'Get along you rascal you! You're a walking orgasm. A living exultation.' 'Whut's dat,

Mist' Alf?' 'Oh never mind about that. Keep up with the pigs'" (50). Although Alf does not mean it that way, Hurston surely slips in an ironic author-reader joke here, since we see clearly that Alf, for all his pride in John, looks at him essentially as less than a man, as a stud—and John's sexual exploits do little more than enable him to "[k]eep up with the pigs" and the other animals in gargantuan sexual appetite. As in François Rabelais and comic writers before and after him, excessive appetite will always have a comic perspective. Still, he tells John, "[D]on't steal and don't get too biggety and you'll get along" (42). We note, as well, that "beget" can evoke "biggity," giving it a punning and sexual dimension, one in keeping with what proves to be John's fatal flaw.

During the first half of the novel, we find John a man among men, linguistically speaking, in various situations. Before his marriage, John seeks work in a tie camp, and his initial appearance causes alarm, for the men are gaming and think he's white, a "buckra" (59). But after John's joking, "[e]veryone laughed except Coon Tyler," who proves to be hostile to John's inclusion. The men say not to mind Coon, that he's just "funnin'," which makes Coon even madder: "Y'all know Ah don't joke and Ah don't stand no jokin'. 'Tain't nothin' in de drug store'll kill yuh quick ez me" (60). Obviously, Coon offers an ugly, aggressive performance of masculinity, one that, unlike John's, operates against the idea of community. His variant of sounding, or verbal insult, includes traditional components, such as provocation, goading, and taunting, but lacks any pleasurable element, and, indeed, ends in violence. Ignoring Coon, John quickly acquires two guides. One, an old man named Ezeriah Hill, provides needed advice, although he's known by "de lady people" as Uncle Dump (60). Uncle becomes yet another father figure for John, a mentor much like Moses's Mentu in *Moses, Man of the Mountain*. The other guide, a younger man, complements and yet paradoxically contradicts Uncle Dump. Called Do-Dirty "because of his supposed popularity with and his double-crossing of women," he teaches John lessons in town vice (60). We see here and in a similar camp in Florida how this backwoods world of men gives John linguistic training in the two realms of his future life, womanizing and preaching, as he also learns to "mark" preachers during this time. He thus learns to "talk sweet" like the minister, using decorum and formality; to "talk broad" like the male workers, employing joking and license; and, presumably, to "talk bad," or obscenely, about women and sexuality, an activity Hurston can only suggest because of the censorship of her day. In a prefiguration of Tea Cake in *Their Eyes*, John quickly becomes the favorite of the camp, partly because of his athletic abilities, but also for his gift for "telling lies" (stories), another example of how male verbal ability equals power. He also wins respect with his first fight.

Later, after John's marital infidelities have forced him to leave Alabama (and for a time, Lucy and his family), his job on a Florida railroad crew parallels this earlier passage and allows Hurston to effortlessly insert her research on the folk culture of railroad camps that is key to *Mules and Men*, including male work songs. Spiking is a submerged sexual joke, for as the men drive the spikes home they sing a song that calls their wives' names. Hurston also initiates us and John into the world of marking, when John mimics the sermon of a preacher for the men: "You kin marks folks," said Blue, "Dass jes' lak dat preacher fuh de world. Pity you ain't preachin' yo'self." This comment leads to the suggestion that John go to the newly formed all-black town nearby to observe and then mark the eccentric Methodist preacher there. Thus John's involvement with the poetry of the sermon mode begins in parody, in a folk setting, the realm of self-expression that shapes his daily intercourse with others, inaugurating John as what Roger Abrahams calls "the man of words," whose performances are "typified by his willingness to entertain and instruct anywhere and anytime," but who also attempts to "amuse and dazzle" (135). Hurston, too, in a contrasting way, discussed the creative aspects of black speech, linking the man on the street and the preacher in "Characteristics of Negro Expression." This important essay, which appeared the same year as *Jonah's Gourd Vine*, features Hurston's comments on the way "[e]very phase of Negro life is highly dramatized" and "acted out"; "[n]o little moment passes unadorned" (1020). Applying these qualities to the black sermon, the preacher creates "prose poetry": "The supplication is forgotten in the frenzy of creation. . . . The beauty of the Old Testament does not exceed that of a Negro prayer" (1022). These patterns are made possible by an innate gift for mimicry, which accepts the basics of English; everything becomes transformed, however, as the black speaker makes it *his* tongue through creative embellishment, which frequently involves the key traits of angularity and asymmetry. Hurston, however, carefully forestalls an interpretation of mimicry as "monkey see, monkey do"; instead, it is "an art in itself. If it is not, then all art must fall by the same blow that strikes it down" (1026). Obviously, all these "characteristics" apply to John, who, by these terms, as both a man of words in the secular realm and a poetic preacher, operates as a consummate artist. And, indeed, that artistic aspect feeds into his other self, the lover, for, as Hurston adds, "Love-making and fighting in all their branches are high arts" (1027).

We may take the meaning of John's parallel talents further; his role in the public realm bifurcates when he runs for mayor, using male humor to make his big voice heard politically with the choral group of men communed on Joe Clarke's porch. John's puffed-up pride leads him to declare for the office right to the face of the incumbent, Sam Mosely, in an extended verbal duel. "You and Clarke ain't had nobody tuh run against, but dis time big Moose done come down from de mountain. [Moose fight over their females.] Ahm goin' tuh run you so hard 'til they can't tell yo' run-down shoe from yo' wore out sock" (113). Joe Clarke comments on the rivalry implicit in even the best of male friendships, like this one: "I God . . . Ah never seen two sworn buddies dat tries tuh out do on 'nother lak y'all do. You so thick 'til one can't turn 'thout de other one, yet and still you always buckin' 'ginst each other" (113). This sexuality-as-power theme also dominates the play Hurston wrote with Langston Hughes, *Mule Bone*, where the best friends Jim and Dave duel linguistically and musically over the affections of Daisy.

These scenes and others show John maturing his various voices. The two public realms would interact in any case, since his overall performance as a preacher depends not only on his relatively formal rhetorical ability in the pulpit but also on his creative ability to freely mix folk expression into his daily conversation with his parishioners. Here the banter largely missing from sermons is a necessary and, indeed, expected ingredient. Proficiency in folk idiom, which would be known as slang in an urban setting, gives the communal leader a constant sense, as Abrahams puts it, of "newness, vitality, and pleasurable aggressiveness" (139), highly masculine qualities naturally associated with sexual identity as well.

John's life after Lucy's death declines sadly; her ability to help him channel his "natchel" energies into his sermons has gone with her, but his friend, Deacon Hambo, stoutly supports him at every juncture. This bluff widower employs his camaraderie and skill at signifying to make John do right and to steer him away from temptation. When John quietly leaves Hambo's house after a brief visit back to Eatonville, without saying goodbye but leaving ten dollars and some new nightshirts as gifts, Hambo's true nature is revealed, first in comic invective but then in human gestures that speak to Hurston's ability to portray male friendship:

> "Well de hen-fired son-of-a-gun done slipped off and never tole me good bye again! Bet de wop-sided, holler-headed———thought Ah wuz gointer cry, but he's uh slew-footed liar!" Whereupon Hambo cried over the stove as he fried his sow-bosom and made a flour hoe-cake. Then he found he couldn't eat. Frog in his throat or something so that even his coffee choked him. (200)

Hambo enjoys a special relationship with John; his rough talk is characteristic of the playful insults of male contemporaries, a way of talking based on the personal friendship and cordiality of the two pals. In Hurston's novel, Hambo's generational link to John combines with the brotherhood of the church and its extended community to form a doubled male bond.

Hurston does not neglect to show John's ironic double standard regarding infidelity. After men in Eatonville kid around about taking Lucy from John, he will not permit any joking about the matter from Lucy; when she teases, "If you tired uh me, jus' leave me. Another man over de fence waitin fuh yo' job." John, who has his gun with him, lays down the law: "lemme tell you somethin' right now, and it ain't two, don't you never tell me no mo' whut you jus' tole me, 'cause if you do, Ahm gon' tuh kill yuh jes' ez sho ez gun is iron" (110). This rather appalling act of dominance and hypocrisy nevertheless stems from his deep love for Lucy and has sources in the community's double standard.

Lucy knows John's enemies have not given up; she advises John to discard the traditional Passover-Communion sermon in favor of a self-condemning piece that nevertheless recounts his good acts. And indeed John preaches a brilliant sermon that reminds his flock that he is just a simple man who functions as the Lord's mouthpiece, a man with seven "younguns" at home, which testifies to the fact that he's a "natchel" man. This subtle approach situates the children as visible and acceptable signs of his sexual appetite, which he knows preys on his parishioners' minds, but with more negative manifestations. His appeal to the parishioners as his "children in Christ" links them with his "natchel younguns." Saying he doesn't always remember things, he appears to compliment his parishioners on their memories as they sit on their porches "passin' nations thew yo' mouf" along with him, asking them to try to remember his good deeds over the years (122). In powerful language, he admits his hands may not be worthy any longer (the cleanliness theme again) to serve Communion, and he shuts the book and makes to step down, but "strong hands were there to thrust him back. The church surged up, a weeping wave about him. Deacons Hambo and Harris were the first to lay hands upon him . . . he was roughly, lovingly forced back into his throne-like seat" (123). Hurston's magnificent, cosmic writing in this scene makes us feel the power of John's presence and his link to holy passion and ritual. And in such moments, Hurston forces us to consider the role of the instrument of God: is a flawed servant perhaps more effective than one wholly clean? The biblical Jonah was such a man; conversely, Lucy, should she mount the pulpit, would certainly be clean. Do the ends (spiritual elevation and salvation of the parishioners) justify the means (the unclean agent)?

As a result of this conundrum, several times the community tries to pull John down to a lower level of existence. As his friend Hambo tells him late in the book, "You know our people is jus' lak uh passle uh crabs in uh basket. De minute dey see one climbin' up too high, de rest of 'em reach up and grab 'em and pull 'im back. Dey ain't gonna let nobody git nowhere if dey kin he'p it" (169). Thus the black man must fight not only the white community but also members of his own as he seeks to rise.

John's final, violent showdown with his second wife, Hattie, who has conjured him, cannot be read with late-twentieth-century values in mind. John is advised to beat "de blood out her. When you draw her wine dat breaks de spell" (162), and he complies. How does Hurston feel about this? It seems obvious that she views Hattie as totally evil. Hattie's portrayal owes much to Hurston's lifelong animus toward her stepmother, clearly Hattie's model.

When John divorces Hattie, his dignity in the white courthouse adds a new dimension to his performance of manhood. In one of the book's great passages, he eloquently insists on the dignity of individual and racial privacy:

> Ah didn't want de white folks tuh hear 'bout nothin' lak dat [the details of Hattie's behavior]. Dey knows too much 'bout us as it is, but dey some things dey ain't tuh know. Dey's some strings on our harp fuh us tuh play on and sing all tuh ourselves. Dey thinks wese all ignorant as it is, and dey thinks wese all alike, and dat dey knows us inside and out, but you know better. Dey wouldn't make no great 'miration if you had uh tole 'em Hattie had all dem mens. Dey spectin' dat. Dey wouldn't zarn 'tween uh woman lak Hattie and one lak Lucy, uh yo' wife befo' she died. Dey thinks all

> colored folks is de same dat way. De only difference dey makes is 'tween uh nigger dat works hard and don't sass 'em, and one dat don't. De hard worker is uh good nigger. De loafer is bad. Otherwise wese all de same. Das how come Ah got up and said, "Yeah, Ah done it," 'cause dey b'lieved it anyhow, but dey b'lieved de same thing 'bout all de rest. (169)

John's greatest sermon at Zion Hope, his last, comes directly from a sermon originally preached by the Reverend C. C. Lovelace of Eau Gallie, Florida, on 2 May 1929. The powerful cosmic poetry of the piece offers compelling proof of the sources of Hurston's cosmic metaphors and how she used the sacred to create a transcendence for the profane. The references to the "hammers of creation" (175), the "anvils of time" (175), the "rim bones of nothing" (178), the "scepter of revolvin' worlds" (177), the sun gathering up "de fiery skirts of her garments" (176) echo in all Hurston's novels and stories, which move us exponentially by the deepening of the frame of reference. They also demonstrate the noble side of John's character, which has deepened in ironic contrast to his sinning.

Significantly, the woman who renews John's faith in himself is named Sally Lovelace, surely after the minister who provided Hurston with John's last sermon. Sally offers John a pitcher of water before setting him before a groaning table, echoing once again the biblical pattern of the woman at the well greeting the stranger who will become her husband. When John hesitates to say he'll join Sally at church, she responds, "You jokin', Ah know." People wasting their God-given talents are a joke, indeed. His confession of what happened in Sanford follows and ends with him sobbing with his head in her lap, "like a boy of four" (189), once again emphasizing the paradoxically childish aspect of this big-voiced and muscular man. Sally's protective and comically worded growl underlines her replication of the maternal: "none of 'em bet' not come 'round here tryin' tuh destroy yo' influence. . . . Ain't doodley squat dey self and goin' 'round tromplin' on folks dat's 'way uhbove 'em" (189). Moreover, their physical postures here refigure the sheltering shade of the pietà-like gourd vine.

Keith Cartwright has noted that John's proposal to Sally—"Less go git married and den got set on de fish pond and ketch us a mess uh speckled perches for supper"—is an example of old styles of Maroons, the bands of escaped slaves who lived off nature; in those cultures, the "carnal intimacies" of masculine modes of hunting and fishing are employed in romance, and of course Tea Cake teaches Janie how to fish in *Their Eyes*.

After marrying Sally, however, and restoring his self-image, John promptly spins in the direction of another woman. Ora pleads for a ride in his car, using sexually charged, doubled language right out of the blues: "Let de wheels roll. Ah loves cars. Ride me 'til Ah sweat" (197). Once Ora has seduced John, she asks for money, and he spurns her after tossing four dollars down, roughly throwing her from the car. One would think the Hurston of *Their Eyes* would be more sympathetic, but her loyalties are with John, who tries so mightily to resist temptation.

His death in a car-train accident after he has betrayed Sally with Ora might be meant as a modern equivalent of black folklore's chariot of fire or, more obviously, the "Judgment Train" prefigured in John's great sermon; those big wheels of justice, like Fortuna's, will inevitably turn. The conclusion also echoes the death of Hurston's father. Speaking of a conversation with her brother, Hurston relates:

> My father had been killed in an automobile accident during my first years at Morgan, and Bob talked to me about his last days. In reality, my father was the baby of the family. With my mother gone and nobody to guide him, life had not hurt him, but it had turned him loose to hurt himself. He had been miserable over the dispersion of his children when he came to realize that it was so. We were all so sorry for him, instead of feeling bitter as might have been expected. Old Maker had left out the steering gear when He gave Papa his talents. (*Dust Tracks* 172)

In his flawed performance of masculinity, John Hurston's fictional counterpart also lacks a steering gear at the climactic moment, when the train bears down on him. The gear equates to the Christian's fortitude in turning away from temptation. Despite the residual anger at the pain her father caused his wife and children, Hurston seems to feel that her parent had remained true to his African roots by not slavishly following the white man's dictum of the division of soul and body. This view is illustrated as the book ends, when a significantly unnamed preacher eulogizes John but with the congregation transmogrified to Africans: "They beat upon the O-go-doe, the ancient drum." The preacher's last words are "nobody knowed 'im but God" (202).

By focusing on these avatars of black manhood, which have many links to American expectations of male gender formation, teachers can begin an inquiry into models of patriarchy, which continue to plague both relations between the sexes and society as a whole yet contain noble, inspiring, socially useful functions as well. Further, John's performance of his masculinity is also a validation of his culture's glorious oral heritage. Hurston had challenged the race in general in a 29 December 1934 article in the *Washington Tribune* to recognize the fact that African American folk expression had an integrity that was every bit as fine as that of Anglo-American culture. After providing parallels and examples from both sides, she issued a clarion call:

> Who knows what fabulous cities of artistic concepts lie within the mind and language of some humble Negro boy or girl who has never heard of Ibsen. . . . Fawn as you will. Spend an eternity standing awe struck. Roll your eyes in ecstasy and ape [the white man's] every move, but until we have placed something upon his street corner that is our own, we are right back where we were when they filed our iron collar off. ("Race")

With *Jonah*, that street corner had been triumphantly filled.

Freedom and Identity in Hurston's *Moses, Man of the Mountain*

Carolyn M. Jones

Zora Neale Hurston's *Moses, Man of the Mountain* is a retelling of the biblical account of the Exodus, the liberation of the Hebrew people, described in Exodus, Numbers, and Leviticus in the Hebrew Bible. Hurston's retelling of this foundational myth of the West was published in 1939, in a world in economic depression and on the verge of World War II. Hurston's telling is significant for what it does and does not emphasize. The Passover, for example, central to a Jewish understanding of identity and of the significance of the story of Moses, is lyrically represented, much like the poetic telling in Exodus, and then is "passed over" and never revisited. Hurston focuses instead on the figure of Moses and on the transformation of the Hebrews into a people. Moses is a figure of increasing freedom and wisdom, a border figure connected to many worlds and at home in none.

In contrast to Moses are the murmuring Hebrews, particularly Aaron and Miriam, whose stories Hurston changes significantly from the biblical account. Aaron and Miriam represent an insight that Hurston explores in the novel: that the impulse to enslave, to exercise power in destructive ways, and, once conditioned into the human being, the impulse to let oneself be enslaved, to cooperate with that power and to desire it for the self, are always at odds with the impulse to seek freedom and wisdom, the right manifestations of power. This tension is at the heart of the novel, in Hurston's exploration of the African American and the human community and in the character of Moses. He is, as many critics have identified him, a hoodoo man, but he is also a figure of the power of human choice to realize freedom. As the novel progresses, God disappears as an active presence, leaving the construction of human community to human choice, and the novel ends with a critical choice by Moses: the choice to die. To choose death is to choose freedom. Moses's choice of freedom is highlighted in relation to Miriam's and Aaron's choices.

In teaching the novel, I focus on four areas. First, I set out the state of the world in 1939, that is, the issues that are pressing to Hurston as she writes. Second, I look at the figure of Moses as a hero. I present the sources available to Hurston in writing her story and discuss the ways that she expands on and changes the sources. Third, I contrast Moses to Aaron and Miriam, focusing on the nature of slavery. This section is important. Miriam and Aaron function as foils to Moses but also as mirrors in which Moses sees his reflection. Their choices limit and destroy them; Moses's choices free him. This section of the discussion is crucial for understanding the violence in the novel—or at least for offering some explanation for it. Finally, I look at Moses and what he represents and the exploration of what freedom means in the tensions between individuals and groups.

Any discussion of Moses must begin with a discussion of the ancient sources. Moses is, as Jonathan Kirsch points out in *Moses: A Life*,

> [t]he most haunted and haunting figure in all of the Bible. To be sure, he is often portrayed as strong, sure, and heroic, but he is also timid and tortured with self-doubt at key moments in his life. He is a shepherd, mild and meek, but he is also a ruthless warrior who is capable of blood-shaking acts of violence, a gentle teacher who is also a magician and a wonder-worker, a lawgiver whose code of justice is merciful except when it comes to purging and punishing those who disagree with him, an emancipator who rules his people with unforgiving authority. . . . He is God's one and only friend, and yet he is doomed to a tragic death by God himself. (2)

This complex picture of Moses comes partly from the biblical account but more fully from his ancient biographers. The details of Hurston's portrait come from Philo's *De Vita Moses* and from Flavius Josephus's *Jewish Antiquities* (2.197–4.331). Details like Moses's marriage to an Ethiopian princess (Josephus 2.252) and his military prowess (the details of which Hurston expands, giving Moses the skills of the ancestors of the Hebrews, from the Arabian desert horsemen to Mentu), and Pharaoh's resistance to a god he cannot see (Philo 1.88; Hurston, *Moses* 22) come from these sources. Indeed, Hurston's characterization of Moses as king, priest, legislator, and prophet and as one who seeks justice in his "self-appointed task to champion the weaker" comes from Philo (1.50–51). Her picture of Moses as one who enters "into the darkness where God [is], that is into the unseen, invisible, incorporeal and archetypal essences of existing things" also follow Philo's depiction (1.158).

Other information comes from Hurston's training as an anthropologist. The Book of Thoth that Moses finds and learns is a legendary set of forty-two papyrus rolls dictated by the god Thoth, the Egyptian god who is a magician and a patron of scribes. The book, as Susan Edwards Meisenhelder tells us in *Hitting a Straight Lick with a Crooked Stick: Race and Gender in the Work of Zora Neale Hurston*, is described in W. M. Flinders Petrie's *Egyptian Tales*, and Hurston follows his account almost directly (125–27). The forty-two rolls include two rolls in praise of Thoth; four roles on astrology and astronomy that list the knowledge of the priests; ten rolls on religious traditions, including festivals and rituals; and ten rolls on priestly obligation and regulations. The rest, the main part of the text, are a meditation on philosophy and medicine. These occult and esoteric papyri, though never recovered, are speculated to be prominent in the interpretation of Egyptian magic (Bunson 264). This background confirms and complicates the picture of Moses as a hoodoo man (J. Holloway 40; Lowe, *Jump* 248). Hurston links him to mysterious and magical Egypt, which, in the ancient world, was a source of "remarkable things" and a nation that "have made themselves the . . . most learned of any nation," as the Greek historian Herodotus puts it (2.35, 77). Hurston also gives Moses the qualities of Thoth himself—learning and wisdom, magic and writing, love of truth and hatred of abomination (Bunson 264). As Melanie J. Wright points out, Hurston links Moses to Africa through Haitian voodoo. With his staff, he is linked to Damballah, though, Wright emphasizes, Hurston prefers the biblical account "refracted" through African American tradition (54, 57).

Hurston uses Jewish legends, as well, particularly those suggesting that Moses is the Shechinah, the spirit of Yahweh, come to earth: "The great I AM took the soul of the world and wrapped some flesh around it and that made you" (105). She also follows Jewish mystical tradition in calling the commandments given to Moses "letters." Moses gets ten letters, Hurston tells us. In Jewish kabbalah, there is the idea that all creation is made up of the letters of the Hebrew alphabet, letters that contain God's own essence. For example, in *Yahweh* the letters YHWH symbolize God's wisdom, understanding, splendor, and majesty (Ariel 118).

Moses, therefore, in Hurston's account as in all the accounts, embodies multiple cultures, ancient and modern, and remains, as he describes himself in Exodus, "a stranger in a strange land" (2.22)—the eternal other who belongs nowhere.[1] Indeed, in true African American style, Hurston leaves a gap in the text surrounding Moses's identity, opening the door for him to embody a variety of cultures and qualities and to be a world hero.

All critics of the novel agree that the figure of Moses involves a meditation on power. Some critics see Moses as a figure legitimately exercising power; others, like Meisenhelder (136–37), see him as becoming more and more a tyrant as the novel progresses. To be sure, power and violence are hand in hand in the novel. Its context—the world in 1939—makes this connection understandable. World War I had been a total war, fought, savagely, with technology that dehumanized and destroyed human beings in horrible ways, along extensive fronts, and in trenches. Arnold Toynbee wrote that, after the war, his generation expected that life throughout the world

> would become more rational, more humane, and more democratic and that, slowly but surely, political democracy would produce greater social justice. We had also expected that the progress of science and technology would make mankind richer, and that this increasing wealth would gradually spread from a minority to a majority. We had expected that all this would happen peacefully. In fact we thought that mankind's course was set for an earthly paradise, and that our approach towards this goal was predestined for us by historical necessity. (106–07)

The shock of the war, however, scarred a generation, and its aftermath set the stage for the Second World War.

For African Americans, this interwar period was the best and worst of times. Returning black GIs did not receive a warm welcome. Many, wearing their uniforms, were lynched. Indeed, lynching and race riots accompanied the increasingly urban population of African Americans, who were in their own exodus, the great migration from the South to the North, which began around 1879, as the South was "redeemed," or returned, politically, to the hands of those who had controlled it before the Civil War. The 1920s saw the Harlem Renaissance, which spread African American creativity and literacy all over the United States. The Great Depression of the 1930s hit African Americans particularly hard. John Hope Franklin, in *From Slavery to Freedom*, says that twenty to forty percent of black Americans in urban centers were on relief. In Atlanta, the percentage was sixty-five; in Norfolk, eighty (384).

The New Deal, however, helped African Americans in many ways, despite the racism of its workings. Still, African Americans did not experience full citizenship. A. Philip Randolph, in "The Crisis of the Negro and the Constitution," argued, "True liberation can be acquired and maintained only when the Negro people possess power" (qtd. in Franklin 402). Power and freedom and their relationship, therefore, were on the minds of all Americans, black and white, at that time.

What the interwar period meditation on power and freedom suggested was significant. Charisma moves toward structure—institution building, as Max Weber puts it. But institutions fail. Politics—living in human community—necessitates practical solutions, law, structures, and order that are often in conflict with charisma and ideals. Indeed, the world between the wars illustrated how dangerous charisma, unchecked, could be, and the more terrible acts of the novel, like the sacrifice of Aaron, may be a warning about the power of the unchecked individual—the *Übermensch*. And violence, even in the service of necessary change, is problematic, as Jose Miguez-Bonino in *The Development Apocalypse* explains:

> An ethic of revolution cannot avoid discussion of the use and justification of violence. This question, nevertheless, needs to be placed in its proper perspective as a subordinate and relative question. It is subordinate because it has to do with the "cost" of desired change—the question of the legitimacy of revolution is not decided on the basis of the legitimacy of violence and vice versa. Violence is a cost that must be estimated and pondered in relation to a particular revolutionary situation. It is relative because in most revolutionary situations . . . violence is already a fact constitutive of the situation. Injustice, slave-labor, hunger, exploitation are forms of violence that must be weighed against the cost of revolutionary violence. (108)

As Robert McAfee Brown suggests, violence is the last resort. Using existing structures to reform the system, employing nonviolent means to challenge the system, and developing new structures to replace the system should be the initial actions (78). Violence is a viable alternative only after these preliminary steps fail. The Hebrews in the novel try all these, meeting with Pharaoh, for example, to discuss their condition. When these measures fail, something else is called for: that is, a man like Moses.

In Moses, Hurston makes a distinction between force and power. Force is without mercy (1)—exemplified in Ta-Phar, for whom force is his "juices and his meat" (36). Power answers the cry for justice and mercy with which the story begins and is exercised by Moses.

Moses quickly loses his taste for force. It is too personal and requires no self-mastery; indeed, it generates self-indulgence, as we see in Ta-Phar. Moses's first blow against the oppression of the Hebrews is his killing the overseer, who is an embodiment of force. The overseer, who wants to impress Moses, chooses the weakest man to beat. In the overseer's face, Moses sees power, cruelty, and greed and realizes that the desire for force and status makes one small and mean (63). Moses is a man engaged in something that is beyond his own personal self: he is a man with a mission, a calling (103–04, 105–06). Here, Hurston injects Christian ideas into the novel. Moses's right hand is not only a sign of his power but also the instrument of a god whose sign, Hurston says, is power. He is a man, yes, but also a tool of destiny. When he sees the mountain, the place of manifestation of Yahweh in Exodus, Moses feels that he is home (84, 91). The god of the mountain has waited for him (105), for, as Jethro tells us, the great I AM put the soul of the world in Moses's flesh: he is the son of the mountain (106).

The mountain, according to Mircea Eliade in *The Sacred and the Profane: The Nature of Religion*, is the universal pillar, the *axis mundi* that is at the center of the world, connecting heaven and earth (38–41). Moses's conjuring, therefore, is a sign of his connection to God and, like Jesus's miracles, is not the mark of a mere wonderworker, the ancient divine man. Jethro, whose role in Hurston's story is much expanded, teaches Moses the way to manipulate power to create what will become the plagues of Egypt. Jethro is priest and magician, and he passes what he knows to Moses. Moses, however, quickly surpasses Jethro. His right hand has the power not just to conjure but also to bring the people into the presence of God: "So when Moses lifted his hand the smoke of the incense ceased to be smoke. It became the Presence. If it was not the actual Presence, then it enclosed and clothed the Presence. Finally the smoke itself was deified. It was not understood so it became divine" (116). As Karla F. C. Holloway points out, Moses's crossing over, probably the most important moment in his development as a hero, is a symbol of what he is: someone who is always breaking boundaries. His first crossing ends with his adopting the physical pose that signifies his spiritual reality. He is simply a man sitting on a rock, a symbol of his relation to the mountain and, since he has lost all external symbols of worldly power, to his own freedom.

His status as hero is not all that sets him apart. Moses's task requires wisdom, self-mastery, and discipline—hence he is constantly "crossing over" (Hurston, *Moses* 78), the wonderful image with which his journey begins. Moses's discipline, wisdom, and self-mastery are qualities that Miriam and Aaron do not develop. The violence in which he engages thenceforth could be called—whether we like it or not—a just war to reclaim a land promised to his ancestor, Abraham. (Philo speaks of the movement of the Hebrews into Canaan as colonization, familiar to his ancient world.) As such, the movement into the land is one of consecration, cleansing, and sacrifice. These, it can be argued, are not ultimately destructive; though they bring an end to one form of life, they release vis, life force, that establishes new life and nourishes it.[2]

Force robs the Hebrews of their identities. Hurston begins the novel with the birth of Moses not only because his birth begins the hero journey-cycle but also because she wants to show us how the force exercised by Pharaoh enters the intimate spaces of the Hebrews' lives. The marriage bed and the birthing bed and relationships between neighbors are violated, and this psychological damage is worse than the physical damage. Slavery—and it is African American slavery in the New World that is one aspect of contemplation for Hurston—takes away everything. The past, the glorious history of the Hebrews in Egypt; the present, privacy, intimacy, voice (Jochebed cannot cry out in childbirth), and meaningful work; and the future, the gods (21), and any hope disappear, fixing the Hebrews in an intolerable and repetitive present. This generation of Hebrews loses the only home they know, since they are branded impure and alien (20). As the net of slavery closes on the Hebrews, they fear to act; their external condition as well as their internal ones change, as the conversation between Amram and Caleb shows us: One is afraid to risk losing the "nothing" one has (5). It is Jochebed who opens a gap in this misery. She, refusing to kill her child to save it, argues that they should take a chance and commits her child to the river. This marvelous symbol encapsulates the African American experience: for, as Vincent Harding has shown us, the African American identity began at rivers (3–5). Appropriating and reversing this image—here the river will take the Hebrews out of slavery—Hurston opens possibilities of freedom.

With the commitment of the child to the river, Hurston leaves a gap in the text that readers must narrate for themselves. Miriam, Moses's sister, does not see the princess take the baby from the river; she sees her take "something" (28). The biblical text is clear that the child is taken from the bustling Nile and into Pharaoh's household: there, the alien becomes intimate with the ways of the other and able, therefore, to use the master's tools to dismantle the master's house. In changing the biblical episode on the rescue of the baby Moses, Hurston makes us question, Is the Hebrew baby rescued or does he perish on the busy Nile, a corridor of commerce and a symbol of the slave trade? Is Moses the hero truly a Hebrew child, or is he something else? If he is Hebrew, he feels the natural compassion for his own kind. If not—and this is important in an isolationist 1939 America witnessing atrocities in other, distant places like Manchuria—his compassion is an impulse against oppression of any kind and an orientation to freedom. I think Hurston wants to emphasize this second option in her novel. She leaves Moses's true identity a mystery and complicates notions of race. As Deborah G. Plant points out in *Every Tub Must Sit on Its Own Bottom: The Philosophy and Politics of Zora Neale Hurston*, if Moses is the son of the princess and her Assyrian husband, he is Semitic West Asian and African (128). Wright argues that in making Moses racially ambiguous, Hurston distinguishes his kind of leadership from that of, for example, Marcus Garvey and aligns him more with models of the Harlem Renaissance (66). Moses, Wright argues, as a liminal figure has the capacity to exercise power independently, without community approval (64–66). Constructed by Hurston as a meeting place of otherness, Moses can feel for those he has never known and imagine a grace, to paraphrase Toni Morrison, for others: a free nation. He will find the tools to make this vision real on a mountain.

In Hurston's story, this uncertainty about Moses's identity functions in two ways. First, it allows legends to grow like grass (35), generating hope in the Hebrews. Second, it corrupts Miriam and Aaron and the other Hebrews as well. Miriam and Aaron have identities constituted partly by oppression and partly by this potential relation in the house of power. They represent a generation of Hebrews that are Egyptianized—enslaved physically and mentally (Howard, *Zora* 125; Plant, *Every Tub* 135–37; Lowe, *Jump* 220–21, 228, 233–39). They are emblems of the rest of the Hebrews who, particularly in the desert, concentrate on their hunger rather than on freedom and who are by turns afraid and proud—"stiff necked," as Yahweh calls them.

In the biblical account, Miriam and Aaron are powerful figures. Miriam is a prophetess, and Aaron is the appointed father of the priestly class. It is Miriam who leads the women in song and dance after the Egyptians are drowned at the Re(e)d Sea:

> Then Miriam, the prophetess, the sister of Aaron, took a tambourine in her hand: and all the women went out after her with tambourines, dancing. And Miriam led them in the refrain: "Sing to the Lord for he is gloriously triumphant; horse and chariot he has cast into the sea."
>
> (Exod. 15.20–21)

Aaron's power, despite his construction of the golden calf, is divinely confirmed in Numbers 18, after the rebellion of Korah (Num. 16–17). Moses takes the staffs of the tribes into the tent of meeting. Yahweh says, "[T]he staff of the man of my choice shall sprout" (Num. 17.20). The next morning, only Aaron's rod has "sprouted and put forth not only shoots, but blossoms as well, and even bore ripe almonds" (Num. 17.23), confirming the Levites as legitimate priests. Miriam and Aaron, together, turn against Moses only one time, over his wife Zipporah. In Numbers 12, Miriam and Aaron speak against Moses because Zipporah is a Cushite, an Arab woman, probably of darker skin color (M. Wright 61–62). One can speculate that Moses's connection to this foreign, non-Hebrew woman lets them raise a question about Moses's purity as a prophet.[3] They thus question Moses's authority as the only prophet: "Is it through Moses alone that the LORD speaks? Does he not speak through us also?" (Num. 12.2). God brings them into the tent of meeting and explains his particular relationship with Moses. To other prophets, God says, he speaks through dreams and visions (Num. 12.6), but with Moses he speaks directly: "[M]y servant Moses . . . bears my trust: face to face I speak to him, plainly and not in riddles. The presence of the LORD he beholds" (Num. 12.7–8). As punishment, Miriam is struck with leprosy and is "as white as snow" (Num. 12.10). She is then cured after seven days.

Hurston expands this struggle over power and uses it throughout her story of the Exodus. Aaron and Miriam are desirous of the outward trappings of power. Aaron, as we see, wants the symbols of wealth and power before he will help Moses free the Hebrews (131, 230). Denied, he tries to block Moses in every way, risking the freedom of a whole people for his own ego. He is a man with desire but without vision. Similarly, Miriam, at the river, is so focused on the princess and her wealth and beauty that she literally loses sight of her brother. Her relationship to Moses from this point forward is about her desired connection to power represented in an image of beauty. Miriam is a tragic character. She and Aaron are imprinted with destructive attitudes about race and class and cannot see beyond them. Hurston suggests that, since the Egyptians strip the Hebrews in slavery of a relationship with god(s), power becomes a substitute for true worship. Both Miriam and Aaron make power—and because he has power, Moses—the god they desire and fear.

Miriam has power of her own; she is a prophetess, but in Hurston's story she never develops this power or her self (134). Instead, she yearns for that image of beauty, leisure, and wealth that she believes power is and that she sees in the princess and envies in Zipporah, despite her color. She, therefore, can never claim her true power and, most important, can never see Moses as brother, as anything but other. At the end of her life, she believes she must ask his permission to die. This scene is sad and disturbing and troubles my students greatly. Miriam, who has been punished with leprosy for her jealousy of Zipporah, feels bound by Moses, as one feels bound by a hoodoo man, a slave master, and a god. She interprets his power as force. She has only been able to see him as access to power, impediment to her power (and so she fights him), or power itself, god and master. Miriam understands that freedom is the thing to seek, but she does not know what it means: "This freedom is more than a notion, Moses. It's a good thing. It's bound to be a good thing 'cause everybody wants it. But maybe I didn't know what to do with it, 'cause I ain't been so happy" (262). Miriam does not know whether Moses is a god or a man, but she does know that she feels his hand on her: "you locked me up inside myself and left me to wait on your hour" (263–64). One can argue that Miriam's voice is silenced slowly by male power (M. Wright 76), but Hurston wants to suggest more than that. Reared a slave, Miriam can only die as one; she cannot be free. The burden of leadership that shapes Moses twists Miriam. Still, Moses sees her importance for the Hebrews and for him. The stumbling of a woman who could not see where she was going set him on his path (266).

More problematic is the death of Aaron. This scene, in my classes, calls into question Moses's character and motives. Hurston follows the biblical story in certain respects. Moses, Eleazar, and Aaron do go up Mount Hor, and there, Moses strips Aaron of his garments and puts them on Eleazar, his son. The biblical account says only, "Aaron died there on the top of the mountain" (Num. 20.28). In a startling move, Hurston has Moses kill Aaron.

Aaron, despite his flaws, is a hero in the Hebrew Bible. He is Moses's voice, and he is the ancestor of the priesthood of Israel. Hurston changes his character significantly; she makes him a small, greedy, and difficult man who wants power above all else. Moses's murder (to rid himself of Aaron) or sacrifice (to free the people more completely) of Aaron, depending on how one sees the action, is one of the most difficult moments in the text. It parallels Abraham's willingness to sacrifice Isaac in Genesis 22, but in that sacrifice, God, in love and mercy, sends a substitute once God knows that Abraham is faithful, that Abraham fears Him. In Hurston's story, Aaron has neither love nor mercy (272), and so Moses exhibits neither toward him. At this moment, Moses seems to exercise pure force. Aaron is one who desires to be served, not to serve, Moses tells him (272), and his life, which could have had meaning, is therefore only the product of a great misunderstanding. Aaron is not called or chosen by God in the beginning; he is chosen by Moses because Moses needs someone "of the Hebrews" (273). Aaron's desire to exercise power during the journey and in the new land and his unwillingness to engage in self-sacrifice for the greater cause are his crimes, crimes that keep him out of the land.

Self-sacrifice is the issue here. Moses reprimands Aaron for being unwilling to pay the required cost of freedom: "I haven't spared myself, Aaron. I had to quit being a person a long time ago, and I had to become a thing, a tool, an instrument for a cause" (274). Indeed, Moses reminds Aaron, no one has been spared to bring this mission to fulfillment: "No Aaron, nothing and nobody has been spared to make this nation great, and since you wouldn't give yourself in any other way, Aaron, you will have to do something for Israel by denial." With this, Moses kills Aaron with his knife, saying, "God will remember your sacrifice and guard your memories" (275).

Moses seems to have a moment of regret for—or, at least, a moment of self-understanding of—his act. This moment is reminiscent of Orestes's, in Aeschylus's *Oresteia*, understanding that killing his mother is both necessary and indefensible: the hero realizes that an action must be done but that he should not be proud of the action, which carries a stain. As he did with Miriam, and with Ta-Phar before her, what Moses sees in Aaron is his own self: Moses looked down on him and wept. He remembered so much from way back. "Is this my brother? Is this pitiful old carcass blood of my blood? Maybe this is myself in other moods. Who am I to judge him?" (275). Indeed, Moses faces moments in which he could embrace the path of force and power. He realizes, as he looks on the body of Ta-Phar, that he could make himself king, become another pharaoh. The death of Aaron is the price for the nation (275). Indeed, the death of Moses's whole generation is the price. What is Hurston's point?

Hurston wants to make several points. First, the nation, the group, and its mission are more important than the individual. Second, freedom is the result of discipline and self-sacrifice, qualities that Moses has developed. He tells Joshua that a nation must speak with one voice and be one (278–79). Third, the role of the leader is not to please the self or to look important but to channel the intentions of men toward freedom (279). Fourth, freedom is not doing what one wants to do; Hurston is clear that such an idea of freedom only cultivates the worst in human beings. Freedom is, finally, life oriented toward the will of God. Such a life is one in which a human being gains the self by losing it. A human being is an instrument of the divine, but that surrender frees one to seek greater knowledge and to increase wisdom.

Hurston comes, I think, to the conclusion that many of the modernists did. Fearing power—the destructive force of the modern—and its potential and trying to redefine it after World War I, Hurston and her generation had to come to see that power is present in all relationships. The question is not whether there is power but how to exercise it justly, without using force. The novel emphasizes that leadership is difficult for Moses too. Throughout the novel, as in the biblical text, he, like the Stoic hero, wants to give it up and lead the quiet contemplative life. He must find a balance between desire and duty, between love and power that can lead to justice. Love without power becomes threatening in its own way. It potentially leads to loss of the boundaries of the self, as one desires to become the other; Miriam experiences this loss, since she wants to be the princess and cannot. Power without love leads to pure force and totalitarianism, another kind of absorption of the other into the self that is cruel and without mercy. Ta-Phar embodies power in the sense of force, as Aaron would like to do.

The balance is justice and peace, which Moses wants to bring to the Hebrews along with the law (233). Freedom and justice go hand in hand, since freedom is the capacity to exercise power and to love while respecting the boundaries of the self and maintaining the boundaries of the other. The generation of Hebrews who come out of slavery cannot strike this balance. Slavery, in the novel, means to be alien, to be without gods, and to labor. Slavery also means to experience a change of mind, to be unable to choose and act out one's uniqueness. To be able to initiate and to sustain action is to be free. This generation, the children of Jochebed and Amram, are saucy and disrespectful. They have the capacity to pose, but they do not have the capacity to act: slavery is all they have ever known.

Food is a symbol of change in attitude in the novel, and it functions, as my students have shown me, in many ways. When, on the Exodus, the Hebrew people are afraid or hungry, they yearn for the safety of slavery, for a life without responsibility and without true selfhood. The Hebrews associate freedom with food, having one's basic and immediate needs met, but freedom, as Moses tells them, is not a barbecue. The golden calf—a symbol of a source of food as well as an idol—also symbolizes how the fear the newly freed people have leads them back to slavery: they yearn for Egyptian gods they can see, sacrifice, and eat.

The episode, which ends with the righteous slaying the transgressors, is a battle of images and truths. Moses, who does not want to believe what he is hearing and seeing, breaks the tablets of law on the golden calf. That the tablets break suggests that this generation, including Aaron, cannot move beyond the calf and its meanings. They do not learn and change; they only come to fear Moses and to alternate between fearful obedience and sullen disrespect.[4]

Because the Hebrews fear loss and death, the ultimate risking of the self to be free, they cannot embrace and change life. They cannot, in the language of the novel, cross over, a term that implies the internal crossing of conversion, the ritual crossing of boundaries between god and man, and the change in personality toward freedom. The Hebrews turn away rather than cross over. They turn away from the promised land because they fear the risk that is necessary to possess it. Crossing over is more than physical movement: it represents spiritual and ontological readiness. The Hebrews have to have shed the old selves of slavery to be able to enter and claim the land. The generation of Miriam and Aaron does not enter the land; slavery is their story, all they know. Moses is the only one of his generation who maintains and develops a tremendous capacity for change. When Moses crosses over, he has been stripped of all that makes him Egyptian. He is, simply, a man ready for the next step in his life. At the end of the novel, as the Hebrews prepare to cross over, Joshua realizes that they are "a people now" (277). The use of "people" and not "nation" suggests unity in diversity, wholeness, and identity.

Moses speculates on what a nation is. A nation is "one," speaking in one voice (278). Yet as Moses sits alone on another rock—Mount Pisgah—he understands that he has both succeeded and failed. He did not make a perfect nation, but perhaps he has planted an idea of freedom: "He had found out that no man may make another free. Freedom was something internal. All you could do was to give the opportunity for freedom and the man himself must make his own emancipation" (282). Freedom, Moses suggests, is not easy: he thinks that he has given the Hebrews another sort of work—the "strife of freedom" (284). Freedom is also taking responsibility for one's own (284). Freedom is like music; the melody is the same for all, for a nation, but the words vary for each individual: "He had given Israel back the notes to songs. The words would be according to their own dreams, but they would sing. They had songs and singers" (283). In a time of imminent national crisis, Hurston envisions a way to balance the nation and the individual.

But the nation will not have Moses. Moses, who has given up force and the desire for power, recoils at the thought of kingship and decides, at the end of the novel, to die. In the biblical text, God refuses to let Moses enter the land because he strikes the rock at the spring of Meribah (meaning "strife," where the Israelites strive against God) instead of calling water from it as Yahweh instructs him (Num. 20.8–11). His death is in secret. In the novel, Moses makes the choice to die. There is nothing for him to do in the land except rule, continuing the dependency of the people on him, and he does not want that role. Moses, in choosing death, chooses ultimate freedom. This capacity to risk is what Moses has tried to instill in the Hebrews from the beginning. Without him, they will be pushed into action. They will have to make a beginning of their own, to add their words to the music that Moses has given them. Moses's choice is spurred by his conversation with the old lizard—a symbol of African knowledge and of reconnection to the ancestors.

Moses goes out in glory in the novel. He becomes part of the hierophany of Yahweh, standing in thunder and lightning. His feet are on the moon, and the planets circle his head. He is transfigured, and the people see, if not Moses himself, the lightning: "Fire and flame played all over the peak where the people could see" (288). With the voice of freedom, the thunder, Moses says good-bye. Moses had told Ta-Phar before the Exodus that "I AM" is "a great answer. It takes in the whole world and the firmaments of heaven" (137). He tells the people, "You will be free when you hear the thunder" (138). Moses hears the thunder, becomes one with it, and enters the I AM, the eternal source of being, identity, and action; hearing the thunder, the Hebrews are free.

Moses is more than a man; he remains a spirit of freedom, wisdom, and power. Moses's path is not for all men and women. He is the exemplary hero who keeps connecting to ancient knowledge, the quest figure who seeks new places, and the wise man who deepens his knowledge of the world and of God. As he disappears—in the novel and in the traditional story—his power remains available to all those who need him, who need the spirit of freedom. This myth is important for African American culture because it is, as I have written in "Moses: Identity and Community in Exodus," the story that is the critique of the story:

> Moses is that "homeless spirit," that demonic (in the Tillichian sense), creative power that Yahweh is, loves, and honors.
>
> For the modern person, particularly for colonized peoples of the new world, Moses' role as homeless spirit represents the promise of liberation and of justice. This story, his story, illustrates the power of signification by the powerless. That is, the Exodus story is the symbol of the master's trope being used to undermine the master's power. The Exodus myth, that central myth of the West, also makes a critique of its most terrible acts. It is the story within what Toni Morrison calls the "master narrative," the ideological script of the West, that, again and again, has been used to symbolize and to encourage the flight of people from and the fight of people against oppression and terror. It is a cry from within: a reminder and a cultural conscience. (C. Jones 381)

Hurston ends her novel in three ways. First, the Hebrews are poised to cross over and to begin their life as a people in a New World. Then, she ends with all human possibility and potential; a cycle begins (see Lowe, *Jump* 247). Moses the man shares in this human dimension and is joyful at the prospect of new adventure. Finally, having Moses step into eternity, Hurston makes his spirit of freedom always accessible, present and available to all, eternally. As the Hebrews move forward in time, Moses moves back, to origins, toward timelessness.

Freedom involves all these things—individual, group, and spirit—and yet its meaning is almost impossible to define. Orlando Patterson, in *Freedom in the Making of Western Culture*, argues that freedom in the West "was generated from the experience of slavery." People came to value freedom, "to construct it as a powerful shared vision of life, as a result of their experience of and response to, slavery or its recombinant form, serfdom, in their roles as masters, slaves, and nonslaves" (xiii). Patterson, who does not discuss the Exodus in this volume but begins with Greece and Rome, argues that freedom has three dimensions. Personal freedom is the individual person's sense that he or she is not "coerced or restrained in doing something desired and, on the other hand, the person's desire to do the same" (3). Thus personal freedom is the "capacity to do as one pleases insofar as one can" within boundaries. Sovereign freedom is the capacity to do as one pleases, regardless of the wishes of others, or the capacity to transgress boundaries. Civic freedom is the "capacity of adult members of a community to participate in its life and governance" (4). One is free in belonging to a community of birth, in having a place in it, and in participating in its governance. Religion raises the additional issue of freedom's including doing what one should do morally and religiously. Freedom is not just having freedom *from* something but also having freedom *for* something—for Hurston, the nation, or for Moses, knowledge and wisdom.[5]

Hurston's Moses is a complicated picture of a free man, and, as such, he does justice to the complicated notion of freedom. The novel was reviewed in widely different ways: some called it a masterpiece, and others criticized it. Its unevenness is what makes it a terrific novel to teach. As Robert E. Hemenway points out in his biography of Hurston, Moses is a central figure in African American culture, a deliverer (*Zora* 258). Hurston's portrait of Moses is not a fully integrated one. She puts side-by-side Moses as Hebrew, African, Semitic, and Asian; as deliverer and hoodoo man (263); and as charismatic leader and lawgiver and free man. Blyden Jackson says in "*Moses: Man of the Mountain*: A Study of Power" that "[a] blend of the human and the extra-human make him what he is" (153). Hurston's final emphasis is on that balance in the individual. Moses is, as many critics have emphasized, a man (Howard, *Zora* 120). In an interview with Nick Aaron Ford in 1936, Hurston said:

> You see . . . I have ceased to think in terms of race; I think only in terms of individuals. I am interested in you now, not as a *Negro* man but as a *man*. I am not interested in the race problem, but I am interested in the problems of individuals, white ones and black ones. ("Study" 8)

The territory of *Moses, Man of the Mountain* is the individual human being in action. For Judaism, Moses is such a hero precisely because he is flawed: that a finite human being can become perfect is the sign that all human beings can become perfect in relation to God.

Hurston's sense of freedom is that freedom is the perfection of the individual. To move to self-awareness while gaining experience is freedom. Such a process is done in relation to other people. A recurring motif in the novel is Moses's looking at the face of a dead intimate and coming to a moment of self-understanding. The face of the other is, finally, the face of the self, either as mirror or as contrast. That these moments of self-definition come in looking at the dead leads Moses to his final embrace of death as freedom. To face and embrace death authentically is to live freely and fully. To be sure, the endings of Hurston's novels are tinged with joy as well as sadness. Janie Crawford, in *Their Eyes Were Watching God*, alone on her porch, throws out her net and is able to bring the world, the creation, to her; Moses steps into eternity, entering the creation. Both say farewell, Janie to Tea Cake and to her friend, and Moses to his people. This capacity to stand alone, to own one's story and connect it with the stories of others, and to develop the power to gesture meaningfully to the cosmos without fear is to be free. Like the "cosmic Zora," her characters experience this world fully to be able to enter another world fully (Hurston, "How" 1010).

NOTES

[1] All quotations from the Bible are taken from *The New Oxford Annotated Bible*.

[2] Some African American thinkers have called for the abandonment of the promised-land model in African American liberation theology, because of the violence involved in its conquest: "It was in the early 1970's . . . that C. Shelby Rooks proposed that blacks should abandon the theme of 'promised land,' along with that of 'the American Dream,' because the former had become tarnished by its crass reformulation into the latter" (D. Williams 36).

[3] Louis Ginzberg, in *The Legends of the Jews*, reports the Jewish legend that the disagreement was over the fact that Moses no longer had sexual relations with Zipporah. Neither Aaron nor Miriam had been forbidden by God to suspend sexual relations with their spouses. Also, both Aaron and Miriam are stricken with leprosy, according to the legend. Aaron's goes away "as soon as he looked upon his leprosy" (3.259). Miriam's lasts longer because she is the one who starts the talk against Moses.

[4] Food has many other functions in the novel. Moses feeds Mentu from Pharaoh's table; food is therefore associated with status but also with love, respect, care, and knowledge. Food is gift: God provides manna and quail in the desert for the grumbling Hebrews. Food is brought out for celebration: when Jochebed thinks that Moses is saved, she makes honey cookies (31). Food is, most important, associated with sacrifice: there are times when the Hebrews who are first enslaved, like Jochebed and Amram, do not eat so that something greater can come to be. Such a moment is the making of the basket for the baby Moses: "So four people forgot hunger that night" (24). The Passover itself involves food: the sacrifice of the Paschal Lamb whose blood, smeared on the door lintel, saves the firstborn of the household, insuring the future. Moses, as hero, transforms the

ordinary—food—into the extraordinary that connects the people to something beyond themselves. It connects them to each other (the nation) and to God (the calling), making associations with wisdom, discipline, and freedom.

5 These definitions follow the basic philosophical arguments that freedom is doing what one desires to do and also having the choice to do otherwise (that is, being able to move beyond determinism), as well as acting in harmony with one's character. Martin Luther, for example, argues that the Christian person has freedom *from* the world and freedom *for* the world. The Christian person would not want the world to be the ultimate object of trust and loyalty; God is that ultimate object. To see oneself as freed from the world and free for God, one can be free in the world but the justification for that being is not the world.

Politics of Self: Individualist Perspectives in *Seraph on the Suwanee*

Deborah G. Plant

In his review essay "Between Laughter and Tears," Richard Wright declared that Zora Neale Hurston's novel *Their Eyes Were Watching God* "carries no theme, no message, no thought" (76). Alice Walker decried *Dust Tracks on a Road* as "the most unfortunate thing Zora ever wrote" (*In Search* 91). Darwin T. Turner, in his *In a Minor Chord*, castigated *Moses, Man of the Mountain* as a mere joke (111). Mary Helen Washington dismissed *Seraph on the Suwanee* as "an awkward and contrived novel, as vacuous as a soap opera" ("Woman" 21). With the exception of Wright's, perhaps, these assessments of Hurston's works are made in context of an overall evenhanded evaluation of Hurston's oeuvre. Even so, later scholars have approached these works from critical perspectives that have allowed them to sound the deep structure of the texts and yield rich interpretations that reflect the multivocal, multivalent dimensions of Hurston's writing. Such analyses have rescued these texts from literary obscurity and oblivion and situated them in the (African) American literary canon. *Seraph on the Suwanee*, however, continues to be neglected by many scholars and teachers. As previous critical evaluations have charged, this novel does not easily lend itself to a feminist-womanist reading, and it is not an apparent celebration of black cultural aesthetics and expression. So why read *Seraph on the Suwanee*? Why teach it? What useful interpretations might this narrative yield?

In 1970, Walker audited a course on black literature. She writes, "I became aware of my need of Zora Neale Hurston's work some time before I knew her work existed. . . . I was writing a story that required accurate material on voodoo practices among rural Southern blacks of the thirties . . ." (*In Search* 83). The material Walker found by white anthropologists proved to be racist, disappointing, and insulting and thus not useful to her. "Fortunately, it was then that I discovered *Mules and Men*, Zora's book on folklore, collecting, herself, and her small, all-black community of Eatonville, Florida" (83). Walker's need for an authentic, positive, and empowering assessment, evaluation, and articulation of African American cultural practice and expression led her to the discovery of *Mules and Men* (just as the need of feminist and womanist scholars and activists for positive images and powerful narratives of black female identity and experience led to the recovery of *Their Eyes Were Watching God*).

"Delighted" by *Mules and Men*, Walker was particularly impressed with Hurston's pride in black folks and her strong sense of self: "She had a confidence in herself as an individual that few people (anyone?), black or white, understood" (*In Search* 85). Scholars and critics of Hurston's life and work continually examine and speculate on the wherefore of her self-confidence and achievement. Her individualist orientation is accounted as a major factor in her success. Hurston's staunch individualism is all the more remarkable given her admitted insecurities and diffident sense of self. In an October 1947 letter to her publisher, Burroughs Mitchell, Hurston spoke to the difficulties of communicating with and relating to someone who has an inferiority complex. She alluded to insecure men who were intimidated by her achievements and to her own personal experiences regarding self-esteem:

> Though brash enough otherwise, I got an overwhelming complex about my looks before I was grown, and it was very hard for a long time for me to believe that any man really cared for me. I set out to win my fight against this feeling, and I did. I don't care how homely I am now. I know that [it] doesn't really matter, and my relations with others are easier.
> (Kaplan, *Zora* 558)

Hurston doesn't explain her struggle or how she won her fight. How does one achieve such self-confidence? How does one come into one's self? How does one develop an empowering politics of self? I suggest that *Seraph on the Suwanee* offers possible answers to these questions and that an interpretation of the novel in the context of individualist perspectives may reward contemporary readers. Hurston's individualist stance is particularly poignant in *Seraph on the Suwanee*. The development of her protagonist, Arvay Henson Meserve, and her journey to selfhood is profound and instructive. As Hazel Carby points out in her foreword to the novel:

> [I]t is the complexity and depth of Arvay's frustrated and unsatisfied desires that make *Seraph on the Suwanee* a very modern text, a text that speaks as eloquently to the contradictions and conflict of trying to live our lives as gendered beings in the 1990's as it did in 1948. (xvi)

Seraph also speaks to the contradictions and conflicts inherent in our effort to live as racialized and social beings, contradictions that, even in the twenty-first century, continue to remain unresolved for many members of our global society. More important, *Seraph* looks at the possibilities of crossing the borders of the contradictory concepts and thought patterns that keep us from simply experiencing the world as human beings.

Through Arvay's character, Hurston explores the politics of race, class, and gender as a self-defeating politics of dualism. The very frustration and dissatisfaction Arvay experiences is, at bottom, the result of a mind divided against itself. This division, projected outward, creates the distorted view of reality that strains her social relations. Arvay's journey, then, becomes a search for psychological wholeness and integrity, a search for her individuality. In *Seraph on the Suwanee*, Hurston's conceptualization of the term *individual* goes beyond the rather superficial notion of someone separate and apart who has unique, distinguishing attributes. Her treatment of Arvay suggests a definition of the term that emphasizes its Latin root *individuus*, meaning "undivided." Arvay's suffering stems from a dualistic worldview that generates a sense of inferiority, a distrust of her own senses, a fear of others, and a fragmented and conflicted thought pattern that renders her deluded, devious, suspicious, and fitful (all aspects of her psychoemotional self personified in her son Earl). Hurston's task, then, is to fuse Arvay's id and ego—feeling and thought, body and mind—to get Arvay back together as a single-minded individual.

Carby notes, "In many ways *Seraph on the Suwanee* was Hurston's most ambitious and most experimental novel to date" (Foreword xiv). In this novel, Hurston brings to bear some of her most significant personal, political, and professional issues and convictions. She addresses theories of cultural relativity and cultural integration, concerns regarding literary conventions, questions of sex and gender equality in heterosexual relationships, personal and political power, individual freedom, and social equanimity. Arvay Henson is the matrix through which these narrative concerns get filtered and resolved. If Hurston's protagonist seems weighted down and overburdened to a point where even Hurston protests, "I get sick of her at times myself" (Kaplan, *Zora* 557), it is because Arvay Henson is "de mule of de world" as constructed in *Seraph*. More representative of philosophical and political standpoints than not, Arvay's character is metaphoric. It is a "sign and symbol" of the confusion of the American mind and its possibilities as much as it is an expression of Arvay's (and Hurston's) personal conflicts. Hurston was in accordance with Ruth Benedict's theory that culture was human "personality writ large": a community or society reflects the norm generated by the majority of the individuals in it (*Patterns* 251). As Benedict expressed it, the corporate behavior is "nevertheless the behavior of individuals" (251). Arvay's dualistic and hierarchical thinking reflects and generates the sociopolitical polarity of American society. Arvay's character, therefore, has a twofold purpose: she is both an articulation of the ills of American society and the solution to those ills. If American society is to be transformed, that transformation must first take place in the minds of individual Americans, who must achieve an authentic individualism, in the sense that one has an undivided mind.

Healthy and authentic individualism is inhibited by the double-consciousness that characterizes American society. Hurston's "'Pet' Negro System" and "Crazy for This Democracy" highlight inveterate and persistent dualities of American social, political, and economic institutions. They point up Hurston's concerns and serve as blueprints for reading and interpreting Hurston's efforts in *Seraph on the Suwanee*. Hurston wrote her publisher of her intent to draw a "true picture of the South" (Kaplan, *Zora* 561). The true picture Hurston presents in *Seraph* upsets the assumed racial and social polarities of her day. Beliefs about blacks and whites and attitudes about the North and the South are challenged. In "The 'Pet' Negro System," Hurston adopts the tone of the black folk preacher and makes use of sermonic rhetoric to delineate the particulars of what she describes as the "pet" Negro system: "the web of feelings and mutual dependencies spun by generations and generations of living together and natural adjustment" (157). The pet Negro, Hurston writes, is someone highly favored and selected by a white person or persons and is granted the privileges and perquisites denied other blacks. Conversely, pet whites are those usually prominent, "quality" white folks in the community to whom the pet Negro attaches him- or herself. They admire and serve each other accordingly and look out for each other's welfare (157–58). Hurston considered race relations, particularly in the South, to be a complex matter. The rigid, antagonistic, and stereotyped views held by outsiders undermined chances of social progress. Only policies and plans that gave attention to particulars and to individuals, Hurston maintained, would make the difference (162).

Hurston fictionalizes her observations about race and her vision of racial relations in *Seraph on the Suwanee*. As the resident head of a turpentine camp in Sawley, Jim Meserve, Arvay Henson's suitor, oversees the business of the camp and its workers. Though highly critical of the men's work, he makes an exception for Joe Kelsey's less-than-perfect performance:

> He had spotted a few cups that Joe had not cleaned out well, but he didn't care too much. That was not so good for the company, but he was not going to kick up a fuss with Joe Kelsey about it at all, because somehow, he liked the man tremendously. (43)

Jim Meserve's relationship with Joe Kelsey is critical: it is a source of Hurston's theories—of individualism and of cultural relativity, cultural transference, and integration—and a key factor in the unfolding drama of the narrative. For instance, feeling insecure and uncertain about Arvay's love for him, Jim has a confidential conversation with Joe, his messenger throughout his courtship of Arvay. After this conversation, Jim Meserve determines his actions with Arvay. "Most women folks will love you plenty if you take and see to it that they do," Joe counseled. "Make 'em knuckle under. From the very first jump, get the bridle in they mouth and ride 'em hard and stop 'em short. They's all alike, Boss. Take 'em and break 'em" (46). Influenced by Joe's philosophy on life and love, Jim forces sexual relations with Arvay, then elopes.[1] Married and settled into one of the cabins at the turpentine camp, Arvay becomes acquainted with Joe and Dessie, Joe's wife, and is made aware of their importance to Jim. "Arvay was a daughter of the South. She knew exactly what to think from that," interjects the narrator. Arvay is familiar with this "underground" institution, and it is she who names the situation: "Joe is your pet, I'll bound you." "Kee-reck!" Jim expounds, "Different from every other Negro I ever did see. He's remarkable. Honest as the day is long. Just mighty damn fine, that's all." "Arvay sympathized and understood" Jim's disposition (60, 61). In the ensuing paragraph, characterized by free indirect discourse, Hurston inscribes the narrative with the tenets of the pet Negro system outlined in her essay.

Family visits keep Arvay restless at the camp. Even in her own home, she feels dominated by her sister, Larraine, who does not allow Arvay "to be head of a single thing." She chafes under Larraine's bossiness. There, she also feels guilty over the mental adultery she engaged in, believing that her brother-in-law, the Reverend Carl Middleton, was meant for her. She is afraid her secret thoughts will be made known (61, 62). So she longs to get away from her family and get away from Sawley. She begs, "Jim, please! Take me on off" (64). Shortly after the birth of their son Earl, Jim and Arvay relocate to Citrabelle. Arvay's loneliness and Jim's debauchery compel Arvay to seek the presence of Jim's pets. "Jim always liked having Joe around, and maybe if Joe was here, Jim could be broken of these new habits" (89). She attributes the stability of the Meserve household to the presence of the Kelseys. Over the years, the families grow socially, economically, and culturally interdependent. Their children share an easy camaraderie, Dessie assists Arvay in her domestic and child-rearing responsibilities, and Joe assists Jim in his agricultural and business ventures. Joe also spends time with Kenny Meserve, Jim and Arvay's younger son, teaching him to play guitar and nurturing his musical inclinations.[2]

Though Arvay seems to get on well enough with Dessie, she never sees herself as an integral part of this family-community. Insecure about her place in it, as she was about her place in the Henson household, Arvay opposed every perceived threat to her fragile sense of self-worth. To bolster her sense of security and boost her feeling of superiority, Arvay castigates the Kelseys and takes advantage of every opportunity to jockey against them for position in Jim's eyes. When Arvay discovers that Joe's daughter, Belinda, and Kenny attract attention at the train depot because Belinda stands on her head, "innocent of underwear," Arvay whips them both but blames Belinda for leading her son astray. When Jim speaks in Belinda's defense, Arvay feels herself losing ground: "Belinda being that no-count Joe's young 'un, I reckon any caper that she might up and cut just have to be put up with. Look like Joe is the boss on this place" (112). Jim convinces Arvay that she is "the most precious thing" he's got, and so Arvay's ire is assuaged: "Long as Joe ain't got more influence over you than I have, Jim, I ain't got a thing against him" (113). Given that the dualism of Arvay's thinking is only assuaged, not resolved, it needs only the next opportunity to express itself anew.

It "fell into Arvay's ears" that Jim was running a whiskey still. As Arvay blamed Belinda for Kenny's "going astray," she blames Joe for Jim's involvement with the still. Despite Jim's defense of Joe Kelsey, or maybe because of it, Arvay is persuaded of Joe's culpability. Though Arvay is forbidden to speak her mind to Joe, her actions speak clearly, and Joe concludes that "Miz' Arvay seemed like she would rather have his space than his company. It would be much more better if he took his family and got off the place" (117). With Joe's banishment, Arvay feels her superiority, but it is a Pyrrhic victory. Arvay's initial happiness quickly dissipates. The emptiness left in the silence of their absence gives rise to tensions in the Meserve household. Arvay's demand for, then her opposition to, Joe's presence bespeaks the nature and strength of the pet system. Jim's dependence on, defense of, and affinity for Joe Kelsey contradicts the belief that "the hand of every white man in the South is raised against his black brother" and affirms that the South lives and thinks in individuals (Hurston, "'Pet' Negro System" 156–57). Hurston writes in *Dust Tracks on a Road* that "the solace of easy generalizations was taken from me, but I received the richer gift of individualism. When I have been made to suffer or when I have been made happy by others, I have known that individuals were responsible for that, and not races" (323). Joe Kelsey's relationship to Jim and his family, specifically Kenny, are rendered as prime examples of the kind of social intercourse possible when individuality is the point of reference. These relationships exemplify Hurston's theories of social equality and cultural fusion and suggest the possibility of a truly integrated American society. The holdback to that possibility, Hurston contends, is a politics of dualism fed by personal insecurity and, in America, expressed as racial prejudice and class consciousness.

Prima facie, Jim's relationship with Joe reflects a respect for the individual, a point of view in accord with Hurston's own philosophy.[3] Arvay's relationship, contradistinctively, places her in the camp of those caught up in the dualism of easy generalizations. In terms of race and class, Arvay's thought and behavior reflect the dominant discourse of her day. She feels herself superior to people of color and behaves accordingly. Though Arvay's racist attitude is only subtly evinced in her relationship with the Kelseys, her objectification of the Kelseys is obvious in her whimsical beckonings and dismissals. She behaves as though they are (her) property to take with her or repulse at will. To the extent that they serve her purposes, they are tolerated. Basically, she conceives of them as heathens. Early on in the novel, in the contemplation of her role as Christian missionary, Arvay envisioned herself as one who would take the word to the "heathens of China, India and Africa" (4–5). Encoded in Arvay's use of the term *heathen* is the assumption of the moral and cultural inferiority of blacks. Any perceived offense affirms her conviction.

Arvay's dualist and hierarchical thinking is clearly seen in her relationship with the Corregio family. Jim informs Arvay that "a white family" will occupy the house left vacant by the Kelseys. Arvay was annoyed when she discovered the ethnic makeup of the family:

> Jim said that they were white folks, but the man turned out to be a Portuguese, and his name was Corregio. That made them foreigners, and no foreigners were ever quite white to Arvay. Real white people talked English and without any funny sounds to it. The fact that his wife was a Georgia-born girl that he married up around Savannah did not help the case one bit, so far as Arvay could see. The woman had gone back on her kind and fallen from grace. (120)

Arvay's assessment of the family and what she could expect from them was telltale. "[W]hat did this Gee know about tending a grove?" Arvay ruminated. "And this Georgia Cracker woman who had lowered herself to marrying a foreigner, was not going to be one bit of service to her around the house" (121).

The less worth Arvay feels, the more petty and crass she and her behavior toward others become. Critics have addressed Jim Meserve's egotism and have duly noted that his self-serving attitude is evident even in his name—Me-Serve. Arvay also believes in her presumed privilege as a white woman to benefit from services provided by others. She is like the "pink-toes" Hurston describes in "Seeing the World As It Is," who think that "everybody else owes him something just for being blond" (*Dust Tracks* 343).

In "Crazy for This Democracy," Hurston rails against Western tyranny over the people of Africa and Asia and calls attention to the lack of practice of democratic values in American society. Balked by Jim Crow laws, she complains of her inability to participate fully in first-class citizenship. Hurston writes:

> These Jim Crow laws have been put on the books for a purpose, and that purpose is psychological. It has two edges to the thing. By physical evidence, back seats in trains, back-doors of houses, exclusion from certain places and activities, to promote in the mind of the smallest white child the conviction of First by Birth . . . No one of darker skin can ever be considered an equal. (167–68)

Jim Crow laws are well in effect in Citrabelle. Colored Town is where blacks live, and Mondays are their market days. The author makes no issue of this, but the dualistic philosophy it promotes is manifested in the mindset and carried out in the thoughts and actions of Arvay Henson Meserve. Arvay steadfastly refuses to associate with the Corregios and holds them in great contempt. She spurns invitations to eat the "Geechy messes" Mrs. Corregio cooks, and she holds them responsible for every perceived and real problem that she has since their arrival. When Earl's behavior becomes progressively antisocial and dangerous, Arvay blames the Corregios. She tells Jim:

> He was all right, and you know it, until you fetched them furriners here on the place. They must have some different scent from regular folks and it maked Earl sick in some way or another. All you got to do is get rid of 'em; and Earl will be all right. (125)

Rarely feeling that she belongs any place she finds herself, Arvay is always betwixt and between, as is her mental disposition. She therefore gives no thought to her habit of dislocating others. Jim, however, refuses to have the Corregios leave and, rather, suggests that they "put the boy away and provide for him" (125). Arvay is thoroughly offended and insulted, given that Jim attributes Earl's condition to her side of the family. Arvay takes this opportunity to express her racist and class-conscious mind in the context of her relationship to Jim Meserve and his lineage:

> I know that you been had it in you to say all the time. I been looking for you to puke it up long time ago. What you stay with me for, I don't know,

> because I know so well that you don't think I got no sense, and my folks don't amount to a hill of beans in your sight. You come from some big high muck-de-mucks, and we ain't nothing but piney-woods Crackers and poor white trash. Even niggers is better than we is, according to your kind. (126)

Arvay is white but feels that she is denied the first-by-birth privilege to which she believes she is entitled. Finding herself on a low rung of the same hierarchical ladder by which she judges others, she is victimized by her own oppositional thinking. Her polarized mindset generates tension, separation, and alienation. "Race Pride is a sapping vice," Hurston writes (*Dust Tracks* 325).

> It has caused more suffering in the world than religious opinion, and that is saying a lot. . . . Race Pride and Race Consciousness seem to me to be not only fallacious, but a thing to be abhorred. It is the root of misunderstanding and hence misery and injustice. (326)

Arvay, unfortunately, combines both race pride and religious opinion. The more insecure and unworthy Arvay feels, the more small-minded and unjust she becomes to others, and the more miserable she becomes. The argument over Earl deepens the divide between Arvay and Jim: "The very air of the home was charged with opposition" (130). Arvay believes that now, "Jim's real feelings were exposed. He had never taken her for his equal. He was that same James Kenneth Meserve of the great plantations, and looked down on her as the backwoods Cracker, the piney-wood rooter" (130). In actuality, Arvay exposes her sense of herself as inferior and inadequate. She can never see herself as Jim's equal because she does not believe in equality.

Arvay's prejudices undermine the possibility of peace in her home as they undermine social harmony in her relations with the Kelseys and the Corregios. Her fractious mindset creates schisms all around her and results in her social alienation. Feeling powerless and excluded from Jim's life and the life of her children, Arvay finds refuge in race pride and class consciousness and the consequent denigration and exclusion of racial others. At the football event, Arvay looks on proudly as her son Kenny and her daughter, Angie, interact with those considered to be of high social status. Her children "seem to be right in with the best they is" (207). She is appalled, however, that Kenny deigned to include Felicia, the Corregios' daughter, in their clique. "She had no right to look for Felicia at a place like this, and certainly not in that kind of clothes. When she did make out who that was with Kenny, she was thunder-struck by lightning" (208). While everyone else is having fun, Arvay's mind is doing battle: "Where and how did Felicia get those clothes that she had on? What was she doing here? Kenny had never mentioned Felicia in a single letter to her, so something underhand was going on" (209). Though Arvay feels outclassed among her children's friends, she still feels her white privilege and resents Felicia's presence in her circle. "She could not enjoy anything, however, for Felicia Corregio was there flashing around the room and stopping close to the band," where Kenny played (211–12). Arvay blames the Corregios for Earl's death, and so Felicia's presence reminds her of that event. But Arvay seems more upset that Felicia is accepted: "Jim and the rest insisted that the Corregios were as white as they were" (212).

Arvay continues to feel like an outsider. After Earl's death, Kenny's decision to pursue his career, and Angie's marriage, Arvay questions her reason for being. She feels as though she can never measure up to anybody's standards, certainly not Jim's. When she stands paralyzed while Jim is in danger of being bitten by the rattler, Arvay is found guilty. Arvay and Jim's subsequent separation forces Arvay to begin to think for herself. She resolves to "go back with her own kind" (131). After all, she consoles herself,

> [t]he Bible said, "Everything after its own kind," and her kind was up there in the piney woods around Sawley. Her family, and the folks she used to know before she fooled herself and linked up with a man who was not her kind. Arvay tossed her head defiantly and rhymed out that she was a Cracker bred and a Cracker born, and when she was dead there'd be a Cracker gone. (271–72)

Race and class pride, Hurston wrote, is "poor nourishment." "Mighty little to chew on. You had to season it awfully high with egotism to make it tasty" (*Dust Tracks* 327). With each return to Sawley, Arvay has less and less to chew on. On her last visit, Arvay's romantic and self-deluded notions about the enchantment of Sawley and the superiority of its "teppentime Crackers" begin to dissipate. Taxiing through town, she witnesses the physical decay of old Sawley juxtaposed against modern hotels and businesses. Her delusions of a loving, peaceful, neighborly citizenry are contradicted by the taxi driver's experience of the townspeople:

> Lady! You must not know this town too good. I moved here fifteen years ago and I done summered and wintered with these folks. I hauled the mud to make some of 'em, and know 'em inside and out. I ain't seen no more goodness and kindheartedness here than nowhere else. Such another back-biting and carrying on you never seen. They hate like sin to take a forward step. Just like they was took out their cradles, they'll be screwed down in their coffins. (274)

Arvay is taken aback to see the driver's words realized in the dilapidated condition of her family homestead and in the "ton of coarse-looking flesh" she recognizes as her sister. Her mother, Maria, lies among rats and filth, awaiting Arvay and awaiting death. In the wake of her mother's passing and in the handling of the details of death, Arvay gradually comes alive. For the first time in her adult life, Arvay is present to what is going on and where she is. Her body and mind are finally in the same place. She realizes that her mother's life would have been her death. She sees the absurdity of feeling inferior to her elder sister, Larraine, and she finally lets go of the fantasy that her brother-in-law is the man of her dreams and the ideal husband she missed having.

With each act of pettiness leveled at her by Carl and Larraine and with each sound of rodents scratching in the walls, Arvay's illusions slip away and her dualistic notions begin to resolve. Arvay looks at the poverty-ridden property her mother left her and sees in it the source of her and her family members' unease. The infectious environment had "twisted the limbs of their minds" (306). She thinks of Larraine and her family with compassion, not judgment. She does not consider herself superior to them, but, rather, lucky to have escaped their fate.

Arvay sets the house afire and, from the safety of the mulberry tree, watches it burn. The burning house symbolizes a ritual purification, a cleaning and clearing away of old patterns of thought and negative ways of being.

> The dry old house burned furiously, and as Arvay watched the roaring and ascending flames, she picked herself over inside and recognized why she felt as she did now. She was no longer divided in her mind. The tearing and ripping and useless rending was finished and done. She made a peace and was in harmony with her life. (308)

The strife of dissension over people, places, and stations in life gives way to balance and calm. Arvay begins to realize herself as an individual, someone psychically healthy and whole. And for once in her life, Arvay knows where she belongs. She confides in her neighbor Miss Hessie, "my husband come along and took me off from that place and planned and fixed bigger things for me to enjoy. Look like I ought to have sense enough to appreciate what he's done, and still trying to do for me, and not be always pulling back here" (309). With a new sense of self, Arvay has the wherewithal to step forward, into her own path. She "knew her own way now" and determines to "do all in my power to take care of things my ownself" (308, 310). This mindset affords Arvay a sense of security and self-worth heretofore painfully missing. It affords her the courage to embrace her life. When she returns to Citrabelle, Joe's son Jeff and Jeff's wife, Janie, are there. As the Kelseys were there in the beginning, they are there in the end. As Janie had Pheoby's ear in *Their Eyes Were Watching God*, Arvay has Jeff and Janie's. Her transformed self is realized through their listening. She makes amends with Jeff, confessing her "narrow-hearted littleness." Appreciative of their presence, she now feels herself a part of them and a part of the Meserve family, as do Jeff and his father. Arvay's sense of self creates in her a humility and generosity of spirit that she desires to extend to everyone. No longer dictated to by a sense of inferiority and antagonistic thought, she can now have easier relations with others. She is not sure of how things will go with Jim, but she has the courage to find out. She also has the courage to take responsibility for whatever transpires. "All that happened to her, good or bad," Arvay understands, "was a part of her own self and had come out of her" (349–50). She is whole. Arvay's choice to remain in her marriage and to mother Jim is a controversial choice among critics, yet it is her choice. As Jim states, Arvay could easily have remained separate from Jim and continued to receive financial support. But just as she begins to understand herself and realize who she is, Arvay begins to understand Jim, his fears, insecurities, and vulnerabilities and to realize who he is to her.

Seraph on the Suwanee may be an awkward and contrived novel, as Washington states. But it is also a novel that deserves scholarly attention. Hurston's protagonist is a complex figure who invites critical analysis. Possibly, though, she is ignored and rejected out of hand because she is not a black character. As Walker bluntly put it, Hurston's later work was reactionary and misguided. She thought this particularly true of *Seraph*, "which is not even about black people, which is no crime, but *is* about white people for whom it is impossible to care, which is" (*In Search* 89–90).

Arvay Henson's journey to psychic integration and individuality is healing and empowering, not only for Arvay, but also for her family and community and, by extension, her society. The wisdom conveyed in Hurston's writing is not always apparent or readily accepted. But since other Hurston texts have been recovered from oblivion and reevaluated, *Seraph on the Suwanee* may be too. "*We are a people. A people do not throw their geniuses away*," writes Walker. "And if they are thrown away, it is our duty *as artists and as witnesses for the future* to collect them again for the sake of our children, and, if necessary, bone by bone" (92), and, I would add, book by book.

NOTES

[1] I, as well as other critics, have taken issue with Hurston's characterization of Arvay's rape as a romantic act. See the discussion of this scene in Plant, *Every Tub*; Meisenhelder; St. Clair.

[2] Though the two families are interdependent, the exchange between them is not equal. Hurston suggests in "The 'Pet' Negro System" that this social structure was feudalistic. As imperfect as it was, she saw some promise in it: "Is it a good thing or a bad thing? Who am I to pass judgment? I am not defending the system, belov-ed, but trying to explain it. The lowdown fact is that it weaves a kind of basic fabric that tends to stabilize relations and give something to work from in adjustments" (160). Idealistically, Hurston chose to see the beauty in the friendships that could result from these relations and thought them "a great and heartening tribute to human nature" (162).

[3] Though Hurston portrays Jim Meserve as a good-hearted progressive liberal, Jim is paternalistic and exploitative. Meisenhelder points out, "Every one of his financial ventures—from his still operation to his turpentining, citrus groves, development projects, and shrimping fleet—depends on the expertise and the efforts of black workers" (113). Their labor realizes Jim's dreams, but they don't participate in them.

Polyvocality and Performance in *Mules and Men*

Kimberly J. Banks and Cheryl A. Wall

Together we have taught and written about *Mules and Men* for three decades. Belonging to different generations and trained in different modes of literary study, we have employed various strategies of classroom presentation. Here we share our respective experiences as teachers, recount some of the responses of our students, as well as provide historical background and critical perspectives that inform our pedagogical approaches. In writing this essay we have tried to enact a measure of the polyvocality that we identify in Zora Neale Hurston's classic text.

The art of *Mules and Men* inheres both in the texts it documents and in its own remarkable form. One tale leads to another in a way that seems completely spontaneous; the effect is to suggest the inexhaustibility of the lore. Hurston believed that African American folklore was fluid and dynamic; as she wrote in her groundbreaking 1934 essay "Characteristics of Negro Expression," it was "not a thing of the past. It is still in the making" (1024). But she worked at creating that effect in *Mules and Men*. Students can appreciate the literary achievement of the volume by noting the careful connections between text and context, marking the rhetorical patterns that impose coherence on the volume, and analyzing the subtly drawn representation of the narrator-protagonist.

In *Mules and Men*, Hurston devises a form that enables her to represent her anthropological informants speaking for themselves at the same time that she represents and reconstructs their cultural world. In the text, the protagonist Zora negotiates her cultural authority with her informants. In writing the text, Hurston negotiates her cultural authority with her readers. The identities produced through these two kinds of negotiations are never static. Instead of being given, these identities are performed. Hurston's enactment of cultural struggle invites a series of questions about both the multiplication of cultural voices and the relation among these voices. *Mules and Men* represents three African American communities: Eatonville, Polk County, and New Orleans. Zora is represented differently in the three communities, each of which has a different central organizing structure. The store porch dominates Eatonville; the jook and the road dominate Polk County; the province of the spirit dominates New Orleans. Hurston's use of place and voice enables her to explore identity as performance and black communities as polyvocal.

Historical Background

Although collections of African American folklore began appearing in the nineteenth century, *Mules and Men* was the first such volume compiled by an African American. Published in 1935, it established Hurston's credentials as a social scientist and added luster to her reputation as a writer. Hurston studied anthropology at Barnard from 1925 to 1928. Her mentor was Franz Boas, who is usually considered the founder of the discipline in the United States. Under his tutelage, Hurston began to collect folklore formally. In December 1927, while still an undergraduate, she took a train from New York to Florida to begin her fieldwork. She spent most of the years from 1927 to 1932 crisscrossing the southeastern United States and traveling to the Bahamas in pursuit of the lore. Of course, as she announces in the introduction to *Mules and Men*, she had known many folktales "[f]rom the earliest rocking of [her] cradle" (1). The first section of the book is set in Eatonville, the all-black Florida town in which she was raised. Hurston drew freely from the lore in the short stories she published in the 1920s, even before she entered Barnard. But her academic training, what she calls "the spy-glass of Anthropology" (1), had given her a new lens through which to view the material she had long claimed as her birthright.

As a student Hurston learned to appreciate the uses of folklore and its functions in people's lives. Folklore is verbal art and, in Hurston's definition, "the arts of a people before they find out that there is any such thing as art" ("Folklore" [1938] 876). Created communally, folklore encapsulates the group's values and beliefs. Unofficial and uncensored, it offers an unusually honest and direct expression of the communal worldview. People share their hopes and fears, desires and doubts, in a free space. Literally and metaphorically, folklore is inside stuff. Members of the community are often loath to share it with outsiders, because it is easily misunderstood. At the same time, it expresses, in Hurston's lyrical phrase, "that which the soul lives by" (*Mules* 2).

While recognizing the difficulties of collecting the lore and noting that rural black southerners were "particularly evasive," Hurston was eager to take on the challenge (2). After a few stumbles, she made swift strides, and by 1932, she found that she had more material than she could use. Three years passed before the work saw print. Indeed, Hurston wrote and published her first novel, *Jonah's Gourd Vine*, before *Mules and Men* appeared.

Hurston's vexed relationship with her patron, Mrs. R. Osgood (Charlotte) Mason, was one cause of the delay in publishing her findings. In a contract signed on 8 December 1927, six days before Hurston boarded the southbound train, Mason agreed to employ Hurston as "an independent agent," who would "collect all information possible, both written and oral, concerning the music, poetry, folk-lore, literature, hoodoo, conjure, manifestations of art and kindred subjects relating to and existing among the North American Negroes" (Hemenway, *Zora* 109–10). The stipend was two hundred dollars a month. Having encompassed every possible aspect of the material, the contract stipulated that whatever Hurston collected would belong to Mason. Charlotte Mason retained control over what could be disseminated, in what form, and to whom.

Perhaps more important was Hurston's difficulty in devising a form for her findings. The first volume of folktales she proposed failed to find a publisher.[1] Although she published articles in scholarly journals, she did not want her work to languish on library shelves. Moreover, she believed that drama and music were the wellspring of the lore. She wanted to present the folklore in context. In January 1932, she staged the first of several concerts in which she did just that. "The Great Day," subtitled "A Program of Original Negro Folklore," was produced on Broadway. Subsequent versions entitled "From Sun to Sun," "All de Live Long Day," and "Singing Steel" were produced elsewhere in New York, Chicago, and Florida. Dramatizing a day in the life of a railroad camp, the concert included scenes such as Waking the Camp, Working on the Railroad, Back in the Quarters (including children's games), Itinerant Preacher in the Quarters, In the Jook, a version of "The Fiery Chariot" (based on Hurston's story written in the folk tradition), and a Bahamian fire dance.[2]

Mason subsidized the first of these concerts and exercised her veto power. She allowed only one performance of a conjure ceremony, believing that its documentation should be saved for Hurston's books. In March 1931, Mason dropped Hurston from her payroll, although she provided funds intermittently for the next eighteen months. Once Mason withdrew her support, Hurston was able to draw freely from the archive that she had compiled and from the experience of making the material come alive onstage. A useful way to understand *Mules and Men* is as a re-creation of the theatrical concerts in prose.[3] The book offers folk texts in the context of everyday life. To give readers a window into that life, Hurston constructs a narrative and reconstructs what she called the "between-story conversation and business" (Hemenway, *Zora* 153). A teacher's chief goal is to make students alert to both the texts and the contexts.

Mules and Men documents diverse cultural performances from singing to signifying, from jokes to toasts, from children's rhymes to courtship rituals, from curses to cures, prayers and sermons, and hoodoo rituals. These all constitute the drama of everyday life in the communities the book represents. At the heart of *Mules and Men*, however, are the stories that Hurston collects from her informants. These stories in and of themselves offer students the opportunity to think about the relation between form and function. What story is told and why is it being told? Who is speaking? Who is listening? What is the context? What is the "between-story conversation and business" that comes before and after the tale?

To help students appreciate the achievement of the storytellers in *Mules and Men*, we ask them, before the first class discussion of the text, to select one story and present it to the class. We emphasize that students are to tell a story rather than read it. Most are surprised by how difficult a task this is. Even when they are able to convey the general plot of the story, they are unable to remember the details that enliven it. If two students choose the same story, we sometimes ask both to tell it. Then we note the details that each remembers. In every class there are one or two gifted performers who can imbue the tales with the drama Hurston's account of storytelling emphasizes. But, for most students, simply telling the story is a struggle. This exercise leads to discussions of the art of storytelling, the mnemonic devices that aid in committing stories to memory, and the inevitable variations in the text. Having attempted to tell the tales, students can begin a discussion of *Mules and Men* with a better understanding of how the ability to tell stories wins respect and status for those fortunate enough to have it.

Students should now be sensitive to the difference between the written and spoken texts. The difficulties of transcription is the theme of the tale "How to Write a Letter" (40–41). Students should discuss what can and cannot be captured on the page. Issues of black vernacular English are important here of course, but so are questions of tone, gesticulation, and other nonverbal modes of communication. The tale of the illiterate farmer whose educated daughter cannot transcribe his speech can occasion an analysis of the ethnographer's role in composing the text. To what extent is the ethnographer mediating our understanding of the folk texts? Consider, too, that this tale is one of a cluster concerned with letters. What do these reveal about the communal attitude toward education? With this tale, it is possible to highlight both the ambivalence around education and the improvisational nature of the storytelling where one story picks up on an element in another story. In the story told before the one about the daughter transcribing the letter, a daughter is looking for a suitable husband. In the story following the letter, a father catches a wired letter on its way to his daughter. As it is with most transitions in the ethnography, the connection between the two stories about letters is only superficially similar.

The transcription story highlights the problem with writing as representation. The father uses a sound and wants the daughter to represent that sound in a letter. The sound is one used to kill a mule. To write "cluck" would be to name the sound rather than construct a phonetic representation. Education is also an issue in the story about a parent who wants his college-educated son to tell him how to keep a cow from kicking (125–27). The father doubts his son's advice but follows it anyway because the son has been "educated." The results are disastrous. These questions of authority between parent and child, uneducated and educated, can be used to reflect on questions of authority in the ethnography as a whole. In the first story, the father refuses to surrender to the limitations of written convention. According to his logic, because he uses an oral equivalent for a sound, that equivalent should translate into a written representation. The second story highlights the expectation that education is a practical instrument. For the father here, education must explain how to accomplish everyday tasks more efficiently. We focus on these two stories because they highlight the limitations of formal education. As a society, we are accustomed to focusing on formal education as a relatively quick way to gain class mobility. The world of *Mules and Men*, however, carries different assumptions, and we, as teachers, must reorient students to the assumptions of this world.

Part 1 of Mules and Men*: The Autobiographical Performance of Zora*

Much of the feminist criticism of *Mules and Men* centers on Hurston's fictive double, Zora, and her role in the Eatonville section of the ethnography. Descriptions of women having "the law in their mouths" or being "Mouth Almighty" evoke the contestation between men and women over power. Two specific tales located in Eatonville take up issues of gender politics, "Why Women Always Take Advantage of Men" (31–35) and "Sue, Sal and That Pretty Johnson Gal" (35–37). But even when male-female relationships are not the subject of the tale, the narrative depicts men and women negotiating for a place in the conversation. What is the relation between text and context here? Does the tale "Why Women Always Take Advantage of Men" challenge or reinforce gender stereotypes? How is the porch, a space that mediates between private and public spheres, an appropriate site for these exchanges? Even as the storytellers vie for the upper hand, they are always conscious of their art, as their use of formulas and bywords indicates. For example, as Mathilda tells her story, she recites an ending formula, "Stepped on a pin, de pin bent / And dat's de way de story went" (34). Hurston's representation of this formula as poetry reinforces its status as art. Before John French begins "How Jack Beat the Devil," he announces, "Ah got to say a piece of litery [literary] fust to git mah wind on" (47). He then recites an introductory poem that could be used for numerous stories as a way of establishing him as a bona fide storyteller.

> Well Ah went up on dat meat-skin
> And Ah come down on dat bone
> And Ah grabbed dat piece of corn-bread
> And Ah made dat biscuit moan. (47)

Throughout storytelling sessions, speakers vie for status. At one point, a child, Little Julius Henry, narrates the tale "Ah'll Beatcher Makin' Money" (42–46), one of the longest stories in the book. This feat wins him praise from his elders, who are proud that he can tell a lie like an adult.

Various voices rise from the store porch in Eatonville, as the narrator drives into town. Certain names recur, such as Armetta and Ellis, Gene and Gold, B. Moseley and Mathilda Moseley, and Charlie Jones. Students should take note of who is speaking and of the ways in which Zora reconfigures the groups who gather to share stories later in this section. In Eatonville, Hurston represents many voices sharing folktales and exchanging banter. People like George Thomas, Richard Jones, Jack Oscar Jones, Ruth Marshall, and Seaboard Hamilton never tell stories, but they listen and provide commentary. The list of new names at the end of chapter 2 suggests a new storytelling context. Hurston presents conflicts between Clara and Jack, who are mates, and between Shug and Bennie Lee, who are siblings. In Eatonville, the ritual of storytelling contains community conflict. The communal context provides an opportunity for families and individuals to perform their conflicts in public without fundamentally altering their relationships.

Zora's presence in Eatonville challenges the social-scientific standard of objectivity prevalent in the early twentieth century. Participant observation was an important method of conducting field research, but the representation of such research only focused on observation, not participation. That *Mules and Men* represents both aspects of research methodology puts Hurston in the forefront of ethnographic innovation. Here, too, the role of Zora is central. She provides the framework through which readers accept Hurston's status as an anthropologist. The introduction to *Mules and Men* is crucial in establishing the difficulty of participating in a specific culture. In the introduction, Hurston establishes a racial community, explaining that when the "white person" asks questions, "[t]he Negro offers a feather-bed resistance. That is, we let the probe enter, but it never comes out" (2). Everyone in the community is anxious to tell Zora lies and include her in their trip to Wood Bridge. Zora's efforts to observe social rituals are taken for granted. She can sit on the store porch and attend a "toe-party" without disrupting the rituals that she has come to observe. Eatonville community members call on Zora: "There was a lot of horn-honking outside and I went to the door. The crowd drew up under the mothering camphor tree in four old cars. Everybody in boisterous spirits" (13). Zora's status as a member of the community is reaffirmed the next night, when "a pinch of everything social [is] mixed with the story-telling" (19). Although the Eatonville community is willing to accept Zora, her sense of belonging to that community is complicated by her need to perform her initiation. She asks Calvin Daniels and James Moseley to explain a "toe-party" (9, 14). She also asks Charlie Jones to explain the drink "coon dick" (15). Furthermore, Zora pretends to be unfamiliar with Polk County as a good place to collect folklore (55). Her role as observer rather than participant is highlighted when Gold and Gene exchange words and Charlie tells them to calm down because "Zora's gittin' restless. She think she ain't gointer hear no more" (24).[4]

Hurston ends the Eatonville section with the folktales "How Jack Beat the Devil" (47–56) and "'John Henry'" (56–57), which serve as effective transitions to the important themes of the Polk County section. "How Jack Beat the Devil" is one of several stories that reveal the ways that religious belief in this community deviates from orthodox Christianity. Through its comparative context, it explains the irreverence with which preacher tales are told on the store porch. It introduces Jack and the Devil as folk heroes involved in a match to outwit each other. A complicated tale, it recounts how Jack is entrusted with a fortune from his father, loses that fortune to the Devil, and then has to outsmart the Devil to keep his life and marry the Devil's daughter. Ironically, it is the name of the Lord that defeats the Devil. He throws down the log, swearing, "Damn it! If Ah had of knowed dat God wuz in dat log Ah never would a picked it up" (53). The Devil then proceeds to cause his own death trying to escape from God. The extravagance of the characters' capabilities and the situations they find themselves in make this folktale compelling. At the moment of truth, when either Jack or the Devil has to lose the encounter, the Devil loses the encounter because of a verbal misunderstanding rather than a conscious outwitting.

There are many stories exploring Jack's conflict with the Devil. The Devil is not demonized; rather, he is an opponent who is to be admired for being crafty, but not as crafty as Jack. Students might discuss the various images of deities in *Mules and Men*. To what extent does the God of the folk imagination resemble the God of the Bible? To what extent is the Devil a heroic figure? How is the representation of the Devil aligned to a more general perspective that subverts the dominant social order? How does that perspective constitute a political critique? Students will probably notice that the Devil is a hero in these folktales. A discussion of the Devil as a heroic figure reinforces the point instructors can make, that subversion of an existing social order appealed to black people because of the prevailing social system of segregation. Black people refused to surrender to dominant ideas that they were inferior or, worse, subhuman and instead developed an alternative system of social value that refuted these charges. This system also established other images as resources, such as John, Jack, and Brer Rabbit.

To some degree Jack is a trickster figure, a protagonist who outwits a more powerful opponent. As such he bears comparison to Brer Rabbit, the best-known trickster in the African American tradition.[5] By turns heroic and duplicitous, Brer Rabbit is the focus of only a few tales in *Mules and Men*. Brer Rabbit helps reinforce the importance of coding and inversion and highlights the strengths and weaknesses of different animals, which have a metaphoric relation to negotiations over cultural authority. We can ask students, Why are the folktales coded? What would happen if storytellers did not couch their sentiments in folktales?

Part 1 of **Mules and Men**: *Lumber Camp Workers as Performers*

Long neglected outside feminist contexts, the Polk County section of *Mules and Men* is now understood in terms of its "daily acts of resistance" that form the basis for greater political change; its ability to reconcile the gap between black people in northern, urban centers and black people in southern, rural spaces; Zora's contemporaneous revulsion toward and embodiment of cultural practices at the work camp; and finally Hurston's awareness of the fascination with primitives and the collection of fading cultures. In this new context, the Polk County section is more than the negotiation of gendered power relationships (as first introduced in the Eatonville section) or the addition of the negotiation of racial and class power relationships. The coded meanings of these representations push readers to move beyond a judgment of Hurston's work as apolitical, conservatively political, or faintly political. As Tiffany Ruby Patterson notes, Hurston chronicles the daily lives of turpentine and sawmill workers, workers in the phosphate-mining industry, and migrant workers in agricultural camps, while exploring the developments in consciousness that these changing modes of labor produced. Both the folk texts that *Mules* collects and the narrative contexts it creates make Hurston's work urgently political both for her time and for ours.

Mules and Men was the first volume of folklore to include the John and master cycle of tales. According to Hurston, John (not to be confused with John Henry) "is the great human culture hero in Negro folklore . . . the wish-fulfillment hero of the race" (247). Most of these tales appear in the chapters set in Polk County, where, according to the blues, the "water drink lak cherry wine" and her neighbors in Eatonville assure Zora "they really lies up a mess" (55). As Zora crosses the Maitland-Eatonville line to signal her entry into the initial setting of the book, twelve miles below Kissimmee, she passes "under an arch . . . mark[ing] the Polk County line" to signal her further immersion into African American culture (59). Gene Oliver, Larkins White, Jim Allen, Cliff Ulmer, James Presley, Joe Willard, Lucy, Ella Wall, and Big Sweet live in the quarters of the Everglades Cypress Lumber Company. Their stories confirm Hurston's claim about John's importance. John's heroic status, like Brer Rabbit's, is open to question. On one level, the John stories participate in a bad man tradition of storytelling, maybe even a tradition of tall tales. On another level, the Polk County storytellers are protesting the conditions under which they worked, conditions that echoed the experiences of their enslaved ancestors. By invoking stories of masters and slaves, black workers were not necessarily affirming the relationship between them. This point helps us reinforce ideas of coding and inversion. Although slavery was over, a racist hierarchy existed in the South, and stories about masters and slaves still held resonance for black lumber camp workers. The message of the John and master stories is not servants, obey your masters, but servants, undermine your masters in ways that do not get you killed. For teachers who assign *Mules and Men* in a course where students also read slave narratives, this method of subversion should seem very familiar. What is the relation between physical liberation, in the movement from slavery to freedom, and linguistic liberation? How many different kinds of linguistic liberations can students list? How might we compare Frederick Douglass, who mastered conventional rhetorical forms, and Hurston, who mastered the representation of vernacular voices on the written page?

In "Member Youse a Nigger" (89–90), the master's two children are caught in a boat out in the ocean, and the mistress is afraid they will drown. John swims out and saves the children, and, as long as he fills the barn during harvest time, he will be granted his freedom. Part of what accounts for the humor in many of the John stories is the master's need to have a high opinion of himself even though he holds another human being in slavery. In many of the slave narratives in the abolitionist period, slaves would be promised freedom on certain conditions, and when those conditions were met, the slaves would not be freed. In "How Jack Beat the Devil," the Devil does not honor his promise of freedom to Jack. In Harriet Jacobs's *Incidents in the Life of a Slave Girl*, Linda's grandmother was promised freedom on her mistress's death, but the family did not honor her wishes and sold the grandmother at the next public sale. The master in "Member Youse a Nigger" tells John, "Well, de day done come that I said I'd set you free. I hate to do it, but I don't like to make myself out a lie. I hate to git rid of a good nigger lak you" (90). After the admission of a need to fulfill a promise, John knows he is free and is looking forward to it. The master, however, wants John to feel some bonds of affection to his family. He tells John how much he and the children love John. At the same time, the mistress cannot love John because of the injunctions against white female–black male relationships, an injunction made more important because of the rampant assaults by white males on black females. So the master reminds John that "Missy *like* yuh!" The master also reminds John, "'member youse a nigger," and John only assents because, regardless of how the master classifies him, he is free and beyond the master's control. In this folktale, John accepts the rules of a corrupt system on the distant hope of gaining freedom, and for once the gamble pays off. Students should discuss the ways in which stories like this comment on the speakers' current situation. In what ways do they offer a direct commentary? How is the social critique coded? Does John have more or less agency than the speaker who tells his tale?

"Why the Porpoise Has His Tail on Crossways" (158) is a creation story that represents God not as an omniscient being but as a being who experiments with creation. In what might be a counterintuitive move for many students, we can ask, What are the comic aspects of religion? Many images of God in *Mules and Men* are in the tradition of tall tales. In the introduction, Hurston tells a folktale about God giving out souls (3–4). Another folktale focuses on God giving out color (29–30). Different kinds of folktales ("lies") get told on the Eatonville store porch: a series of preacher tales and "why" stories that contemplate "why Negroes are black," among other questions. Students might consider the extent to which these stories reveal an understanding of social oppression or of racial self-hatred. As God finishes with creation and only has time left, he tells the sun to race around the earth, which will give him the measure of day and night. The porpoise hears the command, decides he wants to race, and beats the sun by over an hour. God did not realize that the porpoise was faster than the sun, so he chases the porpoise down to remedy the situation. Not only is the porpoise faster than the sun, he is faster than God. After three days God catches up with the porpoise. Animals outsmart one another, and they outsmart God. Instead of being an omnipotent being demanding awe, God becomes a being who adapts to unforeseen circumstances. Although animals like the porpoise are limited, they also have phenomenal skills and potential. Such potential is subject to eruptions even when God designs its elimination.

Storytelling sessions in Eatonville are always juxtaposed against church services, meetings, or songs. The sessions in Polk County are juxtaposed against activities of the jook such as Florida flip, the skin game, drinking corn liquor, and wielding knives. The exposure of interpersonal conflict at the lumber camp, instead of diffusing conflict, is only the prelude for greater eruptions of conflict. All the activities available in the jook are competitive activities compared with the harmonious activities available in Eatonville. A combination dance hall, gambling parlor, and pleasure house, the jook allows women to play more assertive roles than they were allowed on the porch in Eatonville. How does the character Big Sweet, presumably a woman whom Hurston actually met in Polk County, become for the narrator a female wish-fulfillment hero similar to John? Although Big Sweet tells only two folktales, how does the narrative create a space in which Big Sweet's own story can be told?

Not until the men realize they have the day off from the swamp and the mill do the women become significant to the storytelling setting. The women join the men on a day of fishing. Zora's initiation into the Polk County camp reveals a system of escort and individualism that is not significantly interrupted when Big Sweet decides to protect Zora. It is only while the participants are fishing that the multiple voices seem to talk to one another. In the context of other pleasure activities such as dancing and partying, verbal exchanges both hide and reveal suppressed conflict. Figuratively, Zora is passed from Cliffert to Pitts to James Presley and Slim to Big Sweet. Conflict arises from heterosexual relationships and from women's jealousy. Both Big Sweet and Ella Wall are involved with Joe Willard. Only Lucy is involved with Slim, but she fears that Zora has stolen his affection. Not only does Big Sweet swear to protect Zora, but she also confronts Lucy's betrayal of friendship in her reporting to Ella Wall. The relationships are layered and crisscrossed in Polk County in a way that does not happen in Eatonville.

Perhaps as a consequence, Zora is inevitably drawn into conflict. In Polk County, Zora has to invent an identity to gain acceptance. The people there do not automatically open up to Zora, and they are not as homogenous as the Eatonville community. Since Polk County is constructed as a community of outsiders, both outlaws and former outlaws, Zora has to pose as a bootlegger to create an outsider position against her alleged insider position of detective. Her performance as a bootlegger is made possible through her boarding at Mrs. Allen's and driving Mrs. Allen's son, Cliffert Ulmer, to Lakeland. Although Zora claims that she was "taken in" by the community with the story of the bootlegger (61), she was isolated at the pay-night dance. Cliffert takes her to the dance, does not offer her a dance, and refuses to introduce men such as Pitts to her. The second hurdle to gaining acceptance in the Polk County community is Zora's dress. Once Pitts gains the courage to approach Zora, he tells her that everyone thinks she is rich. She regrets her "$12.74 dress from Macy's" among "all the $1.98 mail-order dresses" (63). Her acceptance of Pitts's flirting makes men comfortable enough to send someone to ask her to dance. Her initiation is complete when she sings "John Henry" to the accompaniment of the best guitar player, James Presley.[6] Only after she accompanies James Presley and Slim on gigs in and around Polk County does she feel confident enough to confide her mission to the Polk County community.

Part 2 of Mules and Men*: (Not) Performing Hoodoo*

In part 2 of *Mules and Men*, Hurston reenters the frame of the ethnography. Her entrance is significant in its implication that Zora is initiated into the power of Moses and of Marie Leveau, the famous hoodoo queen of New Orleans. Moses's power with words becomes Zora's power. Marie Leveau's incantations and ceremony come under Zora's control, and Hurston can use them in *Mules and Men*. In an origin story that bridges parts 1 and 2, Hurston describes Moses's study under Jethro. She explains, "Moses was the first man who ever learned God's power-compelling words and it took him forty years to learn ten words. So he made ten plagues and ten commandments" (184). This power quickly becomes aligned with Marie Leveau. Valerie Boyd explains her history:

> Marie Leveau was a celebrated Creole conjurer who lived as a freed woman during the 1800s in New Orleans's famous Vieux Carré. The self-proclaimed "Pope of Voodoo" also was a devout Catholic. . . . According to written and oral accounts, the original Marie Leveau had a daughter who also was a magisterial voodoo priestess. She bore a striking resemblance to her mother and did her work under the name Marie Leveau as well, causing some people to believe the conjure queen's power had given her an ageless beauty and an exceptionally long life. (175)

All the hoodoo doctors in New Orleans, including the seven under whom Zora studies, claimed some relationship to Marie Leveau. The hoodoo doctors—Eulalia, Luke Turner, Anatol Pierre, Father Watson, Dr. Duke, Dr. Samuel Jenkins, and Kitty Brown—do not communicate with one another. Hurston seeks separate initiations and apprenticeships with each doctor. Hurston becomes a student to each master and absorbs all their knowledge. She shares some of the symbolic universe of hoodoo through her descriptions of her initiation with Luke Turner. Hurston explains, "I studied under Turner five months and learned all of the Leveau routines; but in this book all of the works of any doctor cannot be given" (202). Such a position in *Mules and Men* is in direct opposition to Hurston's project in "Hoodoo in America," where she reveals all the Leveau routines that she can possibly recover. Nevertheless, final proof of Hurston's hoodoo power comes from Luke Turner: "One day Turner told me that he had taught me all that he could and he was quite satisfied with me. He wanted me to stay and work with him as a partner. He said that soon I would be in possession of the entire business" (205).

Although there is no explicit delineation of performed identities, the rituals of the hoodoo section confirm the assertions that the text makes about this belief system. The speakers in the text share the disposition that hoodoo is subversive; indeed, even its adherents are reluctant to acknowledge their belief. Outsiders often malign hoodoo as devil worship. But *Mules and Men* makes a counterclaim. It uses the Bible to legitimize hoodoo; in the folktale that relates its provenance, the Ethiopian Jethro crowns his son-in-law Moses. The miracles that the Bible attributes to the Hebrew deity are recast as the manifestations of the world's greatest hoodoo doctor. Moving from the legends of the past to the practices of the present, the volume represents hoodoo rituals as a way of directly using divine energy. Unlike Yoruban or Haitian rituals, which are public, rituals in hoodoo assume a private character. When Zora becomes an initiate, she becomes a reluctant informant. In some ways, Hurston's discussion of hoodoo assumes aspects of chanting and ceremony. The use of repetition both reveals and hides ceremony, initiates and refuses to initiate the reader.

The hoodoo section is important not only for its representations of spirituality but also for its continuation of the book's concern with rural black Americans' responses to modernity. As Leigh Anne Duck argues, Hurston's exemplary representation of intersubjective time in *Mules and Men* is her "juxtaposition of clock time with the transcendent timelessness of hoodoo, when she lies naked, face-down, on a snakeskin, waiting 'sixty-nine hours' while her 'spirit went wherever spirits must go that seek answers never given to men as men'" ("'*Go There*'" 275). John Carlos Rowe is also insistent that we understand Hurston's cultural project in economic and political contexts. In *Mules and Men*, Hurston recovers a buried aspect of America's heritage. Contrary to most critics, who have recovered *Mules and Men* as a postmodern ethnography, Rowe sees the framing devices in the ethnography as efforts to "*control* their unruliness" (261), the unruliness of her subjects. What Hurston provides, according to Rowe, is

> Zora's discovery at once of danger, passionate feelings, and the *existence* of her own body in the midst of a social conflict. As a consequence, she is virtually re-embodied, perhaps even *reincarnated*, in ways that will play ever more central roles in the recovery of her own African-American and African identity. (261)

Although Rowe attempts to explain the contrary political impulses in Hurston's work, he reaffirms her participation in modernism and its fascination with primitivism. He identifies an anti-imperialistic impetus in her effort to account for the power of the United States and the need for economic assistance and incorporation in a democratic vision of community. Such a community should include an ability to communicate across differences, not just dichotomize oppressor and oppressed.

In New Orleans, Hurston's initiation is performed through a declaration of faith in hoodoo. Believers in hoodoo are always willing to deny their faith because of most Americans' resistance to it. The first scholar to investigate the practice, Hurston explains that "the worship [of hoodoo] is bound in secrecy. It is not the accepted theology of the Nation and so believers conceal their faith" (185). Declarations of belief or disbelief in hoodoo are difficult to discern and follow the tactics of "feather-bed resistance." Hurston does not provide readers of *Mules and Men* with an opportunity to see her declarations of belief as simply a way to gain initiation. When Zora arrives in Polk County, Hurston describes in elaborate detail the process of initiation and gaining trust in the lumber camp community. Zora learns to see herself through the eyes of the lumber camp workers, and, although she gains access to tales and songs, she never belongs, as evidenced through her need for an escort. Zora is also not automatically accepted by the Eatonville community, where her lack of knowledge has to be performed. Zora's declaration of faith in New Orleans effectively distances her from readers, who have no access to it. Zora's faith is not characterized as a performed identity; it just is.

As teachers, we can use the final section of *Mules and Men* to reflect on the reader's initiation into African American culture. How does the ethnography accomplish such an initiation and how does it refuse it? Do our courses on African American literature provide a similar dynamic, both offering and withdrawing initiation? At the same time, as the most recent critical literature suggests, how does Hurston's work exemplify the possibilities of negotiating across time and space and across gender, race, and class lines?

Pedagogical Contexts

Their Eyes Were Watching God continues to be a favorite text of Hurston's in a range of classes, and "Sweat" is frequently anthologized, because it prefigures so many of the larger themes in *Their Eyes*. "Sweat" features a married couple, Delia and Sykes, and over the course of their marriage Sykes has taken the beautiful, plump Delia and turned her into a "cane chew." *Their Eyes* uses a much larger framework of marriages, but the middle marriage between Janie and Jody is one where Jody transforms Janie from the girl hanging on the gate post to the middle-aged woman with her hair covered in a bandanna, ridiculed for her lack of intellect and socially isolated. Delia never confronts Sykes directly, but she rebels against his emotional abuse by letting him die from a poisonous snake bite. Janie confronts Jody directly and publicly in his own store, calling attention to his fading masculinity.

Mules and Men does not evoke the domestic aspects of *Their Eyes*, but it highlights cultural contexts, the spaces where the private meets the public. Janie works inside a public space, the store, but is unable to participate in the rituals of its porch. The public spaces of *Mules and Men* include the store porch, the front porch or living room, and a fishing trip. Many social relationships are explored in such spaces, including marriage, exclusive and nonexclusive dating relationships, friendships, relationships between workers and bosses, relationships among workers, and relationships between entertainers and audiences.

The folktales take on meaning in this public framework. Hurston mostly comments on relationships among black people, the exception being black workers and white bosses. Similar tales and contexts exist throughout American literature. Mark Twain's framework in "The Man That Corrupted Hadleyburg" plays with the professional folk comedian and his relationship to folk storytellers. This story is comparable to Hurston's "How to Write a Letter." Charles Chesnutt's Uncle Julius tales offer a literate framework, in which a white, northern couple reads a black, southern man. By framing his stories in this way, Chesnutt provides a way to read *against* the framework of the story. Implicitly, Chesnutt also provides a way to challenge the innocuous representation by Joel Chandler Harris in his Uncle Remus tales. Uncle Remus's audience is a child, while Uncle Julius always targets other adults. In addition, Harris does not imply that the tales are anything other than childish entertainment. Many decades later, out of step with his time, the social scientist Newbell Niles Puckett, in *Folk Beliefs of the Southern Negro*, argues that folklore reinforces the late-nineteenth-century belief held by Harris that black folklore was entertaining for white children. He also argues that folklore is evidence of superstition and black inferiority. Hurston's repository of black southern folktales is not the "aunties" and "uncles" of the southern literary imagination. Her repository is communal, more concentrated in Polk County but also fertile in Eatonville. In *Their Eyes*, Hurston describes the shift from "aunties" and "uncles":

> These sitters [on porches beside the road] had been tongueless, earless, eyeless conveniences all day long. Mules and other brutes had occupied their skins. But now, the sun and the bossman were gone, so the skins felt powerful and human. They became lords of sounds and lesser things. (1)

Here, instead of being extraneous appendages to white families, black characters have their own families and communities.

The idea of the performance event is important to the consideration of Hurston's contemporaries in the social sciences. The performance event applies to both folktale contexts and singing or guitar-playing contexts. Hurston includes an appendix of songs with musical notation and words in *Mules and Men*. Earlier, Howard Washington Odum and Guy Benton Johnson produced a compendium of such songs in *The Negro and His Songs* and *Negro Workaday Songs*. They acknowledged, much like Hurston, the variety and richness of black folk music and its improvisatory nature. At the same time, Johnson saw the songs as derivative. In a letter dated 20 October 1929, collected in Carla Kaplan's *Zora Neale Hurston: A Life in Letters*, Hurston refers specifically to Odum and Johnson's work: "I have been following the works of Odum and Johnson closely and find that they could hardly be less exact. They have made six or seven songs out of one song and made one song out of six or seven" (151). The idea of units to songs and tales and how they are moved around is central to understanding methods of improvisation. Standardized units make folktales and songs serve as mnemonic devices.

Much has been written about the signifying monkey, Brer Rabbit, and Anansi the Spider as trickster figures in the United States, Caribbean, and West Africa. John in Hurston's John and master tales in *Mules and Men* is another important trickster figure. Although a slave, John provides a perfect parallel to agricultural-industrial low-wage workers. John is also a culture hero. This idea of a black culture hero was central to anthropologists in the 1920s and 1930s. Guy Johnson asserted the importance of John Henry as folk hero; Odum fictionalized John Wesley "Left Wing" Gordon in his trilogy on the black Ulysses (*Cold Blue Moon*; *Rainbow*; *Wings*). Unlike Johnson and Odum, Hurston does not depict an exemplary culture hero. Her culture hero John is ordinary; he could very well be anonymous, invisible, or have an *X* for a name. In two stories, "From Pine to Pine Mr. Pinkney" (85–86) and "God an' de Devil in de Cemetery" (86–87), the character Jack is the same as John. Hurston even uses the generalized slave name "Old Cuffee" in one story. There are two other tales focused on Jack, but these tales, "How Jack Beat the Devil" and "Strength Test between Jack and the Devil" (155–56), feature an exemplary culture hero. The placement of these stories—the first as a way for Zora to gain credit for being a supreme storyteller and the second as a farewell gesture from the sawmill camp—suggests variable definitions of culture heroes. Before the second tale, Big Sweet promises to protect Zora from Lucy, and such a position places her in the tradition of the culture hero. Since Big Sweet is the female culture hero in part 1 of *Mules and Men* and her name is largely anonymous, like those of the male culture heroes, Hurston asserts and redefines the politics of black labor and its intersection with gendered labor.

Every Tongue Got to Confess offers a version of the folklore of *Mules and Men* that adheres to the protocols of social science. By contrast, the published version of *Mules and Men* is multidisciplinary and multigeneric. It is interesting to consider how and why Hurston mixes different categories of tales in *Mules and Men*. Improvisation is a key element in folk culture, but one only understands improvisation through comparative knowledge. While communities in *Mules and Men* share a common cultural reserve, the volume's contemporary readers did not share such knowledge. *Every Tongue* provides insight into Hurston's individual improvisations. John Edgar Wideman, in his foreword to *Every Tongue*, makes an important distinction. He calls attention to the tales in *Every Tongue* as "speech acts," in which the occasion, storyteller, and performative context should be imagined (xvii). *Mules and Men* represents "performance events." Hurston provides all the information that would have to be imagined otherwise.

Invented individual identity and performance events emphasize Hurston's repeated attention to situational contexts that necessitate performance. With Hurston's autobiography, *Dust Tracks on a Road*, that context is one of white female patrons. Long unread or disparaged, Hurston's *Dust Tracks* is increasingly important in exploring complex issues of invented and performed identity. Rather than shed any light on the public contexts of folktales in *Mules and Men*, the professed autobiography spends more time on Charlotte Mason's financial support of the project. Hurston's relationships with Mason and Fannie Hurst define the extratextual contexts in which *Mules and Men* and the autobiography should be understood. This extratextual context is worlds away from the store porch and the Eatonville community. Tellingly, the American public continues to insist on the truth value of autobiographies, as underlined by the 2005 scandal surrounding James Frey's memoir *A Million Little Pieces*. Fictive elements of true stories are important ways of exploring the boundaries between truth and fiction, fact and perspective.

The Sis Cat story at the end of the collection (245–46) frames Hurston's knowledge in relation to conventional knowledge. Conventional knowledge and forms are necessary, but they mask other forms of consumption and other possible ways of knowing. While Hurston initiates the readers in different forms of knowledge in Eatonville, Polk County, and New Orleans, those forms of knowledge are predicated on context for meaning. Sis Cat's using her manners needs a sense of place to interpret what those manners mean. To what extent does Hurston provide an adequate context for understanding the significance of folktales and ritual? To what extent does she suspend knowledge and to what purpose?

NOTES

[1] One version of the manuscript that she revised in the late 1920s was published as *Every Tongue Got to Confess: Negro Folk-Tales from the Gulf States*.

[2] See Hill for reproductions of concert programs, including program notes written by Hurston and Alain Locke.

[3] Nicholls explains the significance of Hurston's "everyday acts of resistance," the "hidden transcript" of *Mules and Men*, by contrasting the Polk County section of the ethnography with the musical *Polk County: A Comedy of Negro Life on a Sawmill, with Authentic Negro Music, in Three Acts*. Nicholls explains that, in the musical, "Hurston and her collaborator [Dorothy Waring] frame folklore and blues as commercially viable entertainment rather than as modes of resistance in the lumber camp" (*Conjuring* 477).

[4] Carr and Cooper discuss Hurston's problematic of how to expose and resist the commodification of African American culture. In this respect, she operates "within and against modernism" instead of capitulating to it (288). They explain, "[Hurston] continues throughout the text to explore not only the absorption of the 'probe' by the objects of study, but also the violence and objectification endemic to knowledge projects predicated on this 'probe' and what Boas calls its 'penetrating' action" (297).

[5] If *Mules and Men* is discussed in the context of Pan-African ethnographies, it might be useful to compare Brer Rabbit with Anansi the Spider, a trickster figure common in Jamaican and West African folklore. Ethnographies by Harold Courlander and Melville Herskovits, as well as Hurston's *Tell My Horse*, might be used to explore the Pan-African dimension of *Mules and Men*.

[6] See *The Norton Anthology of African American Literature* companion CD for a recording of "John Henry" (Gates and McKay).

Between Mimesis and Mimicry: Teaching Hurston's *Tell My Horse*

Annette Trefzer

Tell My Horse, Zora Neale Hurston's 1938 book on Caribbean folklore, has not yet received much attention in literature departments and classrooms. The Hurston boom of the 1980s and 1990s concentrated mostly on her fiction, particularly *Their Eyes Were Watching God*, and *Tell My Horse* remains marginalized, for two reasons: it does not clearly fit into an academic discipline or genre, and it requires cultural and historical knowledge on Caribbean-American relations to grasp Hurston's political stance. Many critics initially abstained from commenting on a book that, as Robert Hemenway writes, "is filled with political analysis, often of the naive sort, with superficial descriptions of West Indian curiosities." Hurston, he says, "reports a good deal of public gossip as accepted fact, and she reveals a chauvinism that must have infuriated her Haitian hosts" (*Zora* 249). More recently, however, scholars including John Carlos Rowe, Dorothea Fischer-Hornung, Kevin Meehan, Katherine Henninger, Leigh Anne Duck, Amy Fass Emery, and Leif Sorensen all have contributed to reassessing Hurston's ethnographic work as a deliberate narrative marked by its author's complex self-positioning in discourses of American social idealism, nationalism, ethnography, photography, and globalized modernity.

I approach *Tell My Horse* in the literature classroom as a postmodern ethnography.[1] Situated at the intersection of several genres and discourses including ethnography, political commentary, and personal travelogue, *Tell My Horse* is a collage of impressions and information on Jamaica and Haiti and voodoo. It is a "postmodernist book," writes Ishmael Reed in his foreword to *Tell My Horse*, that is at once "skeptical, cynical, funny, ironic, brilliant, and innovative" (xv). I follow Reed's lead in suggesting postmodernism as a useful context for examining this text, and I ask students to work with Roland Barthes's brief and accessible essay "From Work to Text" before they turn their attention to Hurston. With the help of Barthes's distinctions between the modernist mode of the "work" and the postmodernist "text," students quickly categorize *Tell My Horse* as an open-ended text rather than a work bound by closure. According to Barthes, a text is not limited by its signifier but infinite and alive with variations and "overcrossing" of meanings (902). Building on Barthes, students begin to recognize that Hurston's innovations in content and style result in a text that exceeds its boundaries of genre and meaning. After I point out the slippery ways Hurston positions herself toward her informants and materials, I prompt the class to see that the author is primarily interested not in objective ethnographic documentation but in playing with and "signifying" on her materials.[2] Through the notions of play, performance, and signifying, students then approach Hurston's creatively scientific objectives in *Tell My Horse*.

Hurston's work on voodoo in Jamaica (1936) and Haiti (1937) demanded that she leave her position as an ethnographic observer and become an inside participant. As she tells us in *Mules and Men*, voodoo is a participant ritual that demands initiation, instruction, and even faith; it is an engagement that ruptures clear distinctions between scientist and subject. To study voodoo, Hurston has to take part in it; she cannot remain a neutral observer watching the rituals from the sidelines. As a student of Franz Boas, Hurston learned that "an objective, strictly scientific inquiry can be made only if we succeed in entering into each culture on its own basis" (Boas 205). Boas's attempt to make anthropology an objective science untainted by the perspective of the anthropologist was new in 1928, when *Anthropology and Modern Life* was published. The novelty of Boas's approach to anthropology is summed up by Wade Davis:

> In an era when British social anthropology was still an explicit tool to imperialism, [Boas] rejected arbitrary notions of progress and evolutionary theories that invariably place Western society at the top of a social ladder. Instead he championed the need to study cultures because of their inherent value. (207)

When Hurston traveled to Jamaica and Haiti, she tried to enter these cultures on their terms, recording and documenting folklore, history, and religious beliefs as told by local informants. But Hurston also realized that putting her values and cultural biases aside would be impossible, and it seems that she did not even pretend to aim for objectivity in reporting her findings. As an actor in her own drama, Hurston questions the assumption that scientific method and language can objectively describe another culture. She has no qualms about peppering the book with her own (certainly biased) social and political commentary, even at the cost of breaking with the disciplinary conventions of anthropology. With this daring step, Hurston unmasks "one of the conceits of anthropology [that] lies in its positivist dream of a neutralized language that strips off all its singularity to become nature's exact, unmisted reflection" (Minh-ha 53).

Hurston's language is far from neutral, and her rhetorical strategies do not merely describe or display cultural knowledge but frequently aim to persuade. She knows that fieldwork is more than merely recording facts; it consists in ordering and in this way producing observed cultural reality. As a result, Hurston's observations in *Tell My Horse* reveal a central paradox in her text: on the one hand, she attempts to describe the cultures she is studying on their own terms; on the other hand, she highlights her perspective as a black female ethnographer from the United States. Trinh T. Minh-ha explains the difficult position of all cultural anthropologists who, she says, experience a threefold alienation: from their own culture and society, in the choice of their profession, and in relation to those being studied (58). Such a sense of cultural alienation must have been particularly acute for Hurston, who occupied marginal positions in both American and Caribbean societies and who was a woman in a predominantly male discipline. *Tell My Horse* openly dramatizes Hurston's conflicted subject positions—including her race, gender, and national identifications—that remain essentially unresolved throughout the book but problematize in a productive way central questions of cultural knowledge.

In the classroom, I use the book's first section on Jamaica to illustrate Hurston's struggle with colonial race and gender politics. We begin by discussing Hurston's choice to share not only her materials but also some of the difficulties, frustrations, and dangers of her fieldwork. Because much writing in this section reads like a diary or travelogue, it is a good entry into her conflicted relations with her native informants and into her own self-representation. The Jamaica section of the book also links well with Hurston's race and gender politics in some of her other works. It is helpful to remember here that Hurston wrote *Their Eyes Were Watching God* in Haiti, and it is interesting for students in a Hurston course to discuss her real-life encounters as a woman in the Caribbean with the imagined gender dynamics of her fiction. Once students have an understanding of Hurston's racial and gendered difference in the Caribbean, I use the second section of *Tell My Horse* to discuss her controversial rewriting of Haitian politics. Here I focus on Hurston's experience as an American citizen abroad and how such a national positioning adds to the conflicts produced by her self-identification as a black female ethnographer. In the final section, "Voodoo in Haiti," we return to the idea of the anthropologist's (limited) access to the culture under study and to the close link between ethnographic research and personal experiences.

Hurston arrived in Kingston on 14 April 1936 with the intention to study voodoo practices and compare them with the data she had collected in the southern United States. As a black woman from America, Hurston was immediately struck by cultural differences in Jamaica's understanding of race and gender. What complicated her task of diving into black folk culture was her realization that Jamaican blacks tended to identify openly with the white culture of the European colonizer. She notes that in Jamaica "everybody" wants to "talk English, act English and *look* English" (6). Since the desire is to look white, the color line is sharpest between mulattoes and blacks. As Hurston puts it, "to avoid the consequences of posterity the mulattos give the blacks a first class letting alone" (6). This denial of black racial roots combined with the practice of social segregation among blacks puzzles Hurston. Jamaican race relations, she writes, present a curious spectacle "to the eyes of an American Negro," particularly since "in Jamaica a person may be black by birth but white by proclamation. That is, he gets himself declared legally white" (7). Coming out of the Harlem Renaissance celebration of black culture, Hurston cannot mask her surprise at the white cultural identification of Jamaican blacks, their seeming denial of their native culture and lack of racial pride. Although Hurston explains this phenomenon intellectually, she condemns it personally. She understands that these social realities are a result of a culture that was colonized and occupied. For Hurston, the postcolonial subject's desire for whiteness and the attendant denial of race result in a great cultural loss, the practice of mimicry, and psychological damage to the black culture. Commenting on the colonial mind-set of the Jamaican population, Hurston writes that "colonies always do imitate the mother country more or less" and adds sarcastically, "for instance, some Americans are still aping the English as best as they can even though they have had one hundred and fifty years in which to recover" (6). Hurston's representation of colonial mimicry is reminiscent of Frantz Fanon's psychological portrait in *Black Skin, White Masks* of "the Negro of the Antilles [who] will be proportionately white—that is, he will come closer to being a real human being—in direct ratio to his mastery of the French language" (18). Like Fanon, Hurston recognizes the force of colonialism in constructing and altering racial identities and native cultural traditions.

Although Hurston's embrace of blackness allows her to critique the insecurities of black Jamaican postcolonial society, it also makes her dip into some of the colonizing strategies that she condemns. Hurston's cultural observations begin with an interesting description of Jamaica: "Jamaica, British West Indies, has something else besides its mountains of majesty and its quick green valleys. Jamaica has its moments when the land, as in St. Mary's, thrusts out its sensuous bosom into the sea. Jamaica has its 'bush'" (3). Hurston introduces Jamaica as a female-identified landscape with a "sensuous bosom" and experience with the Indian *kama sutra*, so that Jamaica, according to Hurston's informant, "was prepared to teach continental America something about love" (17). Hurston adopts this gendered imagery that orientalizes and feminizes the island while she simultaneously criticizes the misogyny of her native informants. She confesses that "it is a curious thing to be a woman in the Caribbean after you have been a woman in these United States" and hints that women in Jamaica are primarily respected for their bodies and not their minds (57).

> You meet a lot of darkish men who make vociferous love to you, but otherwise pay you no mind. If you try to talk sense, they look at you right pitifully. . . . It is not that they try to put you in your place, no. They consider that you never had any. (57–58)

In these judgmental lines, we can easily glean Hurston's frustration at not being taken seriously as an intellectual inquirer into Jamaica's cultural practices. Hurston explicitly addresses the limits of her gender when she asks about the apparition of the Three-legged-Horse but gets only laughter from men in the community. She speculates:

> I have the strong belief that the Three-legged-Horse is a sex symbol and that the celebration of it is a fragment of some West African puberty ceremony for boys. All the women feared it. . . . Perhaps under those masques and robes of the male revellers is some culture secret worth knowing. But

> it was quite certain that my sex barred me from getting anything more than the other women knew. (26)

She adds parenthetically and with regret, "I found the 'Société Trois-jambe' in Haiti also but could learn nothing definite of its inner meaning" (26).

Hurston's encounter with gender barriers, male chauvinism, and color consciousness made research in the Caribbean hard for her, and as a modern American woman, she could not refrain from criticizing female oppression. As an anthropologist and intellectual, Hurston tried hard to transcend those gender lines by participating in male rituals such as "curry goat," a "feast so masculine that chicken soup would not be allowed. It must be soup from roosters" (13). But being often unsuccessful in exploring such rituals, she laments the misogynist behavior that colonialism produced. She explains, for instance, how black mothers disappear entirely from Jamaica's social spectrum by dint of their gender and skin color. Hurston sarcastically notes, "You get the impression that these virile Englishmen do not require women to reproduce. They just come out to Jamaica, scratch out a nest and lay eggs that hatch out into 'pink' Jamaicans" (8–9). And as a self-confident African American female observer of Jamaican society, and directly in opposition to her male mentor's advice concerning "objective, strictly scientific inquiry," she forcefully condemns the sexist views of Jamaican men and the society's denial of black racial heritage and prophesies that the "Rooster's Nest is bound to be less glamorous in the future" (10).

Hurston's interpretations and predictions reveal much about her conflicted personal and political positioning as an African American female ethnographer at work in the Caribbean. In the second section of the book, "Politics and Personalities in Haiti," Hurston provides a highly colorful and subjective account of the history of Haiti's revolutions and of the American occupation from 1915 to 1934. Her historical narrative deliberately blurs the boundaries between history and story, fact and fiction, mimesis and mimicry, again approaching the mode of a postmodern text. Because Hurston was interested in recording history the way the people tell it, she leaves out significant dates and other historical signposts that might help students situate the events she addresses. In my experience, a first reading of this section with undergraduate English majors usually yields confusion and plenty of calls for help: What is really going on here? To help students find some historical referents to Haiti's past, I divide the class into six groups and assign each a research topic: Haiti as a French colony in the seventeenth century; the role of Toussaint Louverture and the circumstances under which he came to power after the 1791 uprising; Haiti's rise as an independent republic under Jean-Jacques Dessalines; the Haitian Constitution; the assassination of the president Jean Vilbrun Guillaume Sam; or the United States intervention and occupation of Haiti before Hurston's arrival on the island. I tell my students that this assignment should not yield historical objectivity but a reference point for understanding Hurston's politics. Through shared historical research and group work, students become Hurston's collaborators, expanding on and playing with her text rather than consuming it passively. Following Barthes, the students play the text "as one plays a game, looking for a practice which reproduces it, but, in order that that practice not be reduced to a passive inner mimesis" (904). After students share their collected information, they are ready for a rereading of this section of the book. I ask students to note the ways in which Hurston represents the historical figures and incidents, and I work on a reading that tries to point out Hurston's conflicted ideology as an American citizen confronted with the colonial history and the desperate poverty of Haiti's past and present. Discussing the role of America in Hurston's account of Haitian history and pointing out specific patriotic passages are exercises that nicely yield the paradox at the heart of Hurston's politics: Hurston finds herself trapped in American rhetorical justifications for the occupation, yet she defends local resistance to foreign military control and presents voodoo as one form of such resistance.

Hurston's chapter "Rebirth of a Nation"—an eerie echo of *Birth of a Nation*—may serve as an example. Here Hurston describes Haiti's unsuccessful search for peace: "They sought peace under kingdoms and other ruling names. They sought it in the high cold, beautiful mountains of the island and in the sudden small alluvial plains, but it eluded them and vanished from their hands" (65). In this version of the national narrative, peace is finally brought by American "peacekeeping forces," symbolized by the black plume of the American battleship, the USS *Washington*, against the Caribbean sky. Hurston's patriotic narrative emphasizes the "barbarism" of Haiti as a country torn by revolution: when the Americans landed in 1915, they found "the head of [President] Guillaume Sam hoisted on a pole on the Champ de Mars and his torso being dragged about and worried by the mob" (72). This reading of Haitian history represents the way many Americans understood it: as a succession of struggles and military revolutions, internal political corruption, and bloody massacres that devastated the country after Haiti gained its independence in 1804. Building on this sensationalist historical perspective, Hurston also rehearses American nationalist discourses when she comments on the benefits of the American occupation, which gave Haiti, in her words, "a stable currency, the beginnings of a system of transportation, a modern capitol, the nucleus of a modern army" (74). Hurston's praise of the occupation's progress in the construction of roads, hospitals, and other public service institutions reinforces not only the popular perception of American efforts to "civilize" Haiti but also Hurston's growing disenchantment with political rhetoric as opposed to practical social improvements. Turning her gaze toward her homeland, Hurston pronounces with characteristic exaggeration that American " 'race leaders' are simply obsolete. The man and woman of today in America is the one who makes us believe that he can make our side-meat taste like ham," and she adds, "these same sentiments are mounting in Haiti" (77).

Against the backdrop of such economic pragmatism, reminiscent of Booker T. Washington's polemics and perhaps best understood in the context of the world depression, Hurston mounts a defense of the local culture and local folk heroes in her section on voodoo. In the late 1930s, Hurston's treatment of voodoo as a legitimate religion and a serious subject for ethnographic study represents an uphill battle against both American popular perceptions and domestic denials by the Haitian upper class. During America's occupation of Haiti, sensationalist tales of voodoo worship, cannibalism, witchcraft, zombies, torture, sorcery, and spirit possession painted Haiti as a savage country in need of American order and protection. Joan Dayan poignantly asks, "What better way to justify the 'civilizing' presence of marines in Haiti than to project the phantasm of barbarism?" (33). Hurston, who came to Haiti in the wake of the American occupation, had a difficult time pursuing serious research on topics that served political narratives aimed at representing Haiti as America's exotic and violent other. In the United States, voodoo was commonly considered a barbaric ritual and not a subject of scientific study. In this context it is not surprising that when Hurston published her thesis on the zombie phenomenon, it was ignored in America and scorned in Haiti, where antisuperstition campaigns were under way (W. Davis 214). Hurston locates the negative bias against voodoo in Haiti's social system: "The upper-class Haitian is steeped in voodoo traditions but he will 'lie' to save his own and the national pride" (83). And she finds that "voodoo has more enemies in public and more friends in private than anything else in Haiti" (92). As a result, voodoo rituals are publicly repressed and silenced in Haiti, whereas abroad they serve the construction of a savage image of the black republic with the specific political purpose of justifying the American occupation.

When I approach the voodoo section of *Tell My Horse* in the classroom, we begin by discussing the nature and function of voodoo and its representations in contemporary American culture. Most students are familiar with the capitalist exploitation of voodoo in pop culture and its fetishistic displays ranging from horror movies to stickpin dolls, and they are eager to talk about its commercial and sensationalist images. Given the many misperceptions about voodoo as a cultural practice, students are generally curious about how voodoo might emerge differently under Hurston's ethnographic gaze. Hurston calls voodoo "a religion of creation and life" (113) and defines it in three ways: a belief system shared by a community and celebrated in religious ceremonies; a performance located on the boundary between the visible and the invisible; and a story, a fiction, or as one Haitian intellectual explains, "an all powerful trope" (qtd. in Dayan 35). Hurston would probably agree with Dayan, who argues that voodoo means different things to different people and that it is a religious and cultural performance without stable content or meaning. Dayan urges that "in thinking about vodoun we must inhabit—even if risking that fashionable postmodern device—an indeterminate place, not vague so much as very particularized in its many conversions" (35). Voodoo is an open-ended signifier realized only in particular performances; it is an antinarrative rather than a master narrative whose power and meaning relies on context and circumstance as opposed to fixed essences. Marked by ambiguity, discontinuity, and difference, voodoo is a perfect central metaphor for Hurston's postmodern ethnographic text. As a highly variable and syncretic signifier, voodoo incorporates the religious beliefs and cultural practices of many different peoples: "Cibony, Arawak, and Carib Indians; explorers from Spain; French and English buccaneers; West African slaves; French colonizers; American marines; Catholic missionaries." In Haiti, voodoo is "the embodiment of a tradition of cultural synthesis" with the power to challenge the status quo (M. Anderson 90).

A good place to start discussing the social and historical functions of voodoo is Hurston's chapter on the zombie phenomenon, because zombies are "bodies without souls" (179), figures who clearly illustrate the need for ceremonies that put people in touch with their "spirits." Hurston, the first person ever to photograph a zombie and to posit the plant poison theory as responsible for inducing the zombielike state, notes that resistance to tales about zombies comes primarily from the Haitian elite, who think that "the common people [are] superstitious" and deny the power of such beliefs (181). Yet tales about zombies are not just the wild stuff of superstition and imagination. Hurston finds out that zombies—who have lost their identity, speech, and ability to communicate with the world of the living—are conveniently exploited for slave labor. They become crucial signifiers in the larger historical discourse of slavery and economic exploitation in the Caribbean. Zombies appear in a culture where men sell the souls of others (and their own) for personal economic advancement. Once without souls, victims will die, and a "bocor" (voodoo priest) might sell them to a plantation owner who wants to buy some laborers (182). The zombie phenomenon becomes a trope for the dangers of economic exploitation and the importance of possessing "spirit" and keeping it alive with the help of rituals, altars, and ceremonies dedicated to voodoo gods. Hurston leaves no doubt that, circulated among the poorer classes, these local stories are powerful counterhegemonic narratives with an important social function.

Hurston continues her discussion of the rebellious spirit of the peasants in her title chapter, "Parlay Cheval Ou" ("Tell My Horse"), in which she focuses on Papa Guede, a uniquely Haitian god (or "loa"). She explains that "the people who created Guede needed a god of derision. They needed a spirit which could burlesque the society that crushed him" (220). When possessed or "mounted" by Guede, the spirit rider has the liberty to say many things that he or she could not utter otherwise. For instance, during a possession ritual Hurston witnesses, "a prominent official is made ridiculous before a crowd of peasants" without repercussions to the person who is possessed (221). Guede, who "bites with sarcasm and slashes with ridicule the class that despises him" (220), clearly functions as an important avenue for social critique, resistance, and rebellion that neither foreign occupation nor domestic prohibition can crush. Hurston takes careful note not only of the rituals but also of the resistance to the subversive power of voodoo. When she participated in the "Tete l'eau" ceremony, which involved bathing in a waterfall, the worshippers were greeted at the site by the police sent there by the local (most likely Catholic) priest who did not approve of such "pagan" rituals. Hurston writes that the worshippers "all felt that a police at the waterfall at Saut d'Eau was a desecration, but expressions of fervor were not to be suppressed entirely" (234). Although Hurston was prevented from going into the water by the "houngan" who prepared her for initiation, she witnessed hundreds of people who entered the "eternal mists" and experienced "an ecstasy of worship of the beautiful in water-forms" (234). Hurston's point is that the subversive power of voodoo can be curtailed neither by the local police nor by the military occupation. When the United States Marines destroyed the cave dwelling of a voodoo priest, "the Man of Trou Forban," by dynamiting the great rock that blocked the entrance to his mountain residence, legend tells that "the next morning it was there whole and in place again" (190).

In writing about voodoo, Hurston does not merely chronicle cultural rituals for posterity; she is interested in representing voodoo as a narrative of resistance, a Haitian cultural and religious practice invented and celebrated in often oppositional political contexts. As her narrative choices in *Tell My Horse* reveal and as she announces explicitly, "this work does not pretend to give a full account of either Voodoo or Voodoo gods. It would require several volumes to attempt to cover completely the gods and voodoo practices of one vicinity alone" (131). Faced with an impressively large pantheon of voodoo gods and hundreds of different practices, Hurston readily admits that her study of the field is not exhaustive. Some critics suggest that she may have been prevented from writing more extensively about her findings because voodoo initiates cannot divulge the secrets of the religion. In her chapter "Doctor Reser," Hurston confesses that she is "breaking a promise by writing this" (245). Hemenway suggests that the book looks unfinished because Hurston may have received warnings by local practitioners to abandon her inquiries (*Zora* 248). But I believe an exhaustive record of voodoo in the Caribbean may never have been Hurston's goal.

Judging by the cross-disciplinary shape of *Tell My Horse* and Hurston's prominent presence in it, I think Hurston wanted to give us a sample of what Roger Abrahams calls an "ethnography of experience" (xxx). Hurston comes away from the Caribbean with an impressive list of collected materials: the rudiments of a voodoo pantheon, an appendix of songs of voodoo worship, Jamaican proverbs, records of voodoo ceremonies, local tales, folklore, and even photographs. But by binding these ethnographic findings into the context of her own experiences and travels, Hurston shows that cultural material is inseparable from cultural experience. She makes no effort to take herself out of the field in order to turn herself into an invisible scientific observer; on the contrary, she focuses on the creative cultural interactions between informants and ethnographer, performers and audiences. In the process of inscribing herself into the text, Hurston becomes a cultural performer twice over. A brilliant verbal griot, a true woman of words who dwells comfortably on the border between mimesis and mimicry, Hurston dares us to recognize the postmodern truth, best articulated today by James Clifford, that the authority of scientific disciplines such as ethnography "will always be mediated by the claims of rhetoric and power" (11). Her rhetorical innovations in style and content produce a semantic instability that is ultimately performative and politically postmodern. Unwilling to stop her own verbal dexterity and creativity, Hurston courageously writes herself into *Tell My Horse* and in the process moves from being a recorder of cultural performances to becoming a boisterous performer herself.

NOTES

[1] Although *postmodernism* is a term that suffers from the absence of a scholarly consensus on its definition (Hassan 149), I nevertheless find it useful for discussing Hurston's strategies of literary and political fragmentation, marginality, and plurality that often make it difficult to grasp her meaning.

[2] For an explanation of the theory of signification in the African American tradition, see Gates's *Signifying Monkey*, particularly chapter 2.

Telling Tales in *Dust Tracks on a Road*: Hurston's Portrait of an Artist

Kimberly D. Blockett and Nellie Y. McKay

While *Their Eyes Were Watching God* continues to be widely taught on all college levels, Zora Neale Hurston's autobiography, *Dust Tracks on a Road*, remains neglected by many teachers and critics. Often considered a work of lesser value than the novel, it is rarely taught, left to scholars seeking to understand better Hurston's body of work. In 2003, as we discussed various ways that we have taught *Dust Tracks*, we admitted that we, too, did not particularly *like* teaching it. It had been a less fruitful text for our students than *Their Eyes*. Although it does lend itself to good discussions of textual authority, truth in autobiography, and creations of identity, it left students (and teachers) feeling as if they hadn't experienced the joy of reading the "real" Hurston. Robert Hemenway's introduction to her autobiography includes the expressions "paradoxical," "confusing," "less than candid," and "deliberately ambiguous" (xxxviii, x, xi, xi). In fact, Hemenway states that *Dust Tracks* "fails as an autobiography because it is a text deliberately less than its author's talents, a text diminished by [Hurston's] refusal to provide a second or third dimension to the flat surfaces of her adult image" (xxxix). Most readers have certain expectations of autobiographical writing; it is a well-defined genre, and Hurston's book continually transgresses the boundaries of generic conventions. It's no wonder that students (and instructors) find it less than wonderful.

Nevertheless, Hurston's autobiography—however much it may not give readers what they want—is an important contribution to the fields of life writing and African American literature. Its genius lies not in the exploration of Zora Neale Hurston as friend, lover, wife, or daughter but in the few intimate details that provide a map of Hurston as writer and as conscious scholar of and participant in African American oral and literary traditions. To the same degree that the book fails to tell us much that we can believe about her life experiences, it excels at offering a blueprint of why she wrote, how she wrote, and how her writing attempts to articulate a centripetal theme of African American experience: journeys.

After revamping our approach, we have found that offering students an opportunity to read Hurston's *Dust Tracks* alongside one of her works of fiction has proved much more productive than teaching the autobiography alone and satisfies a few agendas, not necessarily those normally expected of autobiography:

Reading *Dust Tracks* guarantees many questions and lively discussion about veracity, perspective, and the influence of race, class, and gender in autobiography. It asks the question, What is or what counts as autobiography? This, in turn, provides a gentle introduction to literary theory for upper-level classes.

After such lively discussions, students are more willing to read literary criticism. They want to know what the experts think.

Comparing the metaphors in *Dust Tracks* with those in her novels effectively makes the point that literary language is deliberate and purposeful on the part of the author.

The ambiguity of Hurston's autobiography frustrates any student's attempt to put forth what the author intends for us to understand as the only truth a text can offer.

For our class, having students read *Their Eyes Were Watching God* immediately before reading *Dust Tracks* works very well. What follows is a detailed discussion of how and why we connect these two texts, related readings, and specific assignments that help move our students through purposeful yet open discussions.

At the University of Wisconsin, Madison, the Department of Afro-American Studies regularly offers an undergraduate course on black women writers at both the introductory and upper levels. Since the introductory course satisfies a couple of core-curriculum requirements and is offered by a popular department, the classes are consistently overenrolled. Because of the institution's selective status in juxtaposition with its land-grant mission, we have both been privileged to have taught this class to every conceivable type of student, including football stars, children of farmers, first-generation immigrants, prep school valedictorians, working adults, and teenage mothers. Thus our classroom experience with these texts is considerable and varied. Although this essay focuses on the introductory-level, large lecture course, the methodology applies to the small discussion sections that students attend weekly and is readily manipulated for undergraduate seminars.

Because students new to college-level literature can be intimidated or bored by nonfiction, it is easier to begin with the novel. *Their Eyes* tends to have such universal appeal as a work of art that it leaves students feeling open to and interested in Hurston. For many, it is their first time reading anything by a person of color or by a woman. Once students are eager to learn more about the woman who introduced them to Janie, Eatonville, and the horizon, they are ready for the first piece of nonfiction. As a gateway to nonfiction, the essays at the end of *Dust Tracks* (otherwise known as the structural problems of the book) provide good preparation for reading sociohistorical essays as context for the literature. Students begin to understand that even fiction is not written in a vacuum as they discuss Hurston's inclusion of sociopolitical thinking and events as critical to the construction of her self in the autobiography. As they read about Hurston's world, students see how even when a text does not directly address political issues, writing it is often a political act. In this way, *Dust Tracks* serves as an excellent entry to the idea of reading essays about real things alongside books with fictional characters and, later, theoretical essays about abstract things.

First, we want to move from primary to secondary texts. To that end, after completing *Their Eyes* and before reading *Dust Tracks*, we begin a classroom assignment that defines autobiography. As students volunteer phrases, the instructor can write them on the board, creating a list of what they expect to discover in an autobiography, such as how the author grew up, how she became famous or infamous, details about personal relationships and traumas, and so on. We then ask our students to use this list to compile information from Hurston's autobiography. This information, or journal, should include a list of facts about Hurston and some assessment of the book based on the list of expectations that they have created.

After reading the autobiography and discussing their journals, the class begins to question Hurston's textual choices. Students hesitantly ask about her decisions to include some bits of information about her life or feelings but exclude others that would seem obvious. By this point, as instructors, we can feel the discomfort in the classroom. Students had put Hurston on a pedestal in their reading of *Their Eyes* and now feel that critiquing her autobiography is somehow wrong, perhaps disloyal to her. We allow them to struggle with their feelings and find that assigning them a few pieces of literary criticism helps open the floor for the next discussion. Hemenway's introduction provides a useful summary of critical responses to the autobiography (see also N. McKay; P. Walker). After reading critics who agree that the text lacks fundamental autobiographical qualities, students gain confidence in their abilities to read, assess, and critique the text.

With their newfound confidence, students participate in a productive conversation about the problems they have with *Dust Tracks.* After everyone agrees that the text fails to fulfill our expectations of autobiography, we ask students to read Kathleen Hassall's "Text and Personality in Disguise and in the Open: Zora Neale Hurston's *Dust Tracks on a Road.*"[1] In it, Hassall affirms and then complicates their assessments. She suggests:

> [O]ne way to make sense of this problematic text is to recognize it as a series of performances by an actress trained in Eatonville. . . . Alice Walker's choice of the word "pretending" to describe what Hurston does in *Dust Tracks* is telling. *Dust Tracks* seems to be nonconfrontational; it seems to reflect the "powerlessness" of its author. It is possible, however, to read the autobiography differently, to read it as a set of glimpses into the character of an inventive, resourceful, spirited, effective writer—in disguise. Pretense, misdirection, secrecy, and a deliberate, slippery unpredictability—all venerable "confrontational strategies," and all lessons Hurston learned in Eatonville—direct her performances in *Dust Tracks*. . . . Hurston was expected to report and interpret Hurston; instead she *presents* Hurston—or rather she presents an assemblage of fictionalized Hurstons. (160–61)

Here Hassall negotiates Alice Walker's limited assessment of *Dust Tracks*, offering the class a valuable example of the ways in which scholars can disagree while valuing and building on each other's ideas.

Reading literary criticism helps students think about different yet equally valid readings of a text. It inspires multilevel thinking and addresses questions students may have had earlier while reading Hurston's fiction. When discussions about fiction yield multiple readings of a passage, students may complain that literature is too abstract and ask how one is supposed to figure out what it really means. Reading different viewpoints about a nonabstract, nonfiction work can help prepare students to be more open to contradiction and complication.[2]

Now that the class has worked through issues of authenticity, critical viewpoints, and constructions of the self, *Dust Tracks* can also serve as an important gateway to understanding central metaphors in Hurston's fiction. Although we like to have students read *Their Eyes* before *Dust Tracks*, the initial discussion of the novel is purposely limited to plot and entry-level analysis. We ask students to note the recurring images, themes, and metaphors as they read. We then move quickly on to *Dust Tracks* to use the autobiography as a road map when we revisit the novel for deeper exploration.

The first clear benefit of reading an unreliable autobiography is that it clears a path for students to analyze language, as an entity unto itself, without the author's getting in the way. Students of literature, particularly in the introductory courses, often feel a strong desire to link an author's life to the text. As instructors, we are usually much more interested in the analysis of language and thematic foci and thus push students away from trying to determine authorial intent on the basis of the author's psyche. *Dust Tracks* frustrates anyone's attempt to figure out Hurston's id and superego. Yet it serves the more important function of helping students understand how and why Hurston uses particular images, language, and themes in her fiction. While it is not an example of writing about the self (as students want and expect it to be), it is an autobiography that illustrates the self in the act of writing. In addition, usually most students will not have much knowledge of African American history or literature, and Hurston's writing is an excellent vehicle for exploring history and oral traditions as represented by her insistence on journey motifs and metaphors of movement.

Hurston's most notable travel metaphor is, of course, her characterization of her life journey as dust tracks on a road. Hurston then creates a fictionalized autobiography in *Their Eyes Were Watching God* as Janie Starks Woods narrates her life story to her best friend. Both narrations couch major life developments in language that evokes fluidity and mobility. In *Dust Tracks*, Hurston tellingly entitles the chapter detailing her mother's death as "Wandering" and explains, "that hour began my wanderings" (89), again defining herself primarily as a traveler. In fact, the book gives us few intimate details of her life. Yet Hurston does use personal moments to construct her persona, and she articulates those specific constructions of self using language of mobility. Her major life challenges such as poverty and family problems are described as "my vagrancy" (115), and resolving to change her situation is "setting my feet" to move to different spaces of resistance.

In the same way, Hurston uses tropes of movement as a narrative strategy to signal Janie's discontent, her desires, and her decisions to act on those desires. Just as the title of her autobiography announces its intention to privilege movement to construct her life, Hurston tells the reader of *Their Eyes* early on that mobility provides the opportunity and catalyst for theorizing subjectivity. She opens with an interjection from the omniscient narrator that reminds us of the historical nature of movement as being gendered:

> Ships at a distance have every man's wish on board. For some they come in with the tide. For others they sail forever on the horizon, never out of sight, never landing until the Watcher turns his eyes away in resignation, his dreams mocked to death by Time. (1)

Using the first page of the frame tale as a classroom project gives students an opportunity to do close reading together and privileges the importance of paying attention to how and why an author might structure her text in such a way. An instructor might ask the class why we are given this reflection before we are introduced to the heroine or have any sense of her story. A collaborative analysis brings out many points. Students tend to notice immediately that the first phrase of the novel places male desire in the context of travel. Hurston begins by coupling movement and desire in an abstract sense (the ship is a distant spot on the horizon) and genders it male but then declares that for women the realities of time and distance do not obscure the desire: "The dream is the truth. Then they act and do things accordingly" (1). The women, unlike the men, place desire at the forefront and act on it. Only after Hurston situates the story philosophically in the rhetoric of travel does she introduce us to the central story of Janie, "a woman . . . [who] had come back from burying the dead[,] . . . the sudden dead, their eyes flung wide open in judgment" (1). From this setup, the class identifies three important things: she went on a journey; there was a conflict; she was the survivor. Thus the novel is simultaneously situated in the Western literary tradition of the bildungsroman and in the African American literary tradition as a rejection of the "tragic mulatta" motif. As Janie journeys, each relocation is precipitated by discontent, and every location is marked by a new experience from which Janie comes to understand something new about herself and her world.

After comparing the language of the novel to the stories of the autobiography, we begin to outline ways to read the variety of symbols that signal psychological development. Using the journal in which they have recorded metaphors and recurring images, students can see that throughout Janie's quest, Hurston uses the tropes of gates and roads to indicate discontent and desire. They are not simply signals of change but also spaces of waiting and wondering. Each gate—Nanny's, Logan's, and Joe's—represents a liminal space to which Janie goes and waits. The gate functions as a boundary, or border, that emphasizes difference and separation as well as access. The same structure that holds one in and holds others out allows reciprocal movement from one space to another, from private to public or vice versa. At this place of potential entrance or exit, Janie looks to the road as a space that engenders curiosity and wonder. The road offers opportunity.

In Janie's story to Pheoby, the rhetoric of location conflates desire, subjectivity, and travel. Janie's decision that "her conscious life had commenced at Nanny's gate" with a kiss from Johnny Taylor is profound (10). Here she experiences sexual desire and actively pursues satisfaction. On reflection, she equates both the desire and the quest with her consciousness—her ability to begin theorizing her multiple selves, her multiple desires, the liminality of her location—indeed, her subjectivity. Just after experiencing her first orgasm, Janie wonders, "Where were the singing bees for her?" She is "seeking confirmation" and looks to the road for answers:

> Nothing on the place nor in her grandma's house answered her. She searched as much of the world as she could from the top of the front steps and then went on down to the front gate and leaned over to gaze up and down the road. Looking, waiting, breathing short with impatience. Waiting for the world to be made. (11)

This passage highlights the ways in which Hurston privileges the epistemological nature of journey. Her heroine leans over a moving border (the gate), constructs her quest for sex as a thirst for knowing, and determines that location is the key to desire and discernment. Johnny Taylor has transformed from "shiftless" to "a glorious being *coming up the road*" precisely because he can answer her immediate desires and is on the other side of her boundary (11; our emphasis). He is outside Nanny's yard and, therefore, the world; he is coming from somewhere, a wanderer bringing knowledge of another location. In like manner, Janie's first vision of Joe Starks arrives after a disagreement with Killicks, when she "moved everything to a place in the yard where she could see the road. . . . She had been there a long time when she heard [Joe's] whistling coming down the road" (26). Tea Cake does not live in Eatonville and is just passing through on his way to another town. But he is "easy tuh see on Church Street most any day" (94–95), thus claiming his location as unfixed, somewhere on a road, but not living any place specifically. In fact, all the men that Janie chooses for herself (Johnny, Joe, and Tea Cake) are coming down a road from somewhere else, going someplace else. They are all traveling men, and it is the promise of someplace else, something different that intrigues Janie. Janie understands that with each movement, she is allowing herself to be someone slightly different, slightly other. With each shift in location, there is a shifting subjectivity, and the text is engaging different aspects of black female experience as it explores Janie's multiple existence.

In the same way, Hurston identifies herself and other writers as travelers, or "pilgrims on [a] strange road" (*Dust Tracks* 60). Hurston's autobiography insists that any understanding of Hurston must privilege the construction of the writerly self as it shifts and moves along multiple paths, creating multiple selves.

NOTES

1 This article is fairly accessible for undergraduates. For a particularly resistant class, assigning the first few pages that introduce her argument will suffice. A course for English majors should assign the entire article. Pam Bordelon's "New Tracks on *Dust Tracks*: Toward a Reassessment of the Life of Zora Neale Hurston" is another easily read and useful article on veracity in the autobiography.

2 For upper-level courses, we introduce literary theory at this point. Françoise Lionnet's "Autoethnography: The An-Archic Style of *Dust Tracks on a Road*" is an easy-to-read argument that Hurston would never seriously attempt to write any truths about herself. This argument sets up the inherent paradox in autobiography. Lionnet's discussion of the lack or denial of an essential quality in the telling of a tale is exactly what *Dust Tracks* illustrates. It doesn't give the essential Hurston but instead proposes a structure from which to understand the rhythm, or artistry, of Zora Neale Hurston; it instructs us about Hurston as the teller of tales. From there, we might assign Pierre Walker's "Zora Neale Hurston and the Post-modern Self in *Dust Tracks on a Road*" and Sidonie Smith's "Self, Subject, and Resistance: Marginalities and Twentieth-Century Autobiographical Practice." While Smith does not focus specifically on *Dust Tracks*, she does introduce important theoretical ideas about the Cartesian self, subjectivity, and the functions of traditional autobiography.

From Gilded Garden to Golden Anniversary: Teaching Hurston's "The Gilded Six-Bits"

Margaret D. Bauer

"The Gilded Six-Bits," first published in 1933 in *Story*, is now among the most often anthologized of Zora Neale Hurston's works. Robert Bone considers it "representative of [Hurston's] principal achievement in the short story form" (144). I suggest that part of Hurston's achievement with this story is how she recasts in it perhaps the oldest short story of all: the story of Adam and Eve.[1] Teaching it, therefore, offers an opportunity to demonstrate resisting reading that reenvisions texts traditionally presented from a patriarchal perception.[2] In addition, this Hurston short story is an excellent avenue for explaining to students the concept of the *felix culpa*.

Toward both these goals, I try to coax students from their usual initial response to Missie May's affair with Otis D. Slemmons as an unforgivable betrayal of her husband, Joe, to a more compassionate response to this young woman's fall. I begin class discussion by asking students to note the parallels between Hurston's story and the story of Adam and Eve, and then I ask them to identify the major difference: in Hurston's story Adam/Joe is tempted first.

First, we discuss the story's paradisiacal setting and Adam-and-Eve-like couple. The story's opening sentence, which notes the setting to be "a Negro yard around a Negro house in a Negro settlement" (86), suggests that the inhabitants of this home are separated from the racial conflict and oppression we know to have existed in Hurston's day. We discuss the playfulness of the two characters, which begins with Joe's tossing his week's pay in the door and culminates with this scene: "For several minutes the two were a furious mass of male and female energy. Shouting, laughing, twisting, turning, tussling, tickling each other in the ribs" (87). The reference to "male and female energy" suggests that the couple's horseplay has led to sexual relations, but we note that the sexual activity is described in terms of play. Hurston is thereby emphasizing the couple's youth: even in their lovemaking, Joe and Missie May play like children. Students recognize that this couple seems relatively carefree, like Adam and Eve in Eden.

I call to the students' attention the line "It was this way every Saturday afternoon" (87). On the positive side, this sentence tells us that Joe receives regular wages and that he makes enough money for the young couple to get by comfortably, which is also supported by Hurston's earlier idyllic description of their home, by the absence of any reference to Missie May working outside the home, and by the very substantial Saturday dinner Missie May makes and the extra money Joe has for chocolate kisses and ice cream.[3] On the more negative side, the sentence just quoted also emphasizes the sameness of the couple's day-to-day life. I ask students to consider how long such sameness would be enjoyable to them; eventually, wouldn't they get bored with any routine, week after week, no matter how pleasant? Here I introduce the concept of the *felix culpa*, or "fortunate fall," to students: humans are better off for Adam and Eve's having been expelled from Eden. Even Eden would have become boring after a while. Indeed, isn't Joe showing signs of dissatisfaction with the status quo?

In response to this question about Joe, students note his admiration for the worldliness and appearance of the new man in town, which Joe contrasts with his own limited experience and self-image. Examining what Joe says about Slemmons during his conversation with Missie May over dinner leads students to recognize Joe as the first to be tempted by the serpent that has entered this garden.[4] Missie May, in contrast, admires Joe's appearance ("Ah'm satisfied wid you jes lak you is, baby. God took pattern after a pine tree and built you noble" [90]) and is suspicious of Slemmons's stories about his various adventures and accomplishments ("Ah hates to see you so dumb. Dat stray nigger jes' tell y'all anything and y'all b'lieve it" [90]).

Slemmons as dissembler confirms his role as the story's Satan figure. His apparent success and prosperity appeal first to Joe, as Eve was first attracted to Satan's promises of the divine knowledge that would be hers if she ate of the forbidden fruit. The forbidden fruit that Slemmons dangles is his gold jewelry, which he claims was given to him by white women. Slemmons is thereby implying that he has cuckolded the white man—certainly a reason to be admired by black men. One might here recall the association that Joe made earlier between Slemmons and the white man—his build "make 'm look lak a rich white man" (89)—which was meant to be a compliment, despite the white man's role as oppressor in the black man's history.[5]

During the discussion of Slemmons's association with the white man—his reference to receiving gifts from white women as well as Joe's comparison of Slemmons's build to that of a prosperous white man—I have students ponder the significance of Slemmons's use of the word *forty* as an adjective for anything he perceives as being valuable (as in, "Dat wife of yours is jes' thirty-eight and two. Yessuh, she's forte!" [91]). I challenge students to recall various biblical references to the number forty: the forty days and nights of rain sent to wash the earth clean, sparing only Noah and his family; the forty years that the Hebrews had to wander in the desert because of Moses's lack of faith; and the forty days that Jesus fasted in the desert and was tempted by Satan. These examples give the number forty negative connotations, as does a reference to forty in African American history: the forty acres and a mule that were promised to slaves after the Civil War. The allusion to that unfulfilled promise of Reconstruction days reminds us that Slemmons has come south from Chicago, like a carpetbagger,[6] and therefore prepares us for the later discovery that his gold buttons are fake. This allusion also points out to us that the Edenic setting of the story is probably as falsely paradisiacal as the intentions for the Reconstruction South. Together with the presence of the clueless white store clerk at the story's end and the references Joe and Slemmons make to white men within the story, the allusion to the forty acres reminds us of the racial conflict that exists in the world surrounding this domestic scene. Thus the reader is ultimately disturbed by Slemmons's appeal to Joe and Joe's wish to show Missie May off, apparently to get Slemmons's approval.

Sadly, despite Missie May's early perception of Slemmons's speciousness, she, like Adam, is ultimately tempted as well—but like Milton's Adam in *Paradise Lost*, who succumbed to temptation in order to be banished from Eden with Eve rather than remain without her, Missie May falls more because of her love for Joe than because of her own ambition. Before Missie May even sees Slemmons's gold, Hurston foreshadows this fall and prepares us to understand why Missie May cuckolds Joe—even as she questions Joe's admiration of Slemmons and reminds Joe of his own appeal: "Youse a pritty man, *and if Ah knowed any way to make you mo' pritty still Ah'd take and do it*" (90; my emphasis). But after Missie May and Joe have been to the ice cream parlor, while Missie May is still not that impressed with Slemmons ("He'll do in case of a rush" [91]), she is now quite enchanted with the gold money and covets it for Joe: "Dat's de first time Ah ever seed gold money. It lookted good on him sho nuff, but it'd look a heap better on you" (91).

Oddly, on returning from their first evening at the ice cream parlor, Joe, in contrast, is no longer so wishful for himself as he was when he first brought Slemmons up to Missie May; now, in response to *her* reaction to the gold, he says, "Don't be so wishful 'bout me. Ah'm satisfied de way Ah is" (91). Ironically, it is just before Joe catches Missie May in bed with Slemmons that Hurston confirms Joe's dissipated ambition to be like the seemingly more prosperous man. On his way home early to his wife that ill-fated night, Joe ponders his life and reveals to the reader that, instead of being tired of the routine of his married life, he thought

> [t]hat was the best part of life—going home to Missie May. Their whitewashed house, the mock battle on Saturday, the dinner and ice cream parlor afterwards, church on Sunday nights when Missie out-dressed any woman in town—all, everything was right. (92)

How do we account for this change in Joe? I ask students. We note how this role reversal reestablishes the traditional domestic hierarchy: Joe becomes the voice of reason ("Who, me? Missie May youse crazy! Where would a po' man lak me git gold money from?" [91]), while Missie May, who had earlier chastised Joe for being so gullible, now fantasizes about the gold ("Us might find some goin' long de road some time" [91]). The stage is now set for Missie May's fall.

When Joe walks into the bedroom, prepared to defend Missie May from some uninvited intruder, and finds Slemmons struggling to get into his pants, Hurston writes, "The great belt on the wheel of Time slipped and eternity stood still" (93). Note that Hurston says "*eternity* stood still"—this event marks the end of their lives in Eden, where human beings had no awareness of death and thus of time.[7] In discussing the significance of this line, I propose to students a more secular reading of the story of the Garden of Eden than they are perhaps accustomed to: Adam and Eve were mortals and were thus going to die someday whether they ate the fruit or not; but until they ate of the forbidden tree, they (like most children) did not understand what mortality—what death—meant. Considering again Hurston's description of the childlike behavior of Missie May and Joe, we understand that their relationship was still in its honeymoon phase before this tragic event: it had not yet been tested. I bring up again the concept of the *felix culpa* and ask students what might be fortunate about Missie May's fall. I quote from *Paradise Lost* regarding God's explanation for giving human beings free will when he knew they would fail the test: "Not free, what proof could they have given sincere / Of true allegiance, constant Faith or Love" (3.103–04). The point is to show students how the love between Missie May and Joe is not certain until it is tested. Returning to the line referring to the wheel of time, the revelation of Missie May's betrayal of her marriage banishes the couple from Eden and into the realm of time, and the rest of the story will either support the cliché "Time heals all wounds" or reveal that their love is not strong enough to withstand Missie May's mistake.

Whereas students are usually disgusted with Missie May for messing up the paradisiacal situation Hurston had set up in the story's opening frame, I note to them that the injured party, Joe, does not so quickly condemn his wife. We discuss his very adult response to the betrayal: while he cannot forgive her instantly, he does not send her away, leave her, or even chastise her outright. One might argue that his leaving the gilded coins around as payment for sexual relations later in the story is at least a subconscious act of retaliation for the pain she has inflicted on him. Whether subconscious or intentional cruelty, this act serves to humanize Joe, since he otherwise handles himself and the situation with more maturity than most people would be able to summon under such circumstances.

Considering again how Joe was the first to be tempted by the signs of Slemmons's prosperity, perhaps Joe recognizes his part in Missie May's sin.[8] He certainly seems to understand that her infidelity was motivated by her love for him. Turning to Missie May, then, we contrast her development with Joe's: earlier in the story, Joe seemed to be the one dissatisfied with himself; Missie May had not yet reached a stage of wanting more out of life. By the time that Missie May's head is turned by the gold jewelry, Joe seems to have made some adjustment in his values: perhaps having contrasted his wife with Slemmons's jewelry, he has realized that he is the richer man. Both points of contrast suggest that Joe is slightly more mature than his wife, which prepares us for Missie May's naïveté regarding the consequences of an affair. Like Adam and Eve—or any child who has not yet committed a serious transgression—how was she to understand the consequences of such behavior, not yet having experienced any threat to her blissful life?

The compassionate, pensive Joe we see after his discovery of his wife's infidelity is more admirable than the bombastic Joe in the first few pages of the story—which brings us to another reason that the couple's fall can be viewed as fortunate. The class discusses how, once Joe and Missie May know that their marriage can withstand one of the hardest tests of a relationship, they are in a better place than they were before, Joe's awareness of which is reflected in the increased number of candy kisses he buys for Missie May at the story's end. While he resumes the ritual to indicate to his wife that everything is going to be all right, the students agree that Hurston does not mean to indicate that the couple will go back to the status quo; quite the contrary, since by this time they have a baby to take care of.[9] Adults now, rather than two children playing house, they are more ready for this new responsibility than they were before Missie May's affair.

"The Gilded Six-Bits" can be read along with other American retellings of the fall, like Nathaniel Hawthorne's "The Maypole of Merry Mount" and "Young Goodman Brown." Thus, in an American literature survey course, the students see evidence of the continued influence of the Puritan perception of the New World as a new Eden. And in a general introduction to literature or a short story class, the students see how the very earliest stories continue to influence literature throughout time.

In "The Maypole of Merry Mount," two of the maypole revelers are married during the festivities. Immediately following their vows, the two become pensive. Hawthorne's description of their apparent—and mature—recognition of the possible consequences of love reminds us of the postlapsarian Joe and Missie May:

> No sooner had their hearts glowed with real passion than they were sensible of something vague and unsubstantial in their former pleasures, and felt a dreary presentiment of inevitable change. From the moment that they truly loved they had subjected themselves to earth's doom of care and sorrow and troubled joy, and had no more a home at Merry Mount. (45)

Indeed, following their recognition, the merrymakers are interrupted by Endicott and his fellow Puritans, who prepare to punish them for their hedonistic behavior. While in this story, as in his other works, Hawthorne exposes the cruelty of his Puritan ancestors that belied their Edenic analogies of the New World, at the same time, he, like Hurston, reveals the positive side of living in a fallen world. He begins by noting that "never had their [the newlyweds'] youthful beauty seemed so pure and high as when its glow was chastened by adversity" (51), thus also suggesting that virtue must be tested to be assessed. The story proceeds with the husband and then the wife pronouncing their willingness to die for the other. The Puritans recognize the couple's genuine virtue and recruit rather than punish them, and Hawthorne concludes that the couple "returned to [the maypole] no more" and that their lives subsequently led them "heavenward supporting each other along the difficult path which it was their lot to tread" (52).

Reading Hurston's story along with this Hawthorne story reveals the development of Hurston's characters' relationship from an immature, falsely paradisiacal love to a mature love that has withstood a serious test and will thus probably last through the couple's golden anniversary (hence my title for this essay). Hurston's story can also help students see the pride of the title character of "Young Goodman Brown" as the greatest sin, which Hawthorne condemns here. Once students forgive Missie May for her very human mistake and understand Joe's heroism in forgiving her, they are better able to understand Goodman Brown's culpability (whereas they are usually distracted from such understanding by the "devil worshipping" that took place in the woods, much as they are initially compelled to condemn Missie May). Brown, like Joe, is the first to be tempted into the woods, while his wife, Faith, pleads with him to stay with her. But unlike Joe, after finding that his wife, too, has succumbed to temptation (or might have—the whole experience may have been a dream), Brown is not so forgiving. When on emerging from the woods he sees Faith, he "looked sternly and sadly into her face and passed on without a greeting," and we are told that in the years that followed, "often, awaking suddenly at midnight, he shrank from the bosom of Faith, and at morning or eventide when the family knelt down at prayer he scowled and muttered to himself and gazed sternly at his wife and turned away" (71). Brown, unlike Joe, is not able to forgive his wife for succumbing to that which tempted him as well. In contrast to Joe, who seems self-aware, Brown must have determined from his experience in the woods not that he is one among many sinners but that he is the only one in his community who is not a sinner. The "stern . . . sad . . . darkly meditative . . . distrustful . . . man" (71) who emerges from the woods is starkly different from the last we see of Hurston's playful and content, wise and compassionate Joe, returning to his wife and new son with candy kisses.

NOTES

1 Bone (149) and Lillie P. Howard ("Marriage" 263) have also noted Edenic parallels in the story.

2 See *The Resisting Reader*, in which Judith Fetterley argues that "the first act of the feminist critic must be to become a resisting rather than an assenting reader and, by this refusal to assent, to begin the process of exorcizing the male mind that has been implanted in us" (xxii).

3 In their article on this story, Nancy Chinn and Elizabeth E. Dunn refer to its Depression-era setting. They also take note of Joe's steady job, but not without pointing out that the couple owns no luxuries, nothing beyond basic necessities (778).

4 Cheryl A. Wall (Introduction 15), Gayl Jones (162), and Chinn and Dunn (788) also recognize that Joe is the first to have his head turned by Slemmons's apparent prosperity, but other critics overlook this detail. Bone, for example, focuses on how "*the woman* functions as a pivot between two value systems" in the story: "the one urban and 'sophisticated,' the other rural and elemental. At *first she* chooses falsely" (149;

emphasis added). Bone's reference to Missie May as "the woman" and his later reference to Edenic parallels ("As the story opens, Joe and Missie May frolic in prelapsarian innocence" [149]) suggest that his reading of this story is influenced by Milton's emphasis on Eve's culpability.

[5] As Hildegard Hoeller has also pointed out, Otis D. Slemmons anticipates Hurston's Joe Starks of *Their Eyes Were Watching God* (778). Hoeller also notes a comparison between "Gilded Six-Bits" and "Now Cooking with Gas," another Hurston story that examines "the relations between race, money, and sexuality" (779).

[6] Chinn and Dunn also discuss "Slemmons's inventive use of the word 'forte,'" calling it "pure big-city talk" and relating it to his having "sloughed off all that was Southern, rural, and black while he was in the North." His "alien language and habits fascinate *first* Joe and then Missie May," they note, anticipating their reading of the story's conflict emerging when the two main characters "allow corrupt desires to replace their innocent acceptance of their native cultural values" (780; emphasis added).

[7] I tell my students how my professor of Milton at the University of Southwestern Louisiana, Albert Fields, called prelapsarian human beings "divine pets"; to explain this appellation, I compare Adam and Eve before the fall to my own cats, sleeping the day away with no awareness that they only have a limited time on this earth and thus have no need to seize the day. We discuss how the older we get, the more aware we become of the brevity of life, and thus the more we are driven to make the best use of that time.

[8] In his examination of how comedy and tragedy are "intertwined" in this story (75), John Lowe points out Joe's role in Missie May's betrayal: "We readers know . . . (and surely Joe does too, eventually) that he had much to do with it in his oft-expressed yearning for money and power" (*Jump* 77).

[9] Howard reads the ending similarly: "The marriage has come full circle, but it will never be the same. The carefree innocence which characterized the early marriage has been replaced by painfully-gained maturity and knowledge. The lesson has been costly but because the foundation upon which the marriage was built has been strong, the marriage has survived" ("Marriage" 264). Rosalie Murphy Baum writes, "The birth of their son . . . and Joe's efforts to sort and control his overwhelming feelings create a new basis for a less innocent but perhaps deeper relationship" (98).

Africanisms in Hurston's *The First One*, *Color Struck*, and *Mule Bone*

Elizabeth Brown-Guillory

Zora Neale Hurston's novel *Their Eyes Were Watching God*, now an American classic, has overshadowed her plays. The writing of her plays, however, served as training ground for the fiction that would come later. Both her novel and the plays reflect Hurston's humor and spirit of independence. Characters and themes in her plays of the 1920s and 1930s reappear finely honed and multifaceted in *Their Eyes Were Watching God*. One example is Joe Clarke of her plays, who reappears as Joe, or Jody, Starks in the novel. To illustrate Hurston's humorous style, I often read aloud to my students a well-known excerpt from *Their Eyes Were Watching God*: "You big-bellies round here and put out a lot of brag, but 'tain't nothin' to it but yo' big voice. Humph! Talkin' 'bout *me* lookin' old! When you pull down yo' britches, you look lak de change uh life" (79). This slice of humor sets the tone for a discussion of Hurston's commitment to portraying characters whose lives were filled with as much comedy as pathos. Tiffany Ruby Patterson argues that Hurston characterized southern life as more "than unrelenting work, violence, and imprisonment. . . . [T]he South for her and her subjects was also a place of cultural creativity, family, and religion, where everyday life was lived with integrity in the midst of struggle against racial oppression" (*Zora* 9).

After a brief discussion of several main themes in *Their Eyes Were Watching God*—the journey, the image of women as mules of the world, intraracial biases—I introduce my literature students to techniques for studying Hurston's plays. My students generally are more apprehensive about analyzing plays than fiction or poetry, probably because the study of plays has been all but excised from English departments and left to theater departments, where primarily performance aspects are underscored. Sometimes my literature students complain that they are not sure how to critique a play and find themselves distracted while trying to absorb a dramatic text. My task then is to teach them the mechanics of reading a play, using as a starting point Aristotle's *Poetics* to introduce them to character, plot, theme, setting, and dialogue. I especially encourage my students to pay close attention to parenthetical stage directions, wherein stage actions are often as important as dialogue. I find it very helpful to engage students in reading or performing scenes from the plays in class. Following a discussion of Hurston's plays, students are required to write a critical essay, generally a thematic study or a feminist-womanist or postcolonial critique. My non–English majors—about half the class—tend to focus on thematic studies.

Themes in Hurston's plays often suggest that in her roles as anthropologist and literary artist Hurston observed closely the myriad ways of the folk. Her plays reflect "the folk drama tradition in which playwrights attempted artistically to represent the rhythms and patterns of speech common to a particular people, culture, or region" (Stephens 5). She identified strongly with the down-home folks and often felt compelled to dismantle notions of the tragic mulatto, a myth some would say looms large in the literature of the first half of the twentieth century. I find it useful to interweave discussions of Hurston's nonfiction with her dramatic work. Students begin to see connections between Hurston's life and the portrayals of characters in her plays when I read, for example, an excerpt from "How It Feels to Be Colored Me":

> But I am not tragically colored. There is no great sorrow dammed up in my soul, nor lurking behind my eyes. . . . I do not belong to the sobbing school of Negrohood who hold that nature somehow has given them a lowdown dirty deal and whose feelings are all hurt about it. (1009)

Later in the essay we see evidence of Hurston's self-confidence and energy: "Sometimes, I feel discriminated against, but it does not make me angry. It merely astonishes me. How *can* any deny themselves the pleasure of my company? It's beyond me" (1010). Hurston's literary biographer, Robert Hemenway, describes her best when he comments:

> Above all, she was a sophisticated writer who was never afraid to be herself. She was flamboyant and yet vulnerable, self-centered and yet kind, a Republican conservative and yet an early black nationalist. Her personality could seem a series of opposites, and her friends were often incapable of reconciling the polarities of her personal style. Aware of this, she came to delight in the chaos she sometimes left behind. (*Zora* 5–6)

Hurston's dramatic characters mirror her life and are humorous, self-confident, and independent. For a fuller exploration of Hurston's plays, I generally call students' attention to her finely crafted "Characteristics of Negro Expression," which serves as a useful essay to explore Africanisms in three of her published plays: *The First One*, *Color Struck*, and *Mule Bone*.

As an anthropologist, Hurston observed the manners of her people and attempted to draw connections between Negroes in America and their African ancestors. These Africanisms—aspects that make up the African cultural continuum—help us better understand Hurston's characters in all her works, especially her plays. Hurston outlines twelve characteristics that distinguish people of African descent: drama, will to adorn, angularity, asymmetry, dancing, Negro folklore, culture heroes, originality, imitation, absence of the concept of privacy, the jook, and dialect. Though Hurston published her observations of Negro expression in 1934, my black students tend to agree that Hurston's characteristics are accurate and relevant in contemporary society. There's usually an "amen" corner in various pockets of the classroom when we discuss the twelve characteristics. My nonblack students, however, are generally reluctant to offer a critique of the validity of Hurston's observations but do feel comfortable in identifying examples of Hurston's Negro expression in her plays.

Not surprisingly, a close reading of Hurston's plays reveals many Africanisms. Hurston's *The First One* (1927) explores the negative attitude toward blackness, a concept Hurston critiques in her comments about the jook. She describes the jook as a pleasure house associated with women, gambling, fighting, and drinking. She explains that songs in the jook often ridiculed dark-skinned women and labeled them evil. This fear of dark-skinned men and women fuels the plot of *The First One*. Hurston's short play is a retelling of the story of Noah's curse of his son Ham and his descendants as related in Genesis 9 of the Old Testament. Ham is portrayed as a carefree young man who enjoys singing and playing a harp. The wives of his two brothers, however, are jealous of the favors Noah lavishes on Ham and enlist help from their husbands in breaking the deep bond between father and favorite son. They seize an opportunity to discredit Ham during the annual return to the Valley of Ararat to give thanks to God for sparing Noah and his family from the flood. During the celebration, Noah shows his partiality to Ham and refuses to chastise his childish pranks. Mrs. Shem says, "Noah would make [Ham] lord of the earth because he sings and capers" (100). The real source of jealousy is the fear of Noah's daughters-in-law that the patriarch will appoint Ham heir to the vineyards, flocks, and fields and displace them. The plot unfolds as Noah imbibes too much at the celebration and falls asleep naked in his tent. More silly than sinful, Ham laughs at his father's shriveled body and shouts for all to hear, "Our Father has stripped himself, showing all his wrinkles. Ha! Ha! He's as no young goat in the spring. The old Ram, Ha! Ha! He has had no spring for years! Ha! Ha!" (101). Urged on by their wives, Ham's siblings awake Noah and tell him someone has laughed at his nakedness. They stand by horrified, as Noah in a drunken stupor issues a curse without realizing Ham is the culprit. Jennifer Burton suggests that in Hurston's version of the Noah story, the curse of servitude to his beloved Ham and his descendants is but a minor punishment and that it is the curse of blackness that Hurston foregrounds in *The First One*. Burton argues, "Hurston has Noah invoke the 'curse' of blackness, a fate so horrific to the other characters that they overcome their petty greed and jealousy and bond together in an attempt to 'uncurse the curse'" (xxxvi).

One approach to teaching *The First One* is to discuss the religious and historical dramas popularized by pre–Harlem Renaissance playwrights, most notably the works of May Miller. A comparison of Hurston's and Miller's plays underscores the significance of the theme of blackness and establishes Hurston as a major player in black women's theater tradition. Miller's *Graven Images* (1929) echoes Hurston's sentiments about negative attitudes toward blackness. In Miller's play the black son of Moses, Eliezer, suffers abuse because he is different. As the play concludes, he puts his best foot forward and persuades his young enemies he is very much like them, only tanned. Marion politely tells Eliezer, "Black one, you had best hide your shame from the followers of your father and not place your complexion where all may see" (127). Miller's critique of the negative attitude held against blackness resembles closely Hurston's stage directions in *The First One*: "All shrink away from him as if they feared his touch" (106). Noah speaks for his entire (white) family when he banishes his favorite son: "Arise, Ham. Thou art black. Arise and go out from among us that we may see thy face no more, lest by lingering the curse of thy blackness come upon all my seed forever" (106). By linking Hurston to Miller, I am able to establish for my students the importance of blackness in interracial and intraracial relationships in black literature. Hurston satirized this tendency to denigrate blackness in both her fiction and nonfiction.

At this point, I lead my undergraduate students into a discussion of reasons why Ham is ostracized and what it feels like in contemporary situations to be singled out as different. I find it useful to introduce students to two essays, Frantz Fanon's "The Fact of Blackness" and Homi Bhabha's "Cultural Diversity and Cultural Difference." My undergraduates tell me these essays are user-friendly and help them understand Hurston's disenfranchised and dislocated characters. They draw from Fanon and Bhabha a theory to discuss Ham's reaction to the curse and banishment. In the text, Ham is at first stunned and then becomes angry and confused. He is especially wounded when his mother averts her eyes so as not to see his blackness. As Ham is reeling from his mother's rejection, his wife, Eve, enters the stage with their son, also now black, running from other children who are pelting them with sharp objects and jeering at the black child. Only in the stage instructions do we get any indication of how Ham summons up the courage to accept his blackness and exit with dignity. We are told that Ham's eyes light up when he sees his harp and smilingly picks it up. As he exits he says to the family he must leave behind, "Oh, remain with your flocks and fields and vineyards, to covet, to sweat, to die and know no peace. I go to the sun" (106). My students readily accept the interpretation that Hurston's ending suggests that Ham and his descendants are truly the privileged and enlightened ones. This reversal of the myth of black as evil and damned is an example of Hurston's satire at its best. Hemenway notes, "Ham is presented as a lover of dancing and music, a man of joy contrasted with his materialistic brothers" (*Zora* 68).

A significant reversal in the play is the portrayal of Eve. In the biblical story, Eve is a temptress and leads Adam astray. In Hurston's retelling, Eve stands supportive of her now black husband and helps him withdraw from his family with dignity. As she and Ham and their son exit, we are forced to recognize a white Eve as the mother of the African race. This recognition serves as a springboard for a discussion of miscegenation, which is conjured up as students view Eve's whiteness against Ham's new blackness. I generally discuss negative attitudes toward miscegenation in American literature, particularly in other works of the period by both black and white writers. I point out that black and white authors of American literature before the 1950s often killed off characters guilty of miscegenation as a way of signaling disapproval of race mixing. Hurston, however, leads us to believe that Ham and Eve will live happily ever after in the sun, with Ham serenading her and his family and enjoying life while his white family members know no peace. I explain that Hurston downplays miscegenation and cite Hemenway's interpretation of *The First One* as a play that "pokes fun at all those who take seriously the biblical sanctions for racial separation" (*Zora* 68). I then return to Hurston's concept of the jook to point out that Ham's blackness is feared because it represents difference, which is often viewed as evil.

Hurston's play *Color Struck* (1926) also examines attitudes toward blackness and miscegenation. This taut drama centers on Emma, a dark-skinned black woman who has an inferiority complex and feels contempt for Effie, a near-white woman, and for light-skinned black women in general. Emma's distrust and hatred of near-white women grows and deepens, leaving her mentally unbalanced. The play opens with a group of blacks boarding a Jim Crow railway coach bound for a cakewalk contest in Saint Augustine, Florida. Aboard the train, Emma chastises her boyfriend, John, for being friendly with Effie. When he tells her he wasn't flirting with Effie, Emma screams, "Jes the same every time you sees a yaller face, you takes a chance" (81). Later in the dance hall where the contest is to take place, Effie offers a piece of pie to Emma and John. When John accepts the pie, Emma flies into a rage: "Naw, you done ruint mah appetite now, carrying on wid dat punkin-colored ole gal" (85). John tries to comfort her, but Emma becomes even more virulent: "Naw, youse jus' hog-wile ovah her cause she's half-white! No matter what Ah say, you keep carryin' on wid her" (85). Hurston provides no evidence that Emma's jealousy is warranted; instead, we are to read Emma as Hurston's indictment against such destructive jealously between men and women. Emma's paranoia paralyzes her when the time comes for her to join John on the dance floor. She fears that if she and John win the contest, all sorts of yellow girls will start chasing him. Emma's worst fears are confirmed, however, when John enters the contest and wins with Effie, who also has no dance partner. Emma seethes with anger as she shouts, "Oh, them half whites, they gets everything, they gets everything everybody else wants! The men, the jobs—everything! The whole world is got a sign on it. Wanted: Light Colored. Us blacks was made for cobble stones" (87). Hurston, who was very concerned about the negative treatment of dark-skinned people, refers to the creation of stereotypes of dark-skinned women as "disparaging fictitious drama" ("Characteristics" 1030).

Hurston conscientiously addresses the sensitive issue of skin color among African Americans in her portrayal of Emma. I find it helpful to retrace for students an intraracial conflict dating back to slavery. I explain that mulattoes, many of whom were sired by white slave owners and overseers, often worked as house servants, while their dark-skinned counterparts worked as field hands. The house servant–field hand syndrome continued after slavery when the children of former house servants went on to become influential members of the rising black middle class. Hurston uses Emma to express the resentment of standards of beauty based on Nordic features, standards that allowed near-white blacks privileges denied dark-skinned blacks. Hurston's text hints at the animosity felt when near-white blacks crossed the color line and passed for white up North or were favored blacks in the South. While Hurston takes Emma's jealousy to an extreme, she gives voice to intraracial resentment that continues in contemporary communities, as expressed in Spike Lee's movie *School Daze*, which examines conflict between the jigaboos (dark-skinned blacks) and the wannabees (light-skinned blacks). Hurston's *Color Struck* suggests she viewed this obsession with skin color as neurotic. She does, however, offer a sensitive treatment of the subject of passing or crossing the color line.

Hurston's character John links the theme of passing and race migration. John is described as "a light-brown-skinned man," but his complexion does not become an issue until midway through the play, when he disappears after the cakewalk and reappears twenty years later. Emma asks John on his return, "Where you been all these years, up North somewheres? Nobody round here could find out where you got to" (89). John's migration to Philadelphia and his disconnection with his community in the South suggest that, perhaps, he crossed the color line when he left Florida. It is helpful to point out to students that Hurston makes use of the South-to-North theme common in African American literature. She refers to the movement of blacks from South to North in search of a better life during the migration that commenced in the 1870s Reconstruction era and peaked in the 1920s. The ambiguity surrounding John's disappearance makes for a lively discussion about Hurston's commentary on the deplorable conditions and circumstances that forced blacks to uproot themselves from the security of their families in the South. That no one knew John's whereabouts in Philadelphia suggests that he may not have wanted to be found or found out by blacks, as is the case in a similar play about passing, Alice Dunbar-Nelson's *Gone White*. Another point worth mentioning is that when John returns to the South, he comes back well-to-do, which suggests that his passing enhanced his financial status and links him again to the near-white Allan Franklin Cordell in Dunbar-Nelson's *Gone White* as well as to the narrator in James Weldon Johnson's *The Autobiography of an Ex-Colored Man*. Here Hurston suggests that passing was a matter of financial expediency. Evidence that John may have crossed the color line comes when he ignores Emma's accusation that his wife must have been some "high-yaller dicty-doo" (89). Earlier in the play John whispers romantically to Emma, "Ah jus' wants you! You know what they say! De darker de berry, de sweeter de taste!" (84). Interestingly, Hurston makes reference to the berry in "Characteristics of Negro Expression" when she explains the duality that dark-skinned women experience. She argues that they are often simultaneously objects of scorn and desire and offers as evidence a familiar worksong:

> Dat ole black gal, she keep on grumblin'
> New pair shoes, new pair shoes,

> I'm goint to buy her shoes and stockings
> Slippers too, slippers too
> Blacker de berry, sweeter de juice. (1030)

Again, the near-white John mirrors Hurston's observations about the jook and life for dark-skinned women outside the jook in her portrayal of Emma as an object of desire.

Hurston's Emma is multidimensional and serves to illustrate various aspects of black life. Emma's life calls attention to miscegenation and the vulnerability of black women to white men in the rural South of the 1920s. Emma explains that life for her as a cook and washerwoman in white folks' homes was difficult. There is the subtlest of hints that the white doctor who comes to tend to Emma's dying daughter is the girl's father. My students often miss this faint suggestion because so much of the focus is on Emma's jealousy throughout the play. Even in the final scene, when John returns after twenty years to make Emma his wife, her neurotic behavior centers on her fear that John is eyeing her dying near-white daughter. Hurston layers the conflict with the suggestion that Emma succumbed to the advances of her white employer out of desperation. At this point in the play, I direct students to read the stage directions carefully, for much goes unsaid and is indicated by the actions of the characters. When Emma opens the door for the doctor, she blocks his path. When he asks if he may come in, the stage directions tell us Emma steps aside and laughs a little. When he asks her why didn't she come for him earlier—he had instructed her to notify him if there was the least change—she replies, "I did come—I went for the doctor" (94). There is enough innuendo, mystery, and silence between these two to suggest that Emma reacts curiously to the doctor because of the secrecy of their past relationship in a Jim Crow society. If we are misreading the issue of miscegenation, readers can only speculate who might be the father of the near-white child, who is described as having long, flowing hair. We might also speculate about why Emma dallies rather than rushes off for a doctor for her dying daughter. A perceptive student might ask if the play's ending suggests that Hurston was opposed to miscegenation and might recall an earlier discussion about signals of disapproval in texts by American authors, namely the killing off of characters involved in race mixing. After a full discussion of Emma and the question of miscegenation, I propose to my students that Hurston purposely doesn't prescribe how the audience is to react to the play's ending, which finds Emma alone and rocking. David Krasner says of the ending of the play:

> There is nothing verifiable with certainty and this is how it should be. Explanations reduce meaning to mere descriptions, and these descriptions often fail to delineate the unspeakable reality. Emma's story cannot be explained; it is essentially unfinished and without resolution.
> ("Migration" 549)

Color Struck usually elicits a lively discussion as the men and women in class take sides with either John or Emma. Some students insist that John is a lying sneak and Emma has every right to be jealous, an interpretation supported by Krasner, who argues, "John's behavior is hardly innocent: his words and the speed with which he embraces Effie at the dance indicate involvement and desire on a deeper level than surface observations imply" ("Migration" 541). Other students view Emma as someone who needs therapy to help her overcome her color complex. It is helpful to point out to students that Emma so despises her own dark skin that she cannot believe that anyone as handsome as John could love her. Still other students view both John and Emma as characters struggling to make the best of their lives in a Jim Crow society. One theme that permeates *Color Struck* is jealousy, and Hurston's treatment of the subject signals her abhorrence of the chaos this emotion heaps on human beings.

Jealousy is also a central theme in *Mule Bone* (1930), which Hurston wrote with Langston Hughes. The play centers on a song-and-dance team, Jim Weston and Dave Carter, both of whom are pursuing Daisy. During an argument to win Daisy's affection, Jim whacks Dave over the head with a mule bone. Chaos and hilarity follow as the community divides in its determination over how to handle this crime. The Baptists, led by the Reverend Childers, want to have Jim run out of town, and the Methodists, led by Elder Simms, advocate for the building of a jailhouse where Jim can be incarcerated. The Baptists ultimately win, and Jim is ordered to leave town. As fate would have it, Jim meets Daisy on the outskirts of town, where Dave coincidentally joins them. Daisy tries to convince one and then the other to marry her and work for the whites who employ her. Neither Jim nor Dave wants to do menial work for whites, and so neither chooses to marry Daisy; instead, they forgive each other and agree to be friends again and send Daisy on her way to find a gullible mate.

When students raise the issue of the frequency of the theme of jealousy in Hurston's work, I call their attention to the jealousy that colored Hurston's own life. Jealousy seems to be part of the reason Hurston and Hughes ended a deep friendship and fought bitterly over the authorship of *Mule Bone*. There is sufficient evidence that Hurston was jealous of the growing friendship between Hughes and the stenographer Louise Thompson and that Hughes angered Hurston when it was rumored that he had promised to give Thompson a share in the proceeds when the play was produced. Hemenway contends that Hurston broke off the partnership because "she felt, rightly or wrongly, that Hughes was trying to make Thompson a part of their collaborative effort" (*Zora* 138). It is important to review for students the conflict surrounding the play since invariably students have read several versions of the story and wish to understand the battle between Hughes and Hurston, a battle that spread to include other powerful authors, such as Richard Wright, who sided against Hurston. Henry Louis Gates, Jr., argues that "Hurston and Hughes sought to create a work that would undo a century of racist representations of black people" ("Why" 228). It is useful to point students in the direction of Hurston's *Dust Tracks on a Road* and Hughes's *The Big Sea* for these authors' personal accounts of the conflict over *Mule Bone*.

Mule Bone, like *The First One* and *Color Struck*, contains many of the Africanisms Hurston describes in "Characteristics of Negro Expression." Hurston writes in her essay, "The Negro's universal mimicry is not so much a thing in itself as an evidence of something that permeates his entire self. And that thing is drama" (1019). She notes that every phase of Negro life is highly dramatized and acted out, and she calls our attention to the drama that occurs when two opponents meet and threaten to do bodily harm to each other. In *Mule Bone*, there is much drama in the interactions between the two rivals, Jim and Dave, who divide the town with their antics. The Baptists and Methodists engage in verbal dueling as they try to determine whether the mule bone can be considered a weapon. And Lindsay and Mrs. Taylor, two characters in *Mule Bone* who play the dozens and threaten to destroy each other, have this exchange:

> LINDSAY. Go 'head on, Lucy Taylor. Go 'head on. You know a very little of yo' sugar sweetens my coffee. Go 'head on. Everytime you lift yo' arm you smell like a nest of yellow hammers.
>
> MRS. TAYLOR. Go 'head yo'self. Yo' head look like it done wore out three bodies. Talkin' 'bout me smellin'—you smell lak a nest of grand daddies yo'self.
>
> LINDSAY. Aw rock on down de road, 'oman. Ah don't wantuh change words wid yuh. Youse too ugly.
>
> MRS. TAYLOR. You ain't nobody's pretty baby, yo'self. You so ugly I betcha yo' wife have to spread uh sheet over yo' head tuh let sleep slip up on yuh. (105)

Lindsay retaliates with "You fool wid me now an' I'll knock you into doll rags." Not to be outdone, Mrs. Taylor quips, "Hit me! Hit me! I dare you tuh hit me. If you take dat dare, you'll steal uh hawg an' eat his hair" (105). This blowup takes place amid a group of people, not in some private place, and is in keeping with Hurston's observation in "Characteristics of Negro Expression" that there is an absence of the concept of privacy among Negroes. She argues, "Love-making and fighting in all their branches are high arts" and as such are prone to be displayed publicly (1027). Hurston explains that verbal dueling and showmanship on many levels characterize Negro expression. Perhaps it is Hurston's humor that makes her works palatable. In his description of the 1991 Broadway production of *Mule Bone*, John Lowe calls our attention to the ample use of "signifying gesture, tone, song, dance, verbal dueling, and many other conventions of African American humor" (*Jump* 80).

An important characteristic of Negro expression according to Hurston is dancing, which she describes as realistic suggestion. She highlights the importance of dancing in black community life in *Mule Bone*. In several instances Daisy dances suggestively with her two suitors, Jim and Dave. Hurston describes Daisy's movements as rhythmic and sensual. At another point in the play, she writes in the stage directions, "There is dancing, treating, and general jollification. Little children dance the parse-me-la" (84). Song is equally important in Negro life, as Hurston claims in her essay, and she sprinkles several songs throughout *Mule Bone*. The songs, of course, have double meanings. Dave and Jim perform for the community a song that speaks of freedom:

> Got on the train
> Didn't have no fare,
> But I rode some,
> I rode some. (89)

This song speaks to the freedom for which black people yearn in a Jim Crow society. It also has sexual overtones in its reference to riding a train. The music and dancing bring the community together. In Hurston's rural South, dancing and singing served as coping mechanisms, ways for the community members to endure the poverty of their lives.

Hurston as anthropologist understood that a poverty-stricken people necessarily must rely on folklore and culture heroes to sustain them and to offer hope for a better tomorrow. In "Characteristics" Hurston explains that "[t]he rabbit, the bear, the lion, the buzzard, the fox are culture heroes from the animal world" (1024). She might well have added the mule, particularly since the mule figures prominently in *Mule Bone* (Brazzle's mule) and *Their Eyes Were Watching God* (Matt Bonner's mule). In both these works, members of the community sit on or near the infamous store porch telling jokes about the stubborn ole yaller mule. Walter says of Brazzle's mule, "He was too mean to git fat. He was so skinny you could do a week's washing on his ribs for a washboard and hang 'em up on his hip-bones to dry" (53). Head capitalist and owner of the store in *Mule Bone*, Joe Clarke spouts, "I God, Brazzle. Didn't we all go to de draggin' out? More folks went to yo' mule's draggin' out than went to last school closing" (54). To stimulate discussion, I ask my students to suggest some important functions of storytellying in *Mule Bone*. Together we brainstorm, and the class focuses on storytelling as a way of building self-esteem. Someone generally points out that the men on Clarke's porch embellish their stories to make themselves feel powerful. The porch is also where the men denigrate women. Joe Clarke belittles his wife, Mattie, repeatedly and shamelessly. By the time we reach this point in the discussion of Hurston's plays, my students begin to recall an earlier connection I made between Joe Starks from *Their Eyes Were Watching God* and Joe Clarke from *Mule Bone* and sometimes ask me to reread the scene in which Janie verbally destroys Joe Starks's "big voice" by attacking his manhood and sexuality. Janie's mimicking of Joe's impotence devastates him, and he never recovers physically or emotionally.

Hurston explains in her essay that Negroes are famous for mimicry. She counters those who suggest that the Negro imitates from a feeling of inferiority and posits, "He does it as the mocking-bird does it, for the love of it, and not because he wishes to be like the one imitated" ("Characteristics" 1026). Hurston offers as an example her experience of watching "a group of small Negro boys imitating a cat defecating and the subsequent toilet of the cat" (1026). In *Mule Bone*, Small Boy and Small Girl imitate a hawk and a hen. Hurston writes in the stage instructions, "He rises and imitates a hawk flying and trying to catch a chicken" (64). Interestingly, however, the game suggests violence toward females since it is the hawk that manages to capture and subdue the hen and her chicks. The violence of the game of hawk and hen is mirrored in several verbally violent exchanges between men and women in the community. Susan Edwards Meisenhelder notes, "[W]hereas conflicts between males are often innocuous and playful, the ones between men and women are red hot, waged vigorously and heatedly" (25). One can only assume that Hurston seems to be suggesting that the rural South of the 1920s and 1930s was colored by a certain amount of violence that permeated the relationships of all in the community, adults and children alike, but that women also felt the brunt of sexism. To help students articulate a feminist reading of *Mule Bone* and other plays by Hurston, I find it useful to discuss Patricia Hill Collins's landmark books *Black Feminist Thought: Knowledge, Consciousness, and the Politics of Empowerment* and *Black Sexual Politics: African Americans, Gender, and the New Racism.*

The Africanisms Hurston identifies in her essay "Characteristics of Negro Expression" are readily identifiable in her plays. I encourage my students to continue this line of critical inquiry in their research papers, and many of them write lively essays pairing Hurston's essay with her plays to illuminate the conditions of Africans in America.

NOTES ON CONTRIBUTORS

Kimberly J. Banks is visiting professor of English at Fordham University. Her publications include articles on Langston Hughes, W. E. B. DuBois, Jean Toomer, and Jessie Fauset. Her research interests include African American literature, African diasporic literature and film, and American literature. She is working on a manuscript entitled "Diasporic Events: Performing Blackness in African Diasporic Literature between 1917 and 1968."

Margaret D. Bauer was named the first Rives Chair of Southern Literature in 2004 and one of the ten Women of Distinction in 2007 at East Carolina University. She has published *William Faulkner's Legacy: "What Shadow, What Stain, What Mark"*; *The Fiction of Ellen Gilchrist*; and *Understanding Tim Gautreaux*. She has served as editor of the *North Carolina Literary Review* since 1997 and has edited the book *Watering the Sahara: The Legacy of Paul Green from 1894 to 1937* for the deceased author, James R. Spence.

Kimberly D. Blockett is associate professor of English at Penn State University, Brandywine. She teaches courses on nineteenth- and twentieth-century black women writers, travel writing, and theory. Her essay "Writing Freedom: Race, Religion, and Revolution, 1820–40" is forthcoming in "The Cambridge History of African American Literature." She coauthored "Women in the Profession, 2000" for the Modern Language Association, and her articles and reviews have been published in the *Sonia Sanchez Literary Review*, *African American Review*, and *Modern Fiction Studies*. She is working on a manuscript entitled "Race, Religion, and Rebellion: The Life and Travels of Zilpha Elaw, Black Woman Evangelist, 1820–1850."

Elizabeth Brown-Guillory is professor of English, playwright, and performing artist at the University of Houston. Her books include *Their Place on the Stage: Black Women Playwrights in America*; *Wines in the Wilderness: Plays by African-American Women from the Harlem Renaissance to the Present*; *Women of Color: Mother-Daughter Relationships in Twentieth-Century Literature*; and *Middle Passages and the Healing Place of History: Migration and Identity in Black Women's Literature*. Twelve of her plays have been produced, and ten are included in *Black Drama: 1850 to the Present*. A Chautauqua scholar and artist, she regularly performs the life of Zora Neale Hurston.

Carla Cappetti is professor of English at City College, City University of New York. She is the author of *Writing Chicago: Modernism, Ethnography, and the Novel* and has written on Richard Wright, the Federal Writers' Project, and Natalia Ginzburg. Her articles have been published in *MELUS*; *Acoma. Rivista internazionale di studi nordamericani*; *Modern Fiction Studies*; *Against the Current*; the European Writers series; *Rivista di storia contemporanea*; and *Lavoro critico*. She is writing a book entitled "The Beast in the Garden of American Literature."

James C. Hall is director of New College at the University of Alabama, Tuscaloosa, where he specializes in American studies, African American cultural traditions, and religious studies. He has published *Mercy, Mercy Me: African American Culture and the American Sixties* and is writing about the jazz musician Mary Lou Williams, documentary photography in the 1950s, and early twentieth-century culture in Chicago.

Trudier Harris is J. Carlyle Sitterson Professor of English at the University of North Carolina, Chapel Hill. Her books include *Fiction and Folklore: The Novels of Toni Morrison*; *The Power of the Porch: The Storyteller's Craft in Zora Neale Hurston, Gloria Naylor, and Randall Kenan*; *Saints, Sinners, Saviors: Strong Black Women in African American Literature*; and *The Scary Mason-Dixon Line: African American Writers and the South*. She has published a memoir and many articles in journals and anthologies.

Carolyn M. Jones, associate professor of religion, teaches for the Institute for African American Studies at the University of Georgia, Athens. Her interests include religious theory, women's spirituality and literature, ancient and modern literature and ethics, and postmodern and postcolonial theory. She has published articles on Pinkie Gordon Lane, Albert Murray, and African American biblical hermeneutics.

John Lowe is professor of English and comparative literature at Louisiana State University, where he directs the Program in Louisiana and Caribbean Studies and teaches courses on African American, southern, and ethnic literature and theory. He has published *Jump at the Sun: Zora Neale Hurston's Cosmic Comedy* and edited *Bridging Southern Cultures: An Interdisciplinary Approach*; *The Future of Southern Letters*; *Conversations with Ernest Gaines*; and *Louisiana Culture from the Colonial Era to Katrina*. He is writing "Calypso Magnolia: The Carribean Side of the South."

Nellie Y. McKay taught at the University of Wisconsin, Madison. Her research included nineteenth- and twentieth-century African American literature, black women's fiction, and autobiography. She wrote *Jean Toomer, Artist: A Study of His Literary Life and Work* and coedited *The Norton Anthology of African American Literature*, Harriet Jacobs's *Incidents in the Life of a Slave Girl*, *Approaches to Teaching the Novels of Toni Morrison*, and *Toni Morrison's* Beloved*: A Casebook*. She published more than sixty articles on black women writers, black feminist scholars in the academy, the Harlem Renaissance, and black drama.

Deborah G. Plant is associate professor of Africana studies at the University of South Florida, Tampa. Her publications include *Every Tub Must Sit on Its Own Bottom: The Philosophy and Politics of Zora Neale Hurston*; *Zora Neale Hurston: A Biography of the Spirit*; and essays on Africana writers and Africana culture. She has taught courses on Africana literature, women writers, and Zora Neale Hurston. Her current projects are a philosophical biography of Alice Walker and an edition of critical essays on Hurston.

Annette Trefzer is associate professor of English at the University of Mississippi, where she teaches American literature and Native American literature, literary theory, and cultural studies. She is the author of *Disturbing Indians: The Archaeology of Southern Fiction* and coeditor with Kathryn McKee of a special issue of *American Literature*, *Global Contexts, Local Literature: The New Southern Studies*. She is editor with Ann Abadie of *Global Faulkner* and of the forthcoming "Faulkner's Sexualities." Her articles have appeared in *African-American Review*, *Southern Quarterly*, and *Journal of American Studies*.

Cheryl A. Wall is Board of Governors Zora Neale Hurston Professor of English at Rutgers University, New Brunswick, where she specializes in African American literature. She is the author of *Worrying the Line* and *Women of the Harlem Renaissance* and editor of *Changing Our Own Words: Criticism, Theory, and Writing by Black Women*;

Zora Neale Hurston: Novels and Short Stories, Folklore, Memoirs, and Other Writings; *"Sweat": Texts and Contexts*; and Their Eyes Were Watching God*: A Casebook*, as well as coeditor of *Savoring the Salt: The Legacy of Toni Cade Bambara*.

Genevieve West is professor of English and chair of the Department of English, Speech, and Foreign Languages at Texas Woman's University. She has written *Zora Neale Hurston and American Literary Culture*, and her articles have appeared in *Women's Studies* and *Analytical and Enumerative Bibliography*. She is working on a collection of reviews of Hurston's writings.

Gay Wilentz was professor of English and director of ethnic studies at East Carolina University. Her books included *Binding Cultures: Black Women Writers in Africa and the Diaspora* and *Healing Narratives: Women Writers Curing Cultural Dis-ease*. She coedited *Emerging Perspectives on Ama Ata Aidoo* and edited Anzia Yezierska's 1923 novel, *Salome of the Tenements*. Her articles appeared in *Literature and Medicine, College English, African American Review, Research in African Literatures*, and *MELUS*.

Dana A. Williams is associate professor of African American literature at Howard University. She has written *"In the Light of Likeness—Transformed": The Literary Art of Leon Forrest* and has edited *Conversations with Leon Forrest*; *African American Humor, Irony, and Satire: Ishmael Reed, Satirically Speaking*; *Contemporary African American Fiction: New Critical Essays* and coedited *August Wilson: Black Aesthetics*. She is completing a manuscript on Toni Morrison's Random House editorship entitled "The House that Toni Built at Random."

SURVEY PARTICIPANTS

The following scholars responded to the questionnaire on teaching works by Zora Neale Hurston. These responses were very helpful for the "Materials" section of this volume. Except when new information has been offered, the list indicates colleges where the scholars taught when they sent in their responses to the survey.

Vicky Adama, *University of Alabama*
Barbara Baker, *Auburn University*
Kimberly J. Banks, *University of Missouri, Kansas City*
Margaret D. Bauer, *East Carolina University*
Herman Beavers, *University of Pennsylvania*
Kimberly D. Blockett, *Penn State University, Brandywine*
James F. Brown, *Wayne State University*
Elizabeth Brown-Guillory, *University of Houston*
William Cain, *Wellesley College*
Carla Cappetti, *City College, City University of New York*
Frank Louis Cioffi, *Central Washington University*
Elsie Colon, *Touro College*
Bryce Conrad, *Texas Tech University*
Elizabeth DeLoughrey, *University of Maryland, College Park*
Maggie Dunn, *Rollins College*
James C. Hall, *University of Alabama, Tuscaloosa*
David Herman, *North Carolina State University*
Lynda Marion Hill, *Temple University*
Madelyn Jablon, *Philadelphia*
Carolyn M. Jones, *University of Georgia*
Joyce A. Joyce, *Temple University*
Carla Kaplan, *University of Southern California*
Amy Lerman, *University of Kansas*
Lucinda MacKethan, *North Carolina State University*
Norma H. Mandel, *New York*
Nellie Y. McKay, *University of Wisconsin, Madison*
Imafedia Okhamafe, *University of Nebraska, Omaha*
Deborah G. Plant, *University of South Florida, Tampa*
Annye L. Refoe, *Seminole Community College, FL*
Ruthe T. Sheffey, *Morgan State University*
Sarah E. Turner, *Case Western Reserve*
Genevieve West, *Florida State University*
Gay Wilentz, *East Carolina University*
Dana A. Williams, *Howard University*
Jon Woodson, *Howard University*

WORKS CITED

Abrahams, Roger. *The Man-of-Words in the West Indies: Performance and the Emergence of Creole Culture*. Baltimore: Johns Hopkins UP, 1983. Print.

Adams, Edward C. L. *Tales of the Congaree*. 1928. Ed. Robert G. O'Meally. Chapel Hill: U of North Carolina P, 1987. Print.

African American Odyssey: A Quest for Full Citizenship. Exhibit. Lib. of Congress, 2 Sept. 1998. Web. 23 June 2008.

Aidoo, Ama Ata. "Literature, Feminism, and the African Woman Today." Podis and Saaka 15–35.

———. *Our Sister Killjoy; or, Reflections from a Black-Eyed Squint*. New York: NOK, 1979. Print.

Albright, Angela. "Zora Neale Hurston's *Their Eyes Were Watching God* as a Blueprint for Negro Writing." *PAPA* 23.1 (1997): 1–11. Print.

Anderson, Jervis. *This Was Harlem*. New York: Farrar, 1981. Print.

Anderson, Michelle. "Authentic Voodoo Is Syncretic." *Drama Review* 26.2 (1982): 89–110. Print.

Andrews, William, ed. *African American Autobiography: A Collection of Critical Essays*. Englewood Cliffs: Prentice, 1993. Print.

Andrews, William, Frances Smith Foster, and Trudier Harris, eds. *The Oxford Companion to African American Literature*. New York: Oxford, 1997. Print.

Anokye, Akua Duku. "Private Thoughts, Public Voices: Letters from Zora Neale Hurston." *Women: A Cultural Review* 7.2 (1996): 150–59. Print.

Ariel, David S. *The Mystic Quest: An Introduction to Jewish Mysticism*. New York: Schocken, 1988. Print.

Ashcroft, Bill, Gareth Griffiths, and Helen Tiffin, eds. *The Post-colonial Studies Reader*. New York: Routledge, 1995. Print.

Awkward, Michael, ed. *New Essays on* Their Eyes Were Watching God. New York: Cambridge UP, 1990. Print.

Bakhtin, Mikhail. *Rabelais and His World*. Trans. Helene Iwolsky. Bloomington: Indiana UP, 1984. Print.

Baraka, Amiri. "Black Art." L. Jones 116–17.

Barthes, Roland. "From Work to Text." Richter 900–05.

Baum, Rosalie Murphy. "The Shape of Hurston's Fiction." Glassman and Seidel 94–109.

Bell, Bernard. *The African American Novel and Its Tradition: Its Folk Roots and Modern Literary Branches*. Amherst: U of Massachusetts P, 2005. Print.

Benedict, Ruth. *Patterns of Culture*. Boston: Houghton, 1959. Print.

Bethel, Lorraine. "'This Infinity of Conscious Pain': Zora Neale Hurston and the Black Female Literary Tradition." Hull, Scott, and Smith 176–88.

Bhabha, Homi. "Cultural Diversity and Cultural Difference." Ashcroft, Griffiths, and Tiffin 206–09.

Bloom, Harold, ed. *Modern Critical Views: Zora Neale Hurston*. New York: Chelsea, 1986. Print.

———. *Zora Neale Hurston's* Their Eyes Were Watching God. New York: Chelsea, 1999. Print.

Boas, Franz. *Anthropology and Modern Life*. New York: Norton, 1932. Print.

Bone, Robert. *Down Home: A History of Afro-American Short Fiction from Its Beginnings to the End of the Harlem Renaissance*. New York: Putnam, 1975. Print. New Perspectives on Black America Ser.

Bongie, Chris. *Exotic Memories: Literature, Colonialism, and the Fin de Siècle*. Stanford: Stanford UP, 1991. Print.

Bordelon, Pamela, ed. *Go Gator and Muddy the Water: Writings by Zora Neale Hurston from the Federal Writers Project*. New York: Norton, 1999. Print.

———. Introduction. Bordelon, *Go Gator* 3–49.

———. "New Tracks on *Dust Tracks*: Toward a Reassessment of the Life of Zora Neale Hurston." *African American Review* 31.1 (1997): 5–21. Print.

Boyd, Valerie. *Wrapped in Rainbows: The Life of Zora Neale Hurston*. New York: Scribner, 2003. Print.

Brearly, H. C. "Ba-ad Nigger." Dundes 578–85.

Bressler, Charles E. *Literary Criticism: An Introduction to Theory and Practice*. 2nd ed. Upper Saddle River: Prentice, 1999. Print.

Brock, H. I. "The Full True Flavor of Life in a Negro Community: Review of *Mules and Men*." *New York Times Book Review* 10 Nov. 1935: 4. Rpt. in Gates and Appiah 13–15.

Brontë, Emily. *Wuthering Heights*. 1847. New York: NAL, 1959. Print.

Brown, Robert McAfee. *Religion and Violence*. Philadelphia: Westminster John Knox, 1987. Print.

Brown, Sterling A. "Luck Is a Fortune." *Nation* 16 Oct. 1937: 409–10. Print.

———. *The Negro in American Fiction*. Washington: Associates in Negro Folk Educ., 1937. Print.

Brown, William Wells. *Clotel; or, The President's Daughter: A Narrative of Slave Life in the United States*. 1969. Ed. Robert S. Levine. Boston: Bedford, 2000. Print.

Bunson, Margaret. *Dictionary of Ancient Egypt*. New York: Oxford UP, 1995. Print.

Burris, Andrew. "The Browsing Reader: Review of *Jonah's Gourd Vine*." *Crisis* 41.6 (1934): 166–67. Rpt. in Gates and Appiah 6–7.

Burton, Jennifer. Introduction. Gates and Burton xix–lx.

Butler-Evans, Elliot. *Race, Gender, and Desire*. Philadelphia: Temple UP, 1989. Print.

Callahan, John F. *In the African-American Grain: The Pursuit of Voice in Twentieth-Century Black Fiction*. Urbana: U of Illinois P, 1988. Print.

Campbell, Josie P. *Student Companion to Zora Neale Hurston*. Westport: Greenwood, 2001. Print.

Cappetti, Carla. *Writing Chicago: Modernism, Ethnography, and the Novel*. New York: Columbia UP, 1993. Print.

Carby, Hazel. Foreword. Hurston, *Seraph* vii–xviii.

———. "Ideologies of Black Folk: The Historical Novel of Slavery." *Slavery and the Literary Imagination*. Ed. Deborah McDowell and Arnold Rampersad. Baltimore: Johns Hopkins UP, 1989. 125–43. Print.

———. "The Politics of Fiction, Anthropology, and the Folk: Zora Neale Hurston." Awkward 71–93.

———. "The Quicksands of Representation: Rethinking Black Cultural Politics." Carby, *Reconstructing* 163–75.

———. *Reconstructing Womanhood: The Emergence of the Afro-American Woman Novelist*. New York: Oxford UP, 1987. Print.

Card, Caroline, John Hasse, Roberta L. Singer, and Ruth M. Stone, eds. *Discourse in Ethnomusicology II: A Tribute to Alan P. Merriam*. Bloomington: Indiana UP, 1998. Print.

Carr, Brian, and Tova Cooper. "Zora Neale Hurston and Modernism at the Critical Limit." *MFS: Modern Fiction Studies* 48.2 (2002): 285–313. Print.

Cartwright, Keith. "'To Walk with the Storm': Oya as the Transformative 'I' of Zora Neale Hurston's Afro-Atlantic Callings." *American Literature* 78.4 (2006): 742–67. Print.

Chamberlin, John. "Books of the Times: Review of *Jonah's Gourd Vine*." *New York Times* 3 May 1934: 17. Print.

Chesnutt, Charles. *Conjure Tales and Stories of the Color Line*. Ed. William Andrews. 1899. New York: Penguin, 2000. Print.

Chinn, Nancy, and Elizabeth E. Dunn. "'The Ring of Singing Metal on Wood': Zora Neale Hurston's Artistry in 'The Gilded Six-Bits.'" *Mississippi Quarterly* 49.3 (1996): 775–90. Print.

Clark, Winifred Hurston. Annual Zora Neale Hurston Festival. Eatonville, Florida. 24 Jan. 1991. Presentation.

Clarke, John Henrik. Annual Zora Neale Hurston Festival. Eatonville, Florida. 24 Jan. 1991. Presentation.

Clifford, James. "Introduction: Partial Truths." *Writing Culture: The Poetics and Politics of Ethnography*. Ed. Clifford and George E. Marcus. Berkeley: U of California P, 1986. 1–26. Print.

Cole, Jean Lee, and Charles Mitchell. *Zora Neale Hurston: Collected Plays*. New Brunswick: Rutgers UP, 2008. Print.

Collins, Patricia Hill. *Black Feminist Thought: Knowledge, Consciousness, and the Politics of Empowerment*. 2nd ed. New York: Routledge, 2000. Print.

———. *Black Sexual Politics: African Americans, Gender, and the New Racism*. New York: Routledge, 2005. Print.

Connelly, Marc. *The Green Pastures*. 1930. *The Green Pastures*. Ed. Thomas Cripps. Madison: U of Wisconsin P, 1979. 55–190. Print.

Courlander, Harold. *A Treasury of African Folklore*. 3rd ed. New York: Marlowe, 2002. Print.

———. *A Treasury of Afro-American Folklore*. New York: Da Capo, 2002. Print.

Croft, Robert W. *A Zora Neale Hurston Companion*. Westport: Greenwood, 2002. Print.

Cronin, Gloria L., ed. *Critical Essays on Zora Neale Hurston*. New York: Hall, 1998. Print.

Cullen, Countee. "Heritage." Locke, *New Negro* 250–53.

Dance, Daryl. *Shuckin' and Jivin': Folklore from Contemporary Black Americans*. Bloomington: Indiana UP, 1978. Print.

Davis, Gerald L. *I Got the Word in Me and I Can Sing It, You Know: A Study of the Performed African-American Sermon*. Philadelphia: U of Pennsylvania P, 1989. Print.

Davis, Rose Parkman. *Zora Neale Hurston: An Annotated Bibliography and Reference Guide*. Westport: Greenwood, 1997. Print.

Davis, Wade. *The Serpent and the Rainbow*. New York: Simon, 1985. Print.

Dayan, Joan. "Vodoun, or the Voice of the Gods." *Raritan* 10.3 (1991): 32–57. Print.

Delgarno, Emily. "Words without Masters: Ethnography and the Creative Process in *Their Eyes Were Watching God*." *American Literature* 64.3 (1992): 519–41. Print.

Denning, Michael. *The Cultural Front: The Laboring of American Culture*. New York: Verso, 1996. Print.

Docherty, Thomas, ed. *Postmodernism: A Reader*. New York: Columbia UP, 1993. Print.

Dubey, Madhu. *Black Women Novelists and the Nationalist Aesthetic*. Bloomington: Indiana UP, 1994. Print.

DuBois, W. E. B. *The Souls of Black Folk*. 1903. New York: NAL, 1969. Print.

———. "The Talented Tenth." *The Negro Problem*. Ed. Booker T. Washington. N.p.: Wilder, 2008. 11–25. Print.

———. "Two Novels." *Crisis* 25.6 (1928): 202. Print.

duCille, Ann. *The Coupling Convention: Sex, Text, and Tradition in Black Women's Fiction*. New York: Oxford UP, 1993. Print.

———. "The Occult of True Black Womanhood: Critical Demeanor and Black Feminist Studies." *Signs* 19.3 (1994): 591–629. Print.

Duck, Leigh Anne. "'*Go* There tuh *Know* There': Zora Neale Hurston and the Chronotype of the Folk." *American Literary History* 13.2 (2001): 265–94. Print.

———. "'Rebirth of a Nation': Hurston in Haiti." *Journal of American Folklore* 117.464 (2004): 127–46. Print.

Dunbar-Nelson, Alice. *Gone White. The Works of Alice Dunbar-Nelson*. Ed. Gloria T. Hull. 3rd ed. New York: Oxford UP, 1988. 250–80. Print.

Dundes, Alan, ed. *Mother Wit from the Laughing Barrel: Readings in the Interpretation of Afro-American Folklore*. Englewood Cliffs: Prentice, 1973. Print.

DuPlessis, Rachel Blau. *Writing beyond the Ending: Narrative Strategies of Twentieth-Century Women Writers*. Bloomington: Indiana UP, 1985. Print.

Eco, Umberto. *Il superuomo di massa*. Milano: Cooperativa Scrittori, 1976. Print.

Edwards, Thomas, and Elizabeth De Wolfe, eds. *Such News of the Land: U.S. Women Nature Writers*. Hanover: UP of New England, 2001. Print.

Eliade, Mircea. *The Sacred and the Profane: The Nature of Religion*. Trans. Willard R. Trask. New York: Harcourt, 1959. Print.

Ellison, Ralph. *Invisible Man*. New York: Random, 1952. Print.

Emery, Amy Fass. "The Zombie in/as the Text: Zora Neale Hurston's *Tell My Horse*." *African American Review* 39.3 (2005): 327–36. Print.

Empson, William. *Some Versions of Pastoral*. 1935. London: Hogarth, 1986. Print.

Fabian, Johannes. *Time and the Other: How Anthropology Makes Its Object*. New York: Columbia UP, 1983. Print.

Fanon, Frantz. *Black Skin, White Masks*. New York: Grove, 1967. Print.

———. "The Fact of Blackness." Ashcroft, Griffiths, and Tiffin 323–26.

Fauset, Arthur Huff. "American Negro Folk Literature." Locke, *New Negro* 238–44.

Fauset, Jessie Redman. *Plum Bun*. New York: Stokes, 1929. Print.

———. *There Is Confusion*. New York: Boni, 1924. Print.

Felton, Estelle. Rev. of *Jonah's Gourd Vine*, by Zora Neale Hurston. *Opportunity* Aug. 1934: 252–53. Rpt. in Gates and Appiah 4–5.

Feracho, Lesley. "Wandering through the Dust: Textual Statues in *Dust Tracks on a Road*." *Linking the Americas: Race, Hybrid Discourses, and the Reformulation of Feminine Identity*. Albany: State U of New York P, 2005. 183–202. Print.

Ferguson, Sally Ann. "Folkloric Men and Female Growth in *Their Eyes Were Watching God*." *Black American Literature Forum* 21.1-2 (1987): 185–97. Print.

Ferraro, Thomas. *Ethnic Passages: Literary Immigrants in Twentieth-Century America*. Chicago: U of Chicago P, 1993. Print.

Fetterley, Judith. *The Resisting Reader: A Feminist Approach to American Fiction*. Bloomington: Indiana UP, 1978. Print.

Fischer-Hornung, Dorothea. "An Island Occupied: The U.S. Marine Occupation of Haiti in Zora Neale Hurston's *Tell My Horse* and Katherine Dunham's *Island Possessed*." *Holding Their Own: Perspectives on the Multi-ethnic Literatures of the United States*. Ed. Fischer-Hornung and Heike Raphael-Hernandez. Tübingen: Stauffenburg, 2000. 153–68. Print.

Foley, Barbara. *Radical Representations*. Durham: Duke UP, 1993. Print.

Foreman, Gabrielle. "Looking Back from Zora, or Talking Out Both Sides My Mouth for Those Who Have Two Ears." *Black American Literature Forum* 24.4 (1990): 649–66. Print.

Franklin, John Hope. *From Slavery to Freedom*. New York: Knopf, 2000. Print.

Frazier, E. Franklin. *Black Bourgeoisie*. Glencoe: Free, 1957. Print.

Fuller, Hoyt W. "Towards a Black Aesthetic." *Critic* 26.5 (1968). Rpt. in Mitchell 199–206.

Gannett, Lewis. Rev. of *Mules and Men*, by Zora Neale Hurston. *New York Herald Tribune Weekly* 11 Oct. 1935. Rpt. in Gates and Appiah 11–13.

Gates, Henry Louis, Jr. Annual Zora Neale Hurston Festival. Eatonville, Florida. 25 Jan. 1991. Presentation.

———, ed. *Black Literature and Literary Theory*. New York: Methuen, 1984. Print.

———. *The Signifying Monkey: A Theory of Afro-American Literary Criticism*. New York: Oxford UP, 1988. Print.

———. "Why the 'Mule Bone' Debate Goes On." Cronin 225–28.

———. "Zora Neale Hurston and the Speakerly Text." Gates, *Signifying Monkey* 170–216.

Gates, Henry Louis, Jr., and K. A. Appiah. *Zora Neale Hurston: Critical Perspectives Past and Present*. New York: Amistad, 1993. Print.

Gates, Henry Louis, Jr., and Jennifer Burton, eds. *The Prize Plays and Other One-Acts*. New York: Hall, 1996. Print.

Gates, Henry Louis, Jr., and Nellie Y. McKay, eds. *The Norton Anthology of African American Literature*. 2nd ed. New York: Norton, 2004. Print.

Gayle, Addison, Jr., ed. *The Black Aesthetic*. New York: Doubleday, 1971. Print.

———. "Cultural Strangulation: Black Literature and the White Aesthetic." Mitchell 207–12.

———. Introduction. Gayle, *Black Aesthetic* xiii–xxiv.

Ginzberg, Louis. *The Legends of the Jews*. Trans. Henrietta Szold. 7 vols. Philadelphia: Jewish Pub. Soc. of Amer., 1909–38. Print.

Glassman, Steve, and Kathryn Lee Seidel, eds. *Zora in Florida*. Orlando: U of Central Florida P, 1991. Print.

Grant, Nathan. *Masculinist Impulses: Toomer, Hurston, Black Writing, and Modernity*. Columbia: U of Missouri P, 2004. Print.

Gray, Richard. *Southern Aberrations: Writers of the American South and the Problems of Regionalism*. Baton Rouge: Louisiana State UP, 2000. Print.

Gruening, Martha. Rev. of *Jonah's Gourd Vine*, by Zora Neale Hurston. *New Republic* 11 July 1934: 244–45. Rpt. in Gates and Appiah 3–4.

Hapke, Laura. *Labor's Text: The Worker in American Fiction*. New Brunswick: Rutgers UP, 2001. Print.

Harding, Vincent. *There Is a River: The Black Struggle for Freedom in America*. New York: Harcourt, 1981. Print.

Harlem, 1900–1940. Exhibit. Schomburg Center for Research in Black Culture. New York Public Lib., n.d. Web. 23 June 2008.

Harper, Frances Ellen Watkins. *Iola Leroy; or, Shadows Uplifted*. New York: Oxford UP, 1988. Print.

Harris, Joel Chandler. *Uncle Remus: His Songs and Sayings*. 1880. Ed. Robert Hemenway. New York: Penguin, 1982. Print.

Harris, Trudier. *The Power of the Porch: The Storyteller's Craft in Zora Neale Hurston, Gloria Naylor, and Randall Kenan*. Athens: U of Georgia P, 1996. Print.

Harrison, Paul Carter, ed. *Kuntu Drama: Plays of the African Continuum*. New York: Grove, 1974. Print.

Hassall, Kathleen. "Text and Personality in Disguise and in the Open: Zora Neale Hurston's *Dust Tracks on a Road*." Glassman and Seidel 159–73.

Hassan, Ihab. "Toward a Concept of Postmodernism." Docherty 146–56.

Hawthorne, Nathaniel. "The Maypole of Merry Mount." *Twice-Told Tales*. London: Standard, 1931. 41–52. Print.

———. "Young Goodman Brown." *Mosses from an Old Manse*. London: Standard, 1931. 59–72. Print.

Hemenway, Robert E. Introduction. Hurston, *Dust Tracks* ix–xxxix.

———. *Zora Neale Hurston: A Literary Biography*. Urbana: U of Illinois P, 1977. Print.

Henninger, Katherine. "Zora Neale Hurston, Richard Wright, and the Postcolonial Gaze." *Mississippi Quarterly* 56.4 (2003): 579–93. Print.

Herodotus. *The Histories*. Trans. Aubrey De Selincourt. New York: Penguin, 2003. Print.

Herskovits, Melville. *The Myth of the Negro Past*. 1941. Boston: Beacon, 1990. Print.

Hibben, Sheila. "Vibrant Book Full of Nature and Salt: Review of *Their Eyes Were Watching God*." *New York Herald Tribune* 26 Sept. 1937: 2. Rpt. in Gates and Appiah 21–22.

Hill, Lynda Marion. *Social Rituals and the Verbal Art of Zora Neale Hurston*. Washington: Howard UP, 1996. Print.

Hoeller, Hildegard. "Racial Currency: Zora Neale Hurston's 'The Gilded Six-Bits' and the Gold-Standard Debate." *American Literature* 77.4 (2005): 761–85. Print.

Holloway, Joseph E. *Africanisms in American Culture*. Bloomington: Indiana UP, 1990. Print.

Holloway, Karla F. C. *The Character of the Word: The Texts of Zora Neale Hurston*. Westport: Greenwood, 1987. Print.

Holt, Grace Sims. "Stylin' Outta the Black Pulpit." Spradley and Rynkiewich 323–35.

hooks, bell. *Teaching to Transgress: Education as the Practice of Freedom*. New York: Routledge, 1994. Print.

Hopkins, Pauline E. *Contending Forces: A Romance Illustrative of Negro Life North and South*. New York: Oxford UP, 1988. Print.

Howard, Lillie P. *Alice Walker and Zora Neale Hurston: The Common Bond*. Westport: Greenwood, 1993. Print.

———. "Marriage: Zora Neale Hurston's System of Values." *College Language Association Journal* 21 (1977): 256–68. Print.

———. *Zora Neale Hurston*. Boston: Twayne, 1980. Print.

Hughes, Langston. *The Big Sea: An Autobiography*. 1940. New York: Hill, 1963. Print.

Huizinga, Johan. *Homo Ludens: A Study of the Play-Element in Culture*. Boston: Beacon, 1970. Print.

Hull, Gloria T., Patricia Bell Scott, and Barbara Smith, eds. *But Some of Us Are Brave: Black Women's Studies*. Old Westbury: Feminist, 1982. Print.

Hurston, Zora Neale. "Art and Such." Wall, *Zora Neale Hurston: Folklore* 905–11.

———. "Characteristics of Negro Expression." Gates and McKay, *Norton* 1019–32.

———. *Color Struck*. Gates and Burton 79–95.

———. *The Complete Stories*. Ed. Henry Louis Gates, Jr. New York: Harper, 1996. Print.

———. "Crazy for This Democracy." 1945. A. Walker, *I Love* 165–68.

———. *Dust Tracks on a Road: An Autobiography*. 1942. New York: Harper, 1991. Print.

———. *Every Tongue Got to Confess: Negro Folk-Tales from the Gulf States*. Ed. Carla Kaplan. New York: HarperCollins, 2001. Print.

———. *The First One*. Gates and Burton 96–106.

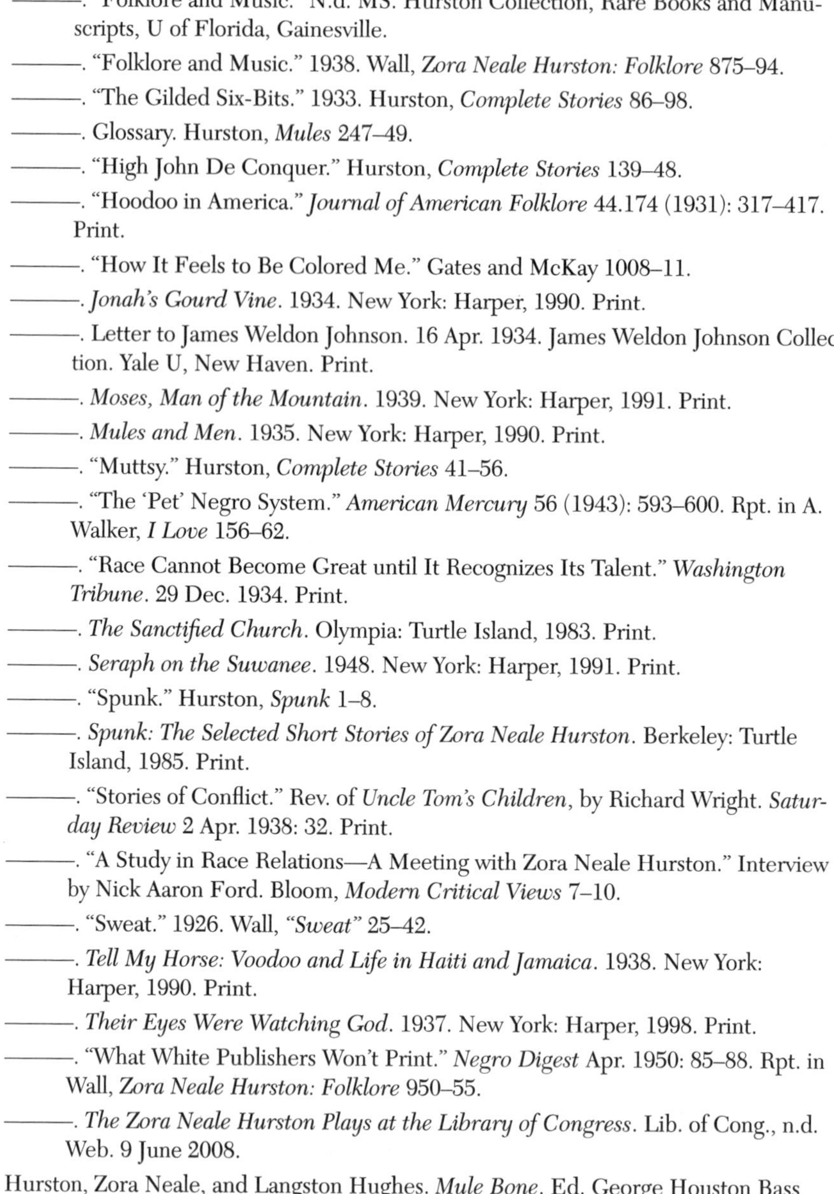

———. "Folklore and Music." N.d. MS. Hurston Collection, Rare Books and Manuscripts, U of Florida, Gainesville.

———. "Folklore and Music." 1938. Wall, *Zora Neale Hurston: Folklore* 875–94.

———. "The Gilded Six-Bits." 1933. Hurston, *Complete Stories* 86–98.

———. Glossary. Hurston, *Mules* 247–49.

———. "High John De Conquer." Hurston, *Complete Stories* 139–48.

———. "Hoodoo in America." *Journal of American Folklore* 44.174 (1931): 317–417. Print.

———. "How It Feels to Be Colored Me." Gates and McKay 1008–11.

———. *Jonah's Gourd Vine*. 1934. New York: Harper, 1990. Print.

———. Letter to James Weldon Johnson. 16 Apr. 1934. James Weldon Johnson Collection. Yale U, New Haven. Print.

———. *Moses, Man of the Mountain*. 1939. New York: Harper, 1991. Print.

———. *Mules and Men*. 1935. New York: Harper, 1990. Print.

———. "Muttsy." Hurston, *Complete Stories* 41–56.

———. "The 'Pet' Negro System." *American Mercury* 56 (1943): 593–600. Rpt. in A. Walker, *I Love* 156–62.

———. "Race Cannot Become Great until It Recognizes Its Talent." *Washington Tribune*. 29 Dec. 1934. Print.

———. *The Sanctified Church*. Olympia: Turtle Island, 1983. Print.

———. *Seraph on the Suwanee*. 1948. New York: Harper, 1991. Print.

———. "Spunk." Hurston, *Spunk* 1–8.

———. *Spunk: The Selected Short Stories of Zora Neale Hurston*. Berkeley: Turtle Island, 1985. Print.

———. "Stories of Conflict." Rev. of *Uncle Tom's Children*, by Richard Wright. *Saturday Review* 2 Apr. 1938: 32. Print.

———. "A Study in Race Relations—A Meeting with Zora Neale Hurston." Interview by Nick Aaron Ford. Bloom, *Modern Critical Views* 7–10.

———. "Sweat." 1926. Wall, *"Sweat"* 25–42.

———. *Tell My Horse: Voodoo and Life in Haiti and Jamaica*. 1938. New York: Harper, 1990. Print.

———. *Their Eyes Were Watching God*. 1937. New York: Harper, 1998. Print.

———. "What White Publishers Won't Print." *Negro Digest* Apr. 1950: 85–88. Rpt. in Wall, *Zora Neale Hurston: Folklore* 950–55.

———. *The Zora Neale Hurston Plays at the Library of Congress*. Lib. of Cong., n.d. Web. 9 June 2008.

Hurston, Zora Neale, and Langston Hughes. *Mule Bone*. Ed. George Houston Bass and Henry Louis Gates, Jr. New York: Harper, 1991. 45–153. Print.

Hurston, Zora Neale, and Dorothy Waring. *Polk County: A Comedy of Negro Life on a Sawmill Camp, with Authentic Negro Music*. New York, 1944. Print.

The Hurston/Wright Foundation. Zora Neale Hurston / Richard Wright Foundation, n.d. Web. 23 June 2008.

Icknigwill, Steve, ed. *Looking Inward / Looking Outward.* Amsterdam: European Contributions to Amer. Studies, 1990. Print.

Jackson, Blyden. "*Moses, Man of the Mountain*: A Study of Power." Bloom, *Modern Critical Views* 151–55.

Jackson, Chuck. "Waste and Whiteness: Zora Neale Hurston and the Politics of Eugenics." *African American Review* 34.4 (2000): 639–60. Print.

Jackson, Joyce Marie. "The Black American Folk Preacher and the Chanted Sermon: Parallels with a West African Tradition." Card, Hasse, Singer, and Stone 205–22.

Jacobs, Harriet. *Incidents in the Life of a Slave Girl.* New York: Penguin, 2000. Print.

Johnson, Barbara. "Metaphor, Metonymy, and Voice in *Their Eyes Were Watching God.*" Gates, *Black Literature* 204–19.

Johnson, Guy. *John Henry: Tracking Down a Negro Legend.* Chapel Hill: U of North Carolina P, 1929. Print.

Johnson, James Weldon. *The Autobiography of an Ex-Colored Man.* 1912. New York: Knopf, 1927. Print.

Jones, Carolyn M. "Moses: Community and Identity in Exodus." *In Good Company: Essays in Honor of Robert Detweiler.* Ed. David Jasper and Mark Ledbetter. Atlanta: Scholar's, 1994. 367–84. Print.

Jones, Gayl. "Breaking Out of the Conventions of Dialect." Wall, *"Sweat"* 153–68.

Jones, Leroi. *Black Magic Poetry, 1961–1967.* New York: Bobbs-Merrill, 1969. Print.

Jones, Sharon Lynette. *Rereading the Harlem Renaissance: Race, Class, and Gender in the Fiction of Jessie Fauset, Zora Neale Hurston, and Dorothy West.* Westport: Greenwood, 2002. Print.

Jordan, Jennifer. "Feminist Fantasies: Zora Neale Hurston's *Their Eyes Were Watching God.*" *Tulsa Studies in Women's Literature* 7.1 (1988): 105–17. Print.

Jordan, June. "Notes toward a Black Balancing of Love and Hatred." 1974. *Civil Wars.* Boston: Beacon, 1981. 84–89. Print.

Josephus, Flavius. *Jewish Antiquities: Books I–IV.* Trans. H. St. J. Thackeray. Cambridge: Harvard UP, 1956. Print. Vol. 4 of *Josephus.* 9 vols. 1926–81.

Kadlec, David. "Zora Neale Hurston and the Federal Folk." *Modernism/Modernity* 7.3 (2000): 471–85. Print.

Kaplan, Carla, ed. *The Erotics of Talk: Women's Writing and Feminist Paradigms.* New York: Oxford UP, 1996. Print.

———, ed. *Zora Neale Hurston: A Life in Letters.* New York: Doubleday, 2002. Print.

Kessler-Harris, Alice, and William McBrien, eds. *Faith of a (Woman) Writer.* New York: Greenwood, 1985. Print.

Kirsch, Jonathan. *Moses: A Life.* New York: Random, 1999. Print.

Klein, Marcus. *Foreigners: The Making of American Literature, 1900–1940.* Chicago: U of Chicago P, 1981. Print.

Konzett, Delia Caparoso. "'Getting in Touch with the True South': Pet Negroes, White Crackers, and Racial Staging in *Seraph on the Suwanee.*" *Ethnic Modernisms: Anzia Yezierska, Zora Neale Hurston, Jean Rhys, and the Aesthetics of Dislocation.* New York: Palgrave, 2002. 69–126. Print.

Krasner, David. *A Beautiful Pageant: African American Theater, Drama, and Performance in the Harlem Renaissance, 1910–1927*. New York: Palgrave, 2002. Print.

———. "Migration, Fragmentation, and Identity: Zora Neale Hurston's *Color Struck* and the Geography of the Harlem Renaissance." *Theatre Journal* 53.4 (2001): 533–50. Print.

Kubitschek, Missy Dehn. "'Tuh de Horizon and Back': The Female Quest in *Their Eyes Were Watching God*." *Black American Literature Forum* 17.3 (1983): 109–14. Print.

Kunitz, Stanley J., and Howard Haycraft. "Zora Neale Hurston." *Twentieth-Century Authors: A Biographical Dictionary of Modern Literature*. Ed. Kunitz and Haycraft. New York: Wilson, 1942. 695. Print.

Ladd, Barbara. *Resisting History: Gender, Modernity, and Authorship in William Faulkner, Zora Neale Hurston, and Eudora Welty*. Baton Rouge: Louisiana State UP, 2007. Print.

Larsen, Nella. *Passing*. New York: Knopf, 1929. Print.

———. *Quicksand*. 1928. New Brunswick: Rutgers UP, 1986. Print.

Lee, Spike, dir. *School Daze*. Forty Acres and a Mule Filmworks, 1988. Film.

Levine, Lawrence. *Black Culture and Consciousness: Afro-American Folk Thought from Slavery to Freedom*. New York: Oxford UP, 1977. Print.

Levy, Valerie. "'That Florida Flavor': Nature and Culture in Zora Neale Hurston's Work for the Federal Writers' Project." Edwards and De Wolfe 85–94.

Lewis, David Levering. *When Harlem Was in Vogue*. New York: Penguin, 1997. Print.

Lieberman, Marcia R. "'Some Day My Prince Will Come': Female Acculturation through the Fairy Tale." *College English* 34.3 (1972): 383–95. Print.

Lillios, Anna. "'The Monstropolous Beast': The Hurricane in Zora Neale Hurston's *Their Eyes Were Watching God*." *Southern Quarterly* 36.3 (1998): 89–93. Print.

Lincoln, C. Eric, and Lawrence H. Mamiya. *The Black Church in the African American Experience*. Durham: Duke UP, 1990. Print.

Lionnet, Françoise. "Autoethnography: The An-Archic Style of *Dust Tracks on a Road*." Andrews 113–37.

Locke, Alain. "Deep River, Deeper Sea: Review of *Mules and Men*." *Opportunity* Jan. 1936: 6–10. Print.

———. "Jingo, Counter-Jingo and Us: Review of *Their Eyes Were Watching God*." *Opportunity* Jan. 1938: 7–11. Rpt. in Gates and Appiah 18.

———, ed. *The New Negro: Voices of the Harlem Renaissance*. 1925. New York: Touchstone, 1997. Print.

Lowe, John. *Jump at the Sun: Zora Neale Hurston's Cosmic Comedy*. Urbana: U of Illinois P, 1994. Print.

———. "Zora Neale Hurston." *The History of Southern Women's Literature*. Ed. Carolyn Perry and Mary Louise Weakes. Baton Rouge: Louisiana State UP, 2002. 379–85. Print.

Lukács, Georg. *The Theory of the Novel*. 1920. Cambridge: MIT P, 1982. Print.

Lyons, Mary E. *Sorrow's Kitchen: The Life and Folklore of Zora Neale Hurston*. New York: Scribner's, 1990. Print.

Marks, Donald R. "Sex, Violence, and Organic Consciousness in Zora Neale Hurston's *Their Eyes Were Watching God.*" *Black American Literature Forum* 19.4 (1985): 152–57. Print.

Marsh-Lockett, Carol P. "Womanism." Andrews, Foster, and Harris 784–85.

Martin, George-McKinley. *The Black Renaissance in Washington, D.C., 1920s–1930s*. D.C. Public Lib., 20 June 2003. Web. 23 June 2008.

Maxwell, William J. "Black Belt / Black Folk: The End(s) of the Richard Wright–Zora Neale Hurston Debate." *New Negro, Old Left: African-American Writing and Communism between the Wars*. Ed. Maxwell. New York: Columbia UP, 1999. 153–78. Print.

McGlamery, Tom. *Protest and the Body in Melville, Dos Passos, and Hurston*. New York: Routledge, 2004. Print.

McGowan, Todd. "Liberation and Domination: *Their Eyes Were Watching God* and the Evolution of Capitalism." *MELUS* 24.1 (1999): 109–29. Print.

McKay, Claude. *Home to Harlem*. New York: Harper, 1928. Print.

McKay, Nellie Y. "The Narrative Self: Race, Politics, and Culture in Black American Women's Autobiography." Stanton and Stewart 74–100.

Meehan, Kevin. "Decolonizing Ethnography: Zora Neale Hurston in the Caribbean." Paravisini-Gebert and Romero-Cesareo 245–79.

Meisenhelder, Susan Edwards. *Hitting a Straight Lick with a Crooked Stick: Race and Gender in the Work of Zora Neale Hurston*. Tuscaloosa: U of Alabama P, 1999. Print.

Miguez-Bonino, Jose. *The Development Apocalypse: Risk*. Geneva: World Council of Churches, 1967. Print.

Miller, May. *Graven Images. Plays and Pageants from the Life of the Negro*. Ed. Willis Richardson. Washington: Associated, 1930. 109–37. Print.

Miller, Monica L., ed. *Jumpin' at the Sun: Reassessing the Life and Work of Zora Neale Hurston*. Spec. issue of *Scholar and Feminist Online* 3.2 (2005): n. pag. Web. 23 June 2008.

Milton, John. *Paradise Lost. Complete Poems and Major Prose*. Ed. Merritt Y. Hughes. New York: Macmillan, 1985. 173–454. Print.

Minh-ha, Trinh T. *Woman, Native, Other: Writing, Postcoloniality, and Feminism*. Bloomington: Indiana UP, 1989. Print.

Mitchell, Angelyn, ed. *Within the Circle*. Durham: Duke UP, 1994. Print.

Moon, Henry Lee. Rev. of *Mules and Men*, by Zora Neale Hurston. *New Republic* 11 Dec. 1935. Rpt. in Gates and Appiah 10.

Morrison, Toni. *Song of Solomon*. New York: Knopf, 1977. Print.

Mules and Men: An E-Text Edition. U of Virginia, n.d. Web. 23 June 2008.

Mullen, Bill, and Sherry L. Linkon. *Radical Revisions: Rereading 1930s Culture*. Urbana: U of Illinois P, 1996. Print.

Nathiri, N. Y., ed. *Zora! Zora Neale Hurston: A Woman and Her Community*. New York: Tribune, 1991. Print.

Neal, Larry. "The Black Arts Movement." *Drama Review* 12.4 (1968). Rpt. in Mitchell 184–98.

Nelson, Cary. *Repression and Recovery*. Madison: U of Wisconsin P, 1989. Print.

The New American Bible. New York: Oxford UP, 1991. Print.

The New Oxford Annotated Bible. Ed. Herbert G. May and Bruce M. Metzger. New York: Oxford UP, 1973. Print.

Newson, Adele S. *Zora Neale Hurston: A Reference Guide*. Boston: Hall, 1987. Print.

Nicholls, David G. *Conjuring the Folk: Forms of Modernity in African America*. Ann Arbor: U of Michigan P, 2000. Print.

———. "Migrant Labor, Folklore, and Resistance in Hurston's Polk County: Reframing *Mules and Men*." *African American Review* 33.3 (1999): 467–79. Print.

Nwankwo, Ifeoma C. K. "Insider and Outsider, Black and American: Rethinking Zora Neale Hurston's Caribbean Ethnography." *Radical History Review* 87 (2003): 49–77. Print.

Odum, Howard W. *Cold Blue Moon: Black Ulysses Afar Off*. Indianapolis: Bobbs-Merrill, 1931. Print.

———. *Rainbow Round My Shoulder: The Blue Trail of Black Ulysses*. 1928. Indianapolis: Indiana UP, 2006. Print.

———. *Wings on My Feet: Black Ulysses at the Wars*. 1929. Indianapolis: Indiana UP, 2007. Print.

Odum, Howard W., and Guy B. Johnson, eds. *The Negro and His Songs: A Study of Typical Negro Songs in the South*. Chapel Hill: U of North Carolina P, 1925. Print.

———, eds. *Negro Workaday Songs*. New York: Negro UP, 1969. Print.

Paravisini-Gebert, Lizabeth, and Ivette Romero-Cesareo, eds. *Women at Sea: Travel Writing and the Margins of Caribbean Discourse*. New York: Palgrave, 2001. Print.

Paris, Renzo. *Il mito del proletario nel romanzo italiano*. Milano: Garzanti, 1973. Print.

Patterson, Orlando. *Freedom in the Making of Western Culture*. San Francisco: Harper, 1991. Print. Vol. 1 of *Freedom*.

Patterson, Tiffany Ruby. *Zora Neale Hurston and a History of Southern Life*. Philadelphia: Temple UP, 2005. Print.

Peters, Pearlie Mae Fisher. *The Assertive Woman in Zora Neale Hurston's Fiction, Folklore, and Drama*. New York: Garland, 1998. Print.

Philo. *De Vita Moses*. Trans. F. H. Colson. Cambridge: Harvard UP, 1929. Print. Vol. 6 of *Philo, an English Translation by F. H. Colson and G. H. Whitaker*. 10 vols. 1929–62.

Pinckney, Josephine. "A Pungent Poetic Novel about Negroes: Rev. of *Jonah's Gourd Vine*." *New York Herald Tribune* 6 May 1934: 6. Print.

Plant, Deborah G. *Every Tub Must Sit on Its Own Bottom: The Philosophy and Politics of Zora Neale Hurston*. Chicago: U of Illinois P, 1995. Print.

———. *Zora Neale Hurston: A Biography of the Spirit*. Westport: Praeger, 2007. Print.

Podis, Leonard, and Yakubu Saaka, eds. *Challenging Hierarchies: Issues and Themes in Colonial and Postcolonial African Literature*. New York: Lang, 1998. Print. Society and Politics in Africa 5.

Poggioli, Renato. *The Theory of the Avant-Garde*. Cambridge: Harvard UP, 1968. Print.

Pondrom, Cyrena. "The Role of Myth in Hurston's *Their Eyes Were Watching God.*" *American Literature* 58.2 (1986): 181–202. Print.

Portelli, Alessandro. *The Text and the Voice: Writing, Speaking, and Democracy in American Literature*. New York: Columbia UP, 1994. Print.

Porter, A. P. *Jump at de Sun: The Life Story of Zora Neale Hurston*. Minneapolis: Carolrhoda, 1992. Print.

Preece, Harold. "The Negro Folk Cult." *Crisis* 43.12 (1936): 364+. Print.

Pryse, Marjorie, and Hortense Spillers, eds. *Conjuring: Black Women, Fiction, and Literary Tradition*. Bloomington: Indiana UP, 1985. Print.

Puckett, Newbell Niles. *Folk Beliefs of the Southern Negro*. 1969. Whitefish: Kessinger, 2003. Print.

Rabinowitz, Paula. *Labor and Desire*. Chapel Hill: U of North Carolina P, 1991. Print.

Reed, Ishmael. Foreword. Hurston, *Tell My Horse* xi–xv.

Rhapsodies in Black: Art of the Harlem Renaissance. Inst. of Intl. Visual Arts, 1997. Web. 23 June 2008.

Richter, David, ed. *The Critical Tradition*. Boston: Bedford, 1998. Print.

Robinson, Beverly. "Africanisms and the Study of Folklore." J. Holloway 211–24.

Rosenblatt, Roger. "Eccentricities." *Black Fiction*. Cambridge: Harvard UP, 1974. 65–97. Print.

Rowe, John Carlos. "Opening the Gate to the Other America: The Afro-Caribbean Politics of Hurston's *Mules and Men* and *Tell My Horse*." *Literary Culture and U.S. Imperialism: From the Revolution to World War II*. New York: Oxford UP, 2000: 253–91. Print.

Sailer, Steve. "The Secret Zora Neale Hurston." *National Review* 47.6 (1995): 58–60. Print.

Schoener, Allon. *Harlem on My Mind: Cultural Capital of Black America, 1900–1968*. New York: New, 1995. Print.

Shange, Ntozake. *For Colored Girls Who Have Considered Suicide When the Rainbow Is Enuf*. New York: Bantam, 1977. Print.

Shulman, Robert. *The Power of Political Art: The 1930s Literary Left*. Chapel Hill: U of North Carolina P, 2000. Print.

Smith, Sidonie. "Self, Subject, and Resistance: Marginalities and Twentieth-Century Autobiographical Practice." *Tulsa Studies in Women's Literature* 9.1 (1990): 11–24. Print.

Sollors, Werner. *Beyond Ethnicity: Consent and Descent in American Culture*. New York: Oxford UP, 1986. Print.

———. "Modernization as Adultery: Richard Wright, Zora Neale Hurston, and American Culture of the 1930s and 1940s." Icknigwill 22–75.

———. "Of Mules and Mares in a Land of Difference; or, Quadrupeds All?" *American Quarterly* 42.2 (1990): 167–90. Print.

Sorensen, Leif. "Modernity on a Global Stage: Hurston's Alternative Modernism." *MELUS* 30.4 (2005): 3–24. Print.

Spradley, James, and Michael Rynkiewich, eds. *The Nacirema: Readings on American Culture*. Boston: Little, 1975. Print.

Stanton, Domna C., and Abigail J. Stewart, eds. *Feminisms in the Academy*. Ann Arbor: U of Michigan P, 1995. Print.

St. Clair, Janet. "The Courageous Undertow of Zora Neale Hurston's *Seraph on the Suwanee*." Cronin 187–212.

Stephens, Judith L. "Lynching Dramas and Women: History and Critical Context." *Strange Fruit: Plays on Lynching by American Women*. Ed. Kathy A. Perkins and Stephens. Bloomington: Indiana UP, 1998. 3–14. Print.

Stepto, Robert. *From Behind the Veil: A Study of Afro-American Narrative*. Urbana: U of Illinois P, 1979. Print.

Sundquist, Eric. *The Hammers of Creation: Folk Culture in Modern African-American Fiction*. Athens: U of Georgia P, 1993. Print.

Thompson, Mark Christian. "National Socialism and Blood-Sacrifice in Zora Neale Hurston's *Moses, Man of the Mountain*." *African American Review* 38.3 (2004): 109–28. Print.

Thornton, Jerome E. "'Goin' on de Muck': The Paradoxical Journey of the Black American Hero." *CLA Journal* 31.3 (1988): 261–80. Print.

Tompkins, Lucy. "In the Florida Glades: Review of *Their Eyes Were Watching God*." *New York Times Book Review* 26 Sept. 1937: 29. Print.

Toynbee, Arnold. *Surviving the Future*. New York: Oxford UP, 1971. Print.

Turner, Darwin T. *In a Minor Chord: Three Afro-American Writers and Their Search for Identity*. Carbondale: Southern Illinois UP, 1971. Print.

Twain, Mark. "The Man That Corrupted Hadleyburg." *The Heath Anthology of American Literature*. 4th ed. Vol. 2. New York: Houghton, 2002. 77–107. Print.

Van Vechten, Carl. *Nigger Heaven*. 1926. Urbana: U of Illinois P, 2000. Print.

Wald, Alan. *Writing from the Left*. New York: Verso, 1994. Print.

Walker, Alice. *The Color Purple*. New York: Harcourt, 1982. Print.

———. Foreword. Hemenway, *Zora* xi–xviii.

———, ed. *I Love Myself When I'm Laughing and Then Again When I'm Looking Mean and Impressive: A Zora Neale Hurston Reader*. Old Westbury: Feminist, 1979. Print.

———. *In Search of Our Mothers' Gardens: Womanist Prose*. New York: Harcourt, 1983. Print.

———. "Looking for Zora." A. Walker, *In Search* 93–116.

———. "Saving the Life That Is Your Own: The Importance of Models in the Artist's Life." A. Walker, *In Search* 3–14.

———. "Zora Neale Hurston: A Cautionary Tale and Partisan View." A. Walker, *In Search* 83–92.

Walker, Pierre. "Zora Neale Hurston and the Post-modern Self in *Dust Tracks on a Road*." *African American Review* 32.3 (1998): 387–99. Print.

Wall, Cheryl A. Introduction. Wall, *"Sweat"* 3–19.

———, ed. *"Sweat": Zora Neale Hurston*. New Brunswick: Rutgers UP, 1997. Print.

———. *Women of the Harlem Renaissance*. Bloomington: Indiana UP, 1995. Print.

———. *Zora Neale Hurston: Folklore, Memoirs, and Other Writings*. New York: Lib. of Amer., 1995. Print.

———. *Zora Neale Hurston: Novels and Stories*. New York: Lib. of Amer., 1995. Print.

———. "Zora Neale Hurston's Essays: On 'Art and Such.'" Monica L. Miller n. pag.

———. *Zora Neale Hurston's* Their Eyes Were Watching God*: A Casebook*. Oxford: Oxford UP, 2000. Print.

Wallace, Margaret. "Real Negro People: Review of *Jonah's Gourd Vine*." *New York Times Book Review* 6 May 1934: 6–7. Rpt. in Gates and Appiah 8–9.

Wallace, Michele. *Invisibility Blues: From Pop to Theory*. New York: Verso, 1990. Print.

Washington, Booker T. *Up from Slavery*. Ed. William L. Andrews. New York: Norton, 1996. Print.

Washington, Mary Helen. Foreword. Hurston, *Their Eyes* ix–xvii.

———. "'I Love the Way Janie Crawford Left Her Husbands': Emergent Female Hero." Gates and Appiah 98–109.

———. Introduction. *Black-Eyed Susans: Classic Stories by and about Black Women*. By Washington. New York: Anchor, 1975. ix–xxxii. Print.

———. *Invented Lives: Narratives of Black Women, 1860–1960*. Garden City: Doubleday, 1987. Print.

———. "A Woman Half in Shadow." A. Walker, *I Love* 7–25.

———. "Zora Neale Hurston: The Black Woman's Search for Identity." *Black World* Aug. 1974: 68–75. Print.

Weber, Max. *Max Weber on Charisma and Institution Building*. Ed. S. N. Eisenstadt. Chicago: U of Chicago P, 1968. Print.

Werner, Craig. "Zora Neale Hurston." *Modern American Women Writers*. Ed. Lea Baechler. New York: Touchstone, 1993. 138–47. Print.

West, Cornel. "Minority Discourse and the Pitfalls of Canonization." *Yale Journal of Criticism* 1.1 (1987): 193–201. Print.

West, Genevieve. *Zora Neale Hurston and American Literary Culture*. Gainesville: UP of Florida, 2005.

Wideman, John Edgar. Foreword. Hurston, *Every Tongue* xi–xx.

Wilentz, Gay. *Binding Cultures: Black Women Writers in Africa and the Diaspora*. Bloomington: Indiana UP, 1992. Print.

———. "Defeating the False God: Janie's Self-Determination in Zora Neale Hurston's *Their Eyes Were Watching God*." Kessler-Harris and McBrien 285–91.

———. "Reading the Critical Writer." *Emerging Perspectives on Ama Ata Aidoo*. Ed. Ada Uzoamaka Azodo and Wilentz. Trenton: Africa World, 1999. 3–10. Print.

———. "Toward a Diaspora Literature: Black Women Writers from Africa, the Caribbean, and the United States." *College English* 54.4 (1992): 385–405. Print.

Williams, Demetrius K. "The Bible and Models of Liberation in the African American Experience." *Yet With a Steady Beat: Contemporary U. S. Afrocentric Biblical Interpretation*. Ed. Randall C. Bailey. Leiden: Soc. of Biblical Lit., 2003. 33–60. Print.

Williams, Raymond. "Base and Superstructure in Marxist Cultural Theory." *Problems in Materialism and Culture: Selected Essays*. London: Verso, 1980. 31–49. Print.

Wilson, Anthony. "The Music of God, Man, and Beast: Spirituality and Modernity in *Jonah's Gourd Vine*." *Southern Literary Journal* 35.2 (2003): 64–78. Print.

Wixson, Douglas. *The Worker-Writer in America*. Urbana: U of Illinois P, 1994. Print.

Wright, Melanie J. *Moses in America: Cultural Uses of Biblical Narrative*. New York: Oxford UP, 2003. Print.

Wright, Richard. "Between Laughter and Tears." Rev. of *Their Eyes Were Watching God*, by Zora Neale Hurston. *New Masses* 5 Oct. 1937: 22+. Rpt. in Cronin 75–76. Rpt. in Gates and Appiah 16–17.

———. *Black Boy*. New York: Harper, 1945. Print.

———. *The Long Dream*. New York: Harper, 1958. Print.

———. "The Man Who Lived Underground." *Eight Men*. New York: Thunder's Mouth, 1987. 27–92. Print.

———. *Native Son*. 1940. New York: Perennial, 1998. Print.

———. *Savage Holiday*. New York: Avon, 1954. Print.

———. *Twelve Million Black Voices*. New York: Viking, 1941. Print.

———. *Uncle Tom's Children*. New York: Harper, 1993. Print.

Zagato, Lauso. *Du Bois e la Black Reconstruction*. Roma: Bibliotheca Biographica, 1975. Print.

Zora! Festival. Association to Preserve the Eatonville Community, n.d. Web. 23 June 2008.

Zuckert, Catherine. *Natural Right and the American Imagination: Political Imagination in Novel Form*. Savage: Rowan, 1990. Print.

INDEX

Modern Language Association of America

Approaches to Teaching World Literature

Achebe's Things Fall Apart. Ed. Bernth Lindfors. 1991.
Arthurian Tradition. Ed. Maureen Fries and Jeanie Watson. 1992.
Atwood's The Handmaid's Tale *and Other Works*. Ed. Sharon R. Wilson, Thomas B. Friedman, and Shannon Hengen. 1996.
Austen's Emma. Ed. Marcia McClintock Folsom. 2004.
Austen's Pride and Prejudice. Ed. Marcia McClintock Folsom. 1993.
Balzac's Old Goriot. Ed. Michal Peled Ginsburg. 2000.
Baudelaire's Flowers of Evil. Ed. Laurence M. Porter. 2000.
Beckett's Waiting for Godot. Ed. June Schlueter and Enoch Brater. 1991.
Beowulf. Ed. Jess B. Bessinger, Jr., and Robert F. Yeager. 1984.
Blake's Songs of Innocence and of Experience. Ed. Robert F. Gleckner and Mark L. Greenberg. 1989.
Boccaccio's Decameron. Ed. James H. McGregor. 2000.
British Women Poets of the Romantic Period. Ed. Stephen C. Behrendt and Harriet Kramer Linkin. 1997.
Charlotte Brontë's Jane Eyre. Ed. Diane Long Hoeveler and Beth Lau. 1993.
Emily Brontë's Wuthering Heights. Ed. Sue Lonoff and Terri A. Hasseler. 2006.
Byron's Poetry. Ed. Frederick W. Shilstone. 1991.
Camus's The Plague. Ed. Steven G. Kellman. 1985.
Writings of Bartolomé de Las Casas. Ed. Santa Arias and Eyda M. Merediz. 2008.
Cather's My Ántonia. Ed. Susan J. Rosowski. 1989.
Cervantes' Don Quixote. Ed. Richard Bjornson. 1984.
Chaucer's Canterbury Tales. Ed. Joseph Gibaldi. 1980.
Chaucer's Troilus and Criseyde *and the Shorter Poems*. Ed. Tison Pugh and Angela Jane Weisl. 2006.
Chopin's The Awakening. Ed. Bernard Koloski. 1988.
Coleridge's Poetry and Prose. Ed. Richard E. Matlak. 1991.
Collodi's Pinocchio *and Its Adaptations.* Ed. Michael Sherberg. 2006.
Conrad's "Heart of Darkness" and "The Secret Sharer." Ed. Hunt Hawkins and Brian W. Shaffer. 2002.
Dante's Divine Comedy. Ed. Carole Slade. 1982.
Defoe's Robinson Crusoe. Ed. Maximillian E. Novak and Carl Fisher. 2005.
DeLillo's White Noise. Ed. Tim Engles and John N. Duvall. 2006.
Dickens's Bleak House. Ed. John O. Jordan and Gordon Bigelow. 2009.
Dickens's David Copperfield. Ed. Richard J. Dunn. 1984.
Dickinson's Poetry. Ed. Robin Riley Fast and Christine Mack Gordon. 1989.
Narrative of the Life of Frederick Douglass. Ed. James C. Hall. 1999.
Duras's Ourika. Ed. Mary Ellen Birkett and Christopher Rivers. 2009.
Early Modern Spanish Drama. Ed. Laura R. Bass and Margaret R. Greer. 2006.

Eliot's Middlemarch. Ed. Kathleen Blake. 1990.
Eliot's Poetry and Plays. Ed. Jewel Spears Brooker. 1988.
Shorter Elizabethan Poetry. Ed. Patrick Cheney and Anne Lake Prescott. 2000.
Ellison's Invisible Man. Ed. Susan Resneck Parr and Pancho Savery. 1989.
English Renaissance Drama. Ed. Karen Bamford and Alexander Leggatt. 2002.
Works of Louise Erdrich. Ed. Gregg Sarris, Connie A. Jacobs, and James R. Giles. 2004.
Dramas of Euripides. Ed. Robin Mitchell-Boyask. 2002.
Faulkner's The Sound and the Fury. Ed. Stephen Hahn and Arthur F. Kinney. 1996.
Fitzgerald's The Great Gatsby. Ed. Jackson R. Bryer and Nancy P. VanArsdale. 2009.
Flaubert's Madame Bovary. Ed. Laurence M. Porter and Eugene F. Gray. 1995.
García Márquez's One Hundred Years of Solitude. Ed. María Elena de Valdés and Mario J. Valdés. 1990.
Gilman's "The Yellow Wall-Paper" and Herland. Ed. Denise D. Knight and Cynthia J. Davis. 2003.
Goethe's Faust. Ed. Douglas J. McMillan. 1987.
Gothic Fiction: The British and American Traditions. Ed. Diane Long Hoeveler and Tamar Heller. 2003.
Grass's The Tin Drum. Ed. Monika Shafi. 2008.
Hebrew Bible as Literature in Translation. Ed. Barry N. Olshen and Yael S. Feldman. 1989.
Homer's Iliad *and* Odyssey. Ed. Kostas Myrsiades. 1987.
Hurston's Their Eyes Were Watching God *and Other Works*. Ed. John Lowe. 2009.
Ibsen's A Doll House. Ed. Yvonne Shafer. 1985.
Henry James's Daisy Miller *and* The Turn of the Screw. Ed. Kimberly C. Reed and Peter G. Beidler. 2005.
Works of Samuel Johnson. Ed. David R. Anderson and Gwin J. Kolb. 1993.
Joyce's Ulysses. Ed. Kathleen McCormick and Erwin R. Steinberg. 1993.
Works of Sor Juana Inés de la Cruz. Ed. Emilie L. Bergmann and Stacey Schlau. 2007.
Kafka's Short Fiction. Ed. Richard T. Gray. 1995.
Keats's Poetry. Ed. Walter H. Evert and Jack W. Rhodes. 1991.
Kingston's The Woman Warrior. Ed. Shirley Geok-lin Lim. 1991.
Lafayette's The Princess of Clèves. Ed. Faith E. Beasley and Katharine Ann Jensen. 1998.
Works of D. H. Lawrence. Ed. M. Elizabeth Sargent and Garry Watson. 2001.
Lazarillo de Tormes *and the Picaresque Tradition*. Ed. Anne J. Cruz. 2009.
Lessing's The Golden Notebook. Ed. Carey Kaplan and Ellen Cronan Rose. 1989.
Mann's Death in Venice *and Other Short Fiction*. Ed. Jeffrey B. Berlin. 1992.
Marguerite de Navarre's Heptameron. Ed. Colette H. Winn. 2007.
Medieval English Drama. Ed. Richard K. Emmerson. 1990.
Melville's Moby-Dick. Ed. Martin Bickman. 1985.
Metaphysical Poets. Ed. Sidney Gottlieb. 1990.
Miller's Death of a Salesman. Ed. Matthew C. Roudané. 1995.
Milton's Paradise Lost. Ed. Galbraith M. Crump. 1986.

Milton's Shorter Poetry and Prose. Ed. Peter C. Herman. 2007.
Molière's Tartuffe *and Other Plays*. Ed. James F. Gaines and Michael S. Koppisch. 1995.
Momaday's The Way to Rainy Mountain. Ed. Kenneth M. Roemer. 1988.
Montaigne's Essays. Ed. Patrick Henry. 1994.
Novels of Toni Morrison. Ed. Nellie Y. McKay and Kathryn Earle. 1997.
Murasaki Shikibu's The Tale of Genji. Ed. Edward Kamens. 1993.
Nabokov's Lolita. Ed. Zoran Kuzmanovich and Galya Diment. 2008.
Poe's Prose and Poetry. Ed. Jeffrey Andrew Weinstock and Tony Magistrale. 2008.
Pope's Poetry. Ed. Wallace Jackson and R. Paul Yoder. 1993.
Proust's Fiction and Criticism. Ed. Elyane Dezon-Jones and Inge Crosman Wimmers. 2003.
Puig's Kiss of the Spider Woman. Ed. Daniel Balderston and Francine Masiello. 2007.
Pynchon's The Crying of Lot 49 *and Other Works.* Ed. Thomas H. Schaub. 2008.
Novels of Samuel Richardson. Ed. Lisa Zunshine and Jocelyn Harris. 2006.
Rousseau's Confessions *and* Reveries of the Solitary Walker. Ed. John C. O'Neal and Ourida Mostefai. 2003.
Scott's Waverley Novels. Ed. Evan Gottlieb and Ian Duncan. 2009.
Shakespeare's Hamlet. Ed. Bernice W. Kliman. 2001.
Shakespeare's King Lear. Ed. Robert H. Ray. 1986.
Shakespeare's Othello. Ed. Peter Erickson and Maurice Hunt. 2005.
Shakespeare's Romeo and Juliet. Ed. Maurice Hunt. 2000.
Shakespeare's The Tempest *and Other Late Romances.* Ed. Maurice Hunt. 1992.
Shelley's Frankenstein. Ed. Stephen C. Behrendt. 1990.
Shelley's Poetry. Ed. Spencer Hall. 1990.
Sir Gawain and the Green Knight. Ed. Miriam Youngerman Miller and Jane Chance. 1986.
Song of Roland. Ed. William W. Kibler and Leslie Zarker Morgan. 2006.
Spenser's Faerie Queene. Ed. David Lee Miller and Alexander Dunlop. 1994.
Stendhal's The Red and the Black. Ed. Dean de la Motte and Stirling Haig. 1999.
Sterne's Tristram Shandy. Ed. Melvyn New. 1989.
Stowe's Uncle Tom's Cabin. Ed. Elizabeth Ammons and Susan Belasco. 2000.
Swift's Gulliver's Travels. Ed. Edward J. Rielly. 1988.
Teresa of Ávila and the Spanish Mystics. Ed. Alison Weber. 2009.
Thoreau's Walden *and Other Works*. Ed. Richard J. Schneider. 1996.
Tolstoy's Anna Karenina. Ed. Liza Knapp and Amy Mandelker. 2003.
Vergil's Aeneid. Ed. William S. Anderson and Lorina N. Quartarone. 2002.
Voltaire's Candide. Ed. Renée Waldinger. 1987.
Whitman's Leaves of Grass. Ed. Donald D. Kummings. 1990.
Wiesel's Night. Ed. Alan Rosen. 2007.
Works of Oscar Wilde. Ed. Philip E. Smith II. 2008.
Woolf's To the Lighthouse. Ed. Beth Rigel Daugherty and Mary Beth Pringle. 2001.
Wordsworth's Poetry. Ed. Spencer Hall, with Jonathan Ramsey. 1986.
Wright's Native Son. Ed. James A. Miller. 1997.